Colorado's
Best Wildflower Hikes
VOLUME 3: **The San Juan Mountains**

TEXT BY
PAMELA IRWIN

PHOTOGRAPHY BY
DAVID IRWIN

WESTCLIFFE PUBLISHERS
westcliffepublishers.com

ISBN-10: 1-56579-538-5
ISBN-13: 978-1-56579-538-9

TEXT COPYRIGHT: Pamela D. Irwin, 2006. All rights reserved.
PHOTOGRAPHY COPYRIGHT: David Harlan Irwin, 2006. All rights reserved.
MAPS COPYRIGHT: Rebecca Finkel, 2006. All rights reserved.

EDITOR: Jennifer Jahner
DESIGN: Rebecca Finkel, F + P Graphic Design
PRODUCTION MANAGER: Craig Keyzer

PUBLISHED BY: Westcliffe Publishers, Inc.
P.O. Box 1261
Englewood, Colorado 80150
westcliffepublishers.com

PRINTED IN CHINA THROUGH: World Print, Ltd.

LIBRARY OF CONGRESS CATALOGING-IN-PUBLICATION DATA:

Irwin, Pamela D., 1942-
　　Colorado's best wildflower hikes : volume 3 : the San
Juan mountains / text by Pamela Irwin ; photography by
David Harlan Irwin.
　　　p cm.
　　Includes index.
　　ISBN-13: 978-1-56579-538-9
　　ISBN-10: 1-56579-538-5
　　1. Hiking—Colorado—Guidebooks. 2. Wild flowers—
Colorado—Guidebooks. 3. Colorado—Guidebooks
I. Title
GV199.42.C61794　　2006
917.88'0434—dc22
　　　　　　　　　　　　　　　　　　　　　2006001347

PLEASE NOTE:
Risk is always a factor in backcountry and high-mountain travel. Many of the activities described in this book can be dangerous, especially when weather is adverse or unpredictable, and when unforeseen events or conditions create a hazardous situation. The author has done her best to provide the reader with accurate information about backcountry travel, as well as to point out some of its potential hazards. It is the responsibility of the users of this guide to learn the necessary skills for safe backcountry travel, and to exercise caution in potentially hazardous areas, especially on glaciers and avalanche-prone terrain. The author and publisher disclaim any liability for injury or other damage caused by backcountry traveling, or performing any other activity described in this book.

The author and publisher of this book have made every effort to ensure the accuracy and currency of its information. Nevertheless, books can require revisions. Please feel free to let us know if you find information in this book that needs to be updated, and we will be glad to correct it for the next printing. Your comments and suggestions are always welcome.

For more information about other fine books and calendars from Westcliffe Publishers, please contact your local bookstore, call us at (800) 523-3692, or visit us on the Web at **westcliffepublishers.com**

COVER PHOTO:
American Basin in July is peak season for wildflowers.

Acknowledgments

Colorado is full of warm, interested, and interesting people. When writing a guidebook such as this, one meets a wide range of helpful folks. Some pass you by on a trail, enthusing about something that excites them as they hike. Others spread maps and respond to inquiries. Rangers rummage through files to pull up plant lists or through their memories for good wildflower trails. To each of these lovers of the outdoors, including volunteers and those that maintain the trails, a grand thanks.

Keep close to nature's heart, yourself; and break clear away, once in a while, and climb a mountain or spend a week in the woods. Wash your spirit clean... —JOHN MUIR

Then there are those who are responsible for *Colorado's Best Wildflower Hikes Volume 3: The San Juan Mountains* coming to fruition. The staff at Westcliffe Publishers deserves kudos and a debt of gratitude: John Fielder, Westcliffe owner-publisher and renown photographer whose love for the San Juans got this book off the starting block; Linda Doyle, copublisher and lovely lady who ably midwifed the three books in the *Colorado's Best Wildflower Hikes* series; Jenna Browning and Jennifer Jahner, gracious editors par excellence; and Craig Keyzer and Rebecca Finkel, who get it all colorfully put together.

The world is but a canvas to the imagination. —THOREAU

Appreciation is due the folks who accompanied the author and photographer on occasion: Brett and Mark Irwin, Sydney Hobson, Pat and Lloyd Whittall, and Peggy and Buzz Angeli.

"Just living is not enough," said the butterfly. "One must have sunshine, freedom, and a little flower." —HANS CHRISTIAN ANDERSEN

And even more thanks is due you, the reader of *Colorado's Best Wildflower Hikes Volume 3: The San Juan Mountains*.

Happiness depends, as nature shows, less on exterior things than most suppose.
—WILLIAM COWPER

A special thank-you goes to my mother, Elizabeth Robinson, for gifting me with a love of nature and its beauty, not to mention with my very existence.

...come from a rushed and noisy world into still country. —ISAK DINESEN

Another special thank-you goes, of course, to my dedicated photographer husband who wore out as many boot soles as I did hiking hundreds of trails.

May your mind run, transported, upon a fresh deep green track. —ISAK DINESEN

And lastly and most importantly, to the Creator of wonderment, a gratefully bowed head.

Dedication

Colorful fireweed and great views can be found on the Clear Lake hike.

To David with love,

for forging silver days into golden years

❧

And to friends, family, and folks

who love being...*out there....*

Colorado's

Best Wildflower Hikes

VOLUME 3: The San Juan Mountains

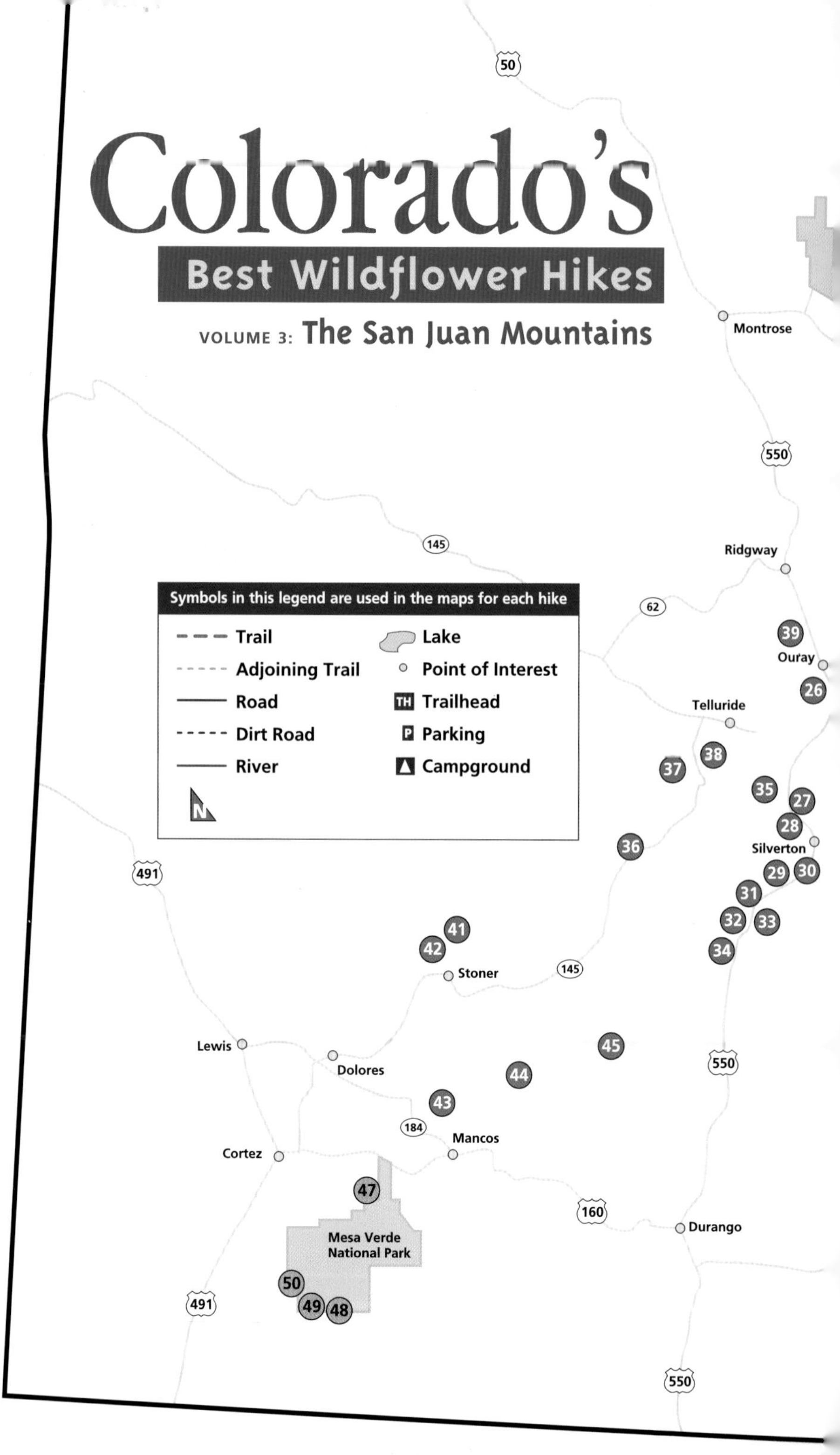

50
Montrose
550
145
Ridgway
62
Symbols in this legend are used in the maps for each hike
Trail
Adjoining Trail
Road
Dirt Road
River
Lake
Point of Interest
TH Trailhead
P Parking
Campground
N
39
Ouray
26
Telluride
38
37
35
27
28
Silverton
36
29
30
31
32
33
34
491
41
42
Stoner
145
Lewis
Dolores
45
44
550
43
184
Mancos
Cortez
47
160
Durango
Mesa Verde National Park
50
49
48
491
550

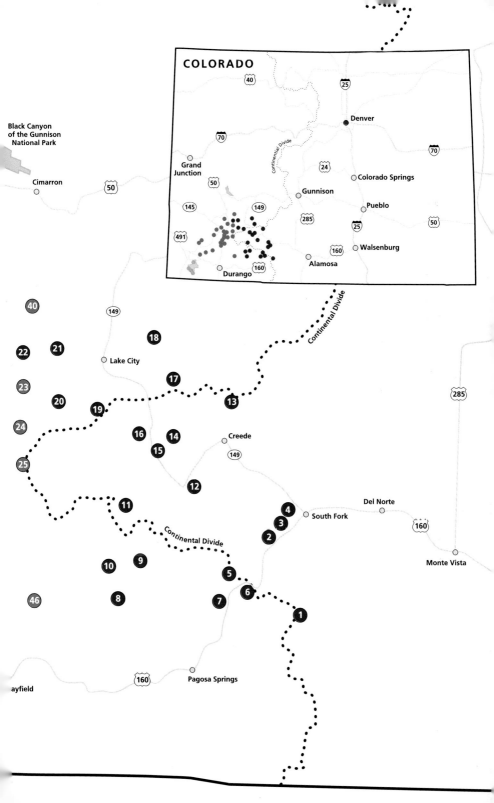

Table of Contents

MESA VERDE NATIONAL PARK

Wildflower Profiles (arranged alphabetically)

Common name (*Latin name*)

Lush flora in the San Juan Mountains

Introduction

The mountains are calling and I must go.
—JOHN MUIR

Rivaling Europe's majestic Alps or our own Grand Tetons, the 12,000 square miles encompassing the San Juan Mountains of southwestern Colorado exemplify high-country grandeur. Boasting a mean elevation of 10,400 feet, this young range also offers some of the most diverse and exciting wildflower viewing in the state.

Formed by magma and ash over millions of years, these mountains bear witness to volcanic activity on a grand scale. The collateral effect, gold and silver, brought many hopefuls to the San Juans in the 19th century. Today, a portion of this wild country is sustained in wilderness areas, national parks and forests, and state wildlife areas, beckoning those modern-day hopefuls who value the intangible wealth of wilderness. Among these treasures are the half million acres of the Weminuche Wilderness, an area larger than Colorado's four extant national parks and crisscrossed by over 475 miles of trails. Also protected are the Uncompahgre, Lizard Head, and La Garita Wildernesses. Trails, often hard-won, bear plentiful rewards as they showcase dramatic scenery, abundant flowers, and breathtaking views.

In contrast to the Rocky Mountains' north-south orientation, the San Juan Mountains run east-west, catching a generous share of storm moisture that results in sparkling lakes, fast streams, and plunging waterfalls. Recreationists can expect thriving wildlife, fine fishing, deep forests, open tundra, and quaking aspens wearing spring's bright green and autumn's gold.

Frequent storms and significant snowfall also translate to bountiful wildflowers, especially west of the Continental Divide, which runs through this land like a contorted tuning fork. Exploring both the drier east side of the Continental Divide and the wetter west side affords a diverse variety of flora. Geology helps make the area floristic as well, contributing a wide variety of substrates—limestone, volcanic rock, and sandstone.

The hikes listed here are only 50 of the myriad trails accessing the San Juans. They cover a diverse area ranging from the South Fork region in the east to the Dolores River country in the west, and from the Gunnison Basin in the north to Mesa Verde National Park in the Four Corners area. These hikes allow visitors to explore some of Colorado's best wildflower displays, and ensure a broad mix of montane, subalpine, alpine, and foothills life zones. But most importantly, they introduce you to the marvelous complexity and rugged beauty of the San Juan Mountains, so that from these 50 hikes, you can search out countless more. Whether finding your way to a waterfall or an ancient cliff dwelling, the San Juan region provides adventure for every skill and ambition level.

Human history is always putting its mark on the wilderness, in the form of mining structures, roads, and the trails featured in this book. But it is a rare treat to visit Mesa Verde National Park, a World Heritage Site that preserves 14 centuries of human civilization, manifested in the renown cliff dwellings scattered about the park's 80 square miles. For those interested in

Dramatic scenery in the San Juan Mountains

Mesa Verde National Park's interesting flora, a quartet of unique hikes can be found within these pages.

The San Juan Mountains offer wide spaces and high places, cradled valleys and folded, volcanic ravines. The largest range in the Rocky Mountains, the San Juans garner devotion even as they demand respect for their challenging topography and capricious weather. Trekking this region can involve everything from a riverside saunter to an aerobic climb. In addition, Colorado's famous fourteeners are numerous, affording peak-bagging opportunities for amateurs as well as seasoned mountaineers.

Keep in mind that the gorgeous mountain vistas awaiting you also leave you vulnerable to the weather. As with all high-country travel, be alert to building afternoon thunderstorms and plan to get an early start on your hikes.

Heed the call of the high, wide, and handsome San Juans. In return, the extraordinary San Juan experience will sustain you through days and months and years of everyday life. If ever there were a depository of extraordinary wildflower wealth, it is found in the generous San Juan Mountains.

Happy hiking among Colorado's munificent wildflowers!

—PAMELA IRWIN

How to Use This Guide

REGIONAL DESIGNATIONS AND HIKE LOCATIONS

The hikes in this guidebook are divided according to three major regions: the east San Juans, the west San Juans, and Mesa Verde National Park. Within each of these areas, trails are grouped by proximity, shared access points, and nearby towns. Refer to the regional map for a general sense of where the hikes are located, but keep in mind that this book should not substitute for more detailed maps of the San Juan Mountains. Whenever you travel into the backcountry, make sure you come prepared with a gazetteer, highway maps, and/or Forest Service maps, as well as trail brochures and information from the local ranger districts. United States Geological Survey (USGS) topo maps are recommended as well.

For exploring the San Juans, the most detailed maps include Trails Illustrated's *Map 139*, *Map 140*, *Map 141*, and *Map 142* for the Weminuche Wilderness, La Garita and Cochetopa Hills, South San Juan/Del Norte, and Silverton, Ouray, Telluride, and Lake City areas. The *Durango, Colorado, Recreation Topo Map* produced by Latitude 40° and DeLorme's *Colorado Atlas & Gazetteer* are also helpful resources. A map of Mesa Verde National Park is available from the National Park Service to all visitors.

HIKE DESCRIPTIONS

Each hike provides a narrative description of the trail, with wildflower species and other flowering plants highlighted in bold. An introduction at the beginning of each description offers information on topography, parking availability, and featured flowers. All hikes also include the following information:

Trail rating: Ratings range from easy to difficult based on elevation change, distance, and unusual features like stream crossings or especially rugged terrain. Be sure to read the full hike description when determining its suitability.

Trail length: Mileages are approximate, based on Trails Illustrated contour maps and trail signs. Each hike provides a round-trip distance, either out and back from the trailhead, or along a loop.

Location: These locations are general. For specific contact information within the San Juan National Forest or various wilderness and recreation areas, see Appendix B, p. 281.

Paintbrush color the foreground at Highland Mary Lakes.

Elevation: These figures reflect the elevation at the trailhead followed by either the high or low point of each hike. Some trails have numerous ascents and descents that might not be reflected in the final elevation figures. These hikes are noted and their ratings adjusted to reflect the added difficulty.

Bloom season: Each hike description provides a general estimate of when to see wildflower colors. The bloom season will vary from year to year depending on winter and spring snow accumulations and summer weather conditions. Certain hikes also travel through grazing areas, and in these cases, an early-season trip might help you beat the herbivore competition.

Peak bloom: Peak bloom times vary according to species and year-to-year conditions, but each hike has its own window of opportunity for best viewing. It is well worth aiming for the peak bloom season, since these weeks offer truly dazzling color.

Directions: Each hike description provides instructions to get to the trailhead. Be sure to have your own topographic and highway maps for additional reference.

WILDFLOWER VIEWING AND IDENTIFICATION

Common names for wildflowers may appear more than once throughout a hike, since a species may be fading in one place but still blooming at high elevations or in shelter. If you miss a sighting early in a hike, this repetition may allow you to spot the flower at a later point.

Wildflowers against a stunning mountain backdrop

Keep in mind, too, that wildflower common names are many and varied—a species can have various names depending on region, tradition, and the person who is identifying it. The descriptions in this book sometimes give alternate common names for a particular species, and you may know the plant by still other names.

This book is a guide to wildflower hikes, not wildflower identification. If you want more than a casual acquaintance with the region's flora, get a wildflower identification book that appeals to you. A simple picture guide may suffice, or you may wish to use a key guide that turns you into a true plant sleuth. William Weber and Ronald Wittmann's *Colorado Flora: Western Slope* is the guide for serious flora aficionados who like to key their way to a plant's identity.

Along with your enthusiasm and curiosity, don't forget to bring along a hand lens for close observation. A 10X-magnification lens is often best, but choose according to your eyes and interest.

Whether you're hoping for in-depth identification or passing familiarity, it helps to learn some basic terms for flower parts. This guide refers to plant parts like corollas, anthers, stamens, and different kinds of petals, as well as varieties of leaves, such as pinnate and palmate. Knowing this vocabulary can help enhance your wildflower experience.

Each hike also includes profiles of one or two featured flowers. These provide a more detailed description of the flower for those who are curious and looking for more information.

LIFE ZONES

The elevation of a hike determines what sorts of flowers you'll find along the way. All of the hikes pass through one or more of the following life zones:

FOOTHILLS: 6,000–8,000 FEET

Semidesert scrub, grasslands, and scrub oak offer a good variety of spring wildflowers while higher elevations are still shaking off winter.

MONTANE: 8,000–10,000 FEET

This zone rises from the foothills' scrub oak, narrowleaf cottonwoods, and piñon-juniper to the ponderosa belt. On cooler north aspects, you can find Douglas firs, alders, and, up higher, aspens.

SUBALPINE: 10,000–11,500 FEET

Many of the showiest wildflowers dwell in the subalpine life zone, often among lush forbs and grasses. Here, spring flows seamlessly into summer and vegetation benefits from water coursing down from the high country.

ALPINE: 11,500–14,000 FEET AND ABOVE

The San Juans' treeline is higher than that in the northern mountains, and marks the boundary of vast tundra stretches producing carpets and crannies of short-season wildflowers. Hardy alpine flora have only six to eight weeks to emerge, bud, bloom, find pollinators, and set seed—often in harsh conditions—before the brief summer gives way to fall and the inevitable snows of winter.

TRAIL ETIQUETTE AND PRECAUTIONS

Even if you're only planning a short day hike, it is important to act responsibly on the trail. Following the Leave No Trace guidelines helps preserve the lovely San Juan trails for future generations:

- Plan ahead and prepare
- Travel on durable surfaces
- Dispose of waste properly
- Leave what you find
- Minimize impact
- Respect wildlife
- Be considerate of other users

More information on trail use is available from the Leave No Trace Center for Outdoor Ethics at www.lnt.org.

It goes without saying that you should never pick flowers along a hike. Collecting wildflowers in national parks is against the law. Please allow these lovely natural resources to mature and live out their bloom season so that others might enjoy them, too.

WHAT TO BRING

Make sure you always hike with plenty of potable water. Sampling from streams, rivers, and lakes is not safe. Other essential items to bring include sunscreen, maps, compass, hat, sturdy hiking boots, and weather-wise gear.

Yellow-bellied marmots are often seen in the San Juan backcountry.

WEATHER

Summer in the Colorado high country is also thunderstorm season. Weather changes quickly, and a perfect day can become dark, stormy, and dangerous in minutes. Don't take the threat of lightning lightly when you are hiking in the mountains, especially in exposed areas or above treeline. Watch the skies and listen for thunder. Make sure you're under cover if a storm strikes. Better yet, start your hike early so that you can be out of harm's way by early afternoon.

TRAIL OBSTACLES

Severe weather can change a trail. Rock- or mudslides, erosion, washouts, downed timber, or even late-melting snow can alter or block a route. Forest Service personnel and volunteers clear obstacles as soon as possible, but it is a good idea to check with a local ranger district for reports of any problems.

Use caution and common sense when negotiating stream crossings. Especially when water levels are high, creeks present some risk. Choose your crossing carefully.

TRAVELING IN THE BACKCOUNTRY

Hiking in the San Juans requires both perseverance and a sense of adventure. Some of the trailheads are difficult to get to, requiring good navigational skills, a high-clearance and/or four-wheel-drive vehicle, and a competent driver. Don't leave home without detailed road maps of the areas, and don't attempt roads that look unsafe or impassable. Once you get to your destination, be prepared for some of the most spectacular wildflower displays you can imagine.

Several of the best routes are not even on trails at all, but rather follow four-wheel-drive jeep routes. Since these roads may see some vehicle or ATV traffic, use caution when hiking. Many are also crisscrossed with spur roads, ATV tracks, and abandoned routes that can be confusing to navigate. The hike descriptions steer you in the right direction, and a compass will help, too.

Most of all, bring your enthusiasm and curiosity. You are hiking through some of the most pristine, dramatic, and inspiring land in this country. See you on the trail!

I will be the gladdest thing under the sun,
I will touch a hundred flowers and not pick one.
—EDNA ST. VINCENT MILLAY

Wildflower Hike 1

Crater Lake Trail

The Crater Lake Trail offers high mountains, wide meadows, and handsome wildflower displays.

Trail Rating	easy to moderate
Trail Length	3 miles out and back
Location	Rio Grande National Forest, east and south of South Fork
Elevation	11,600 to 12,100 feet
Bloom Season	July to August
Peak Bloom	late July to early August
Directions	From South Fork, head west on US 160 for approximately 7.5 miles, taking a left (south) onto FR 380. Follow this road 15 miles, bearing right (south) at the Summitville/South Fork junction. Continue on FR 380 just over 4 miles to the trailhead for Crater Lake Trail No. 707. Park to the left at the South Fork pullout and sign.

With abundant wildflowers and stunning scenery, the Crater Lake Trail is the ideal short and sweet San Juans hike. The moderate rating is due to high altitude rather than elevation gain, which is gradual from the trailhead to the wilderness boundary.

The trail begins roadside and leads up through spruce forest, soon opening to wide vistas. It continues a gentle ascent before crossing a steep, loose-soiled slope, then heads across meadows, passing a small pond before a short descent to a rocky tundra patch near the South San Juan Wilderness boundary. This description ends at the halfway point to Crater Lake. The lake, frequented by anglers, is gained by descending into a steep, forested canyon.

Late July or early August is the best time to explore this trail, as the wildflowers are breathtaking. Parking is limited to a wide spot on a signed curve along the dirt access road and across from the trailhead itself.

Flowers abound even before you begin this hike. A spruce grove at the pullout is full of subalpine wildflowers species that appreciate the cool, moist shade, such as **tall chimingbells**, **Coulter daisy**, and both **rayless** and **daffodil senecio**.

Across the road, Crater Lake Trail begins in a boggy area, angling up to pass wildflowers like small-flowered, blue **alpine speedwell**, **wild geranium**, **false hellebore**, and **little pink elephants**, accented by the bright gold rays of **subalpine arnica**. Choose your footing well as you approach a post marked No. 707. Continue up the sloping meadow, where moist conditions encourage a blue, white, and gold meadow of **sawtooth senecio**, **subalpine larkspur**, and more white Coulter daisy, a native named for an adventurous young botanist with the Hayden Survey of the late 1800s.

Wild strawberry thrives in spruce shade as Crater Lake Trail rises to a seep sporting cheery **yellow monkeyflower**, **homely buttercup**, and five-petaled **cinquefoil**. Another yellow denizen is **aspen sunflower**. **Yarrow**, appropriately once called **woundwort**, joins **Whipple** or **dusky penstemon**'s wine-colored tubes.

ALPINE DUSTY MAIDEN
Chaenactis alpina

Like soft, coarse feathers divided three times, the leaves of alpine dusty maiden, also called alpine pincushion, surround single heads of tubular disk flowers. Rising from a long taproot, the off-white florets, tipped in dusty pink, are long blooming. Preferring alpine scree, these 4- to 8-inch mounded wildflowers are also called morning brides. The crushed foliage was once used as a poultice to reduce swelling and to relieve chapped hands and insect bites.

As the elevation gain eases, the lavender-blue blooms of **delicate Jacob's ladder** appear under spruces. Openings feature **white geranium, American bistort**, and more spirited Coulter daisy. A snag guards a damp swale where **king's** and **queen's crown** reign. On the left, look for nodding daffodil senecio among cool pink heads of **subalpine daisy**. Even more showy are vivid red bracts of **paintbrush**, often a species cross.

As the trail opens into meadows, brilliant but small **Brandegee clover** dangles deep, magenta-pink florets. Named for another Hayden Survey botanist, this high-elevation inhabitant is fragrant, like all clovers. Nearby is false hellebore, also known as **cornhusk lily**. No matter the name, this robust plant is toxic to its core. Here, too, **northern paintbrush** presents palest yellow bracts, modified leaves, and green, toothpicklike flowers.

Between conical spruces, the trail continues west. A keen eye may spot tiny, deep yellow heads of **golden draba**, a mustard family member. Moist soil supports **triangleleaf senecio** and soft-leaved subalpine arnica, as well as tall

Paintbrush

Porters lovage, a veritable pharmacy for early peoples. This parsley clan member, with its fernlike foliage and off-white umbellate heads, is sometimes confused with similar-appearing poison hemlock.

In the high-country meadow scene before you, northern paintbrush joins a subtle palette of more American bistort, yarrow, Coulter daisy, subalpine arnica, aspen sunflower, and the smooth, barrel heads of rayless senecio. Trailside, **prickly mountain currant** bushes border the ascending trail as it aims toward elegant **Colorado blue columbine**.

The grade increases as does the rocky footbed, passing **redstem cinquefoil** and **red-berried elder** bushes. The alpine scenery is hard to drop your eyes from, but in late summer the silky, mauve-pink points of **little rose gentian** bloom at your feet. Brandegee clover and vibrant, pink-violet **Halls penstemon** add to the pink tones here.

As you climb out of a small bowl, native **subalpine dock** is common. Willows signal a seep on the left where yellow monkeyflower flourishes. Royal purple-blue **subalpine larkspur's** showy inflorescences add to the gorgeous view.

Continuing on a gently rising grade, the trail passes copper-colored **orange agoseris**; lowland specimens have burnt orange rays. An outcrop sports **yellow stonecrop, alpine sandwort, purple fringe, pinnate-leaf daisy**, draba, and cinquefoil. In the pale gray gravel, **sky pilot** and **alpine phlox** greet early-season hikers.

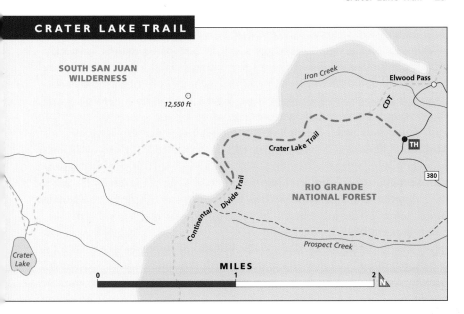

CRATER LAKE TRAIL

SOUTH SAN JUAN
WILDERNESS

Iron Creek

Elwood Pass

12,550 ft

CDT

Crater Lake Trail

TH

RIO GRANDE
NATIONAL FOREST

380

Continental Divide Trail

Prospect Creek

Crater
Lake

MILES

0   1   2

Gravelly tread leads past earlier blooming alpine plants, and summer showcases **pussytoes** and **many-rayed goldenrod**, as well as brassy **alpine avens**, a rose family cousin of cinquefoil. A creek on the left supports yellow monkeyflower, **pink willowherb**, and **marsh marigold**. Joining them are little pink elephants, snowy **bittercress**, queen's crown, small blue **alpine violet**, and **tall scarlet paintbrush**.

From the ravine, the trail curves, passing bowed spruce stands called krummholz to expose Brandegee clover and Halls penstemon, the latter is in honor of the mid-19th-century plant collector Elihu Hall. More water means more wildflowers, and the next rivulet repeats the previous array, adding lacy **cowbane** and, up on the next tier, a serpentining parade of little pink elephants. **Stitchwort**'s tiny white bursts take an observant eye, though cousins **alpine chickweed** and the ubiquitous **mouse-ear chickweed**, or **mouse-ears**, appear trailside. Along the flow, look for **brook saxifrage** on wiry red stems. Big, rosy globes of **Parry clover** also appear.

The trail cuts up through the blue-green foliage of rock-anchored king's crown. To the south, 12,866-foot Long Trek Mountain is visible, while the sloped peaks of the Summitville Mine region fill the landscape to the northeast. Lookout Mountain's level top stands at 12,448 feet, while jutting peaks define the eastern view.

On the right, a little pond nurtures marsh marigold and, perhaps, vivid **Parry primrose**. **Alpine parsley**'s yellow blooms abound on the rise beside the pond, and sky pilot and **single-headed daisy** add complementary tints. Nearby, the Continental Divide Trail meets and crosses the Crater Lake Trail, with the CDT hemmed in by thick tundra grasses.

As the trail narrows to traverse a steep, shifting slope, be sure to pause for wildflowers. To the right, **black-tipped senecio** is easily recognized by its big, rubbery, mint green leaves, but even more showy is the vibrant, violet-pink Halls penstemon. Thriving in the lithic soil are purple fringe and **alumroot**, as well as butter-colored **wallflower** and **slender-tipped clover**. **Greenleaf sage**, **harebell**, and clumps of Colorado blue columbine also grow in the loose volcanic soil. Mounds of **rock senecio** highlight **alpine dusty maiden**, or **alpine pin-cushion**, a pinkish-gray scree hugger with disk flowers. King's crown is quite abundant here. In sheltering vegetation, the soft pink buds of **pink-headed daisy** appear, as do Colorado blue columbine and purple fringe.

On the far side of the slope, look for pinwheels of creamy **Parry lousewort** accompanying little rose gentian. **Stemless goldflower** may be visible near a stone cairn signaling rockier tread.

The trail descends, passing **alpine bistort**, alpine sandwort, and bright pink **moss campion**. Light yellow **western paintbrush** and spruce krummholz line the route, and in late summer, **Rocky Mountain gentian** blooms in vivid royal blue.

At the sign announcing the boundary of the South San Juan Wilderness, the trail bends down to a low knoll on the left, paved with broken, iron oxide–stained rock. Here grow alpine sandwort, or **sandywinks**, **blueleaf cinquefoil**, moss campion, goldflower, and stonecrop. Tucked into the rocks is **whiplash saxifrage** with its red runners and little gold cups. The corolla features a pistil that is lime green before pollination and red after. Further searching may turn up **snowlover**, a short penstemon relative indicating a late snowmelt, and the small petals of blue-lavender **moss** or **compass gentian**. This small area features an array of tundra flora, including ground-hugging **snow willow** and, in August, **Arctic gentian**, its purple-streaked, translucent white buds signaling coming snow. Be alert for ptarmigan in the vicinity as well. On the lusher, north side of the trail, look for purple **star gentian** among the willows, as well as short purple **monkshood**. **Snowball saxifrage** also grows here, resembling lollipops.

This makes a good turnaround point. From here, the trail drops into a forested ravine on its way to Crater Lake.

Once back at your vehicle, consider a side trip to the Summitville Mine area. While the infamous modern mine cleanup site is off-limits, the weathered old wooden structures of historic Summitville across the road are worth exploring.

Big Meadows Reservoir Loop

Wildflower Hike 2

Many wildflowers species appear along easygoing Big Meadows Reservoir Loop.

easy	**Trail Rating**
3-mile loop	**Trail Length**
Rio Grande National Forest, west of South Fork	**Location**
9,350 feet	**Elevation**
June to August	**Bloom Season**
late June to early July	**Peak Bloom**
From South Fork, head west on US 160 for 11 miles, turning right (west) on FR 410, which is also named Big Meadows Rd. Continue 1.75 miles to the South Fork Trailhead on the northeast side of the reservoir. Park at the Archuleta Trailhead.	**Directions**

This 3-mile loop encircles Big Meadows Reservoir, which looks, except for the dam, like a naturally occurring lake. The trail is easygoing, passing through several habitats and offering a startling variety of wildflowers. It isn't everywhere in the mountains that you can see so many species on a nearly flat walk.

The parking area is shared by anglers and hikers and manages to accommodate both, especially early in the morning. More parking is available on the east side of the dam, but there is a fee. Keep an eye out for thunderstorms, especially since you'll be in the vicinity of the lake.

The trailhead is located beyond the restroom and sign kiosk, and from here, hikers head right to encircle the lake counterclockwise. After signing the trail register, start along the north shore where **beauty** and **silvery cinquefoil** and their hybrid progeny dot the way with yellow, as do **mountain parsley** and **many-rayed goldenrod**.

The trail passes dangling purple **harebell** and little cups of **red globe anemone**, whose seedheads look like oversized cotton swabs. Traveling evenly above the shore, the trail enters spruce forest where **wild geranium** and **wild rose** bloom in pink. Open skies highlight **scarlet gilia** and **Rocky Mountain penstemon**, robust in blue and violet. **Golden aster** follows the route back down to lake level.

Northern bedstraw's froth of fragrant white flowers is visible in the shoreline meadow, along with **shrubby cinquefoil**. Damp areas feature **tall chimingbells** and pale yellow **northern paintbrush**. **Black-tipped senecio** is found near a footbridge crossing of Black Creek. Check here for **twinberry honeysuckle** and **cow parsnip**'s wide umbels. Beyond, in red and soft yellow, is **western red columbine**, backed by sunny **subalpine arnica**

LITTLEFLOWER PENSTEMON

Penstemon confertus ssp. *procerus*

Blooming midsummer in rich pigments from blue to violet, little-flower penstemon's tubes angle slightly downward. Another common name, clustered penstemon, describes the crowded and separated whorls or groupings of the tubes. Reasonably moist meadows in montane, subalpine, and even lower alpine zones from Alaska to Colorado are places to look for littleflower penstemon. Latin *confertus* means "crowded," while the subspecies *procerus* means "tall," even though littleflower penstemon grows only from 4 to 12 inches high.

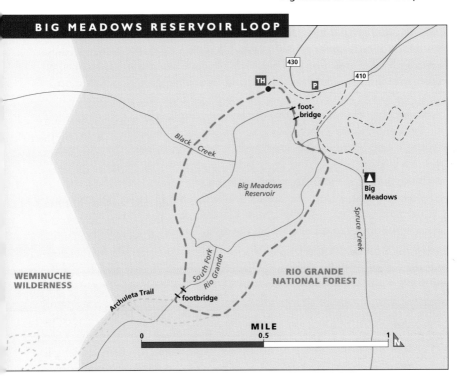

and wild geranium. By the stream, look for **yellow avens**, tall chimingbells, airy **brook saxifrage**, and **bittercress**, or **brookcress**, in white. Closer observation with a hand lens may turn up **green mitrewort**, or **bishop's cap**, displaying minute blossoms with maroon tracery.

The flat path finds white-starred **spergulastrum**, or **rock starwort**. **Littleflower penstemon** precedes a small cove guarded by shoreline outcrops. In the thick grass, northern paintbrush, **green bog orchid**, and **pink plumes**, a nodding member of the rose family, flourish in the moist soil.

As the tread grows rockier, **meadowrue**, **monkshood**, gray-green mats of **pussytoes**, and fuzzy-leaved subalpine arnica are visible. Near a pair of boulders on the uphill side of the trail, look for the hanging blossoms of western red columbine and, in front of it, meadowrue, which is also called **false columbine**. Examining the leaves of these neighbors explains the latter name.

A shallow-rooted spruce sends the route uphill, then quickly down to wander among shrubby cinquefoil, accented by **orange sneezeweed**. Fingers of the reservoir reach west into plush grasses where littleflower penstemon and **orange agoseris** grow.

Cross a boggy area on stones to enjoy **little pink elephants**. At their feet, are tiny blue **alpine veronica**, or **alpine speedwell**; about the same size is **alpine bistort**. Monkshood pops up, as does the somewhat uncommon **western Jacob's ladder** in lavender, complemented by yellow northern paintbrush.

On drier ground now, the trail rises into forest. Keep an eye on the ground in a search of **rattlesnake plantain orchid**, a small orchid surrounded by flat leaves with white midribs. This plant was once used to treat rattlesnake bites. Another orchid, **spotted coralroot orchid**, is unable to produce chlorophyll. Each tiny flower on the stalk sports a red-spotted lip; the miniature orchid blossoms soon morph into inflated, rust-colored tubes.

A sign indicating Archuleta Trail straight ahead sends the Big Meadow Reservoir loop left toward an inlet creek. A little garden of scarlet gilia, gold **New Mexico senecio**, and yellow mountain parsley attracts broad-tailed hummingbirds and mourning cloak butterflies.

The swift stream is the South Fork of the Rio Grande. Tall-growing **twistedstalk**, each bell suspended from a kinked pedicel, or stem, appears as hikers approach a rugged outcrop on the right. Later in the summer, **fireweed** will shoot up magenta-flamed spires.

The trail turns east over a sturdy footbridge. Shade-loving **baneberry**'s filmy bottlebrush inflorescences will mature into racemes of glassy, toxic berries that are typically red, though an occasional mutant may be white. Near running water is the place to find bittercress and tall chimingbells. **Subalpine daisy**, a showy fleabane with lavender-pink ray flowers and golden disk flowers, also appreciates damp soil. This is all seen from the bridge.

Coming off of the bridge, more baneberry is visible, along with the glossy green alternating leaves of **false Solomon's seal**, which follow an arced, unbranched, zigzag stem to a terminal cluster of creamy stars. Note a red and gold display on the left; the right features **parrot's beak lousewort**, or **rams-horn**, in white, and the showy glow of western red columbine.

As you leave the spruce shade, enjoy the short willows and **potentilla** bushes that foreground the lake waters, along with western Jacob's ladder and **false hellebore**, poisonous in all parts, even, reportedly, to its pollinating bees.

A footbridge spanning a gentle creek leads hikers up to a log-flanked trail section. Tiger swallowtails flit in the open before woods take over, presenting **green gentian** and little **blue** or **hooked violet**. Back in spruce shade, watch for dainty **twinflower** with its paired bells. Poking out of rotting duff on a curve, green mitrewort calls for hand lens examination. **Mountain death camas**' toxic white stars may be found in the same vicinity.

The meadow edges up to the reservoir as the trail aims somewhat north, curving to overlook a small beaver dam. The wet area behind it sees the delicate heads of **subalpine valerian**, pale pink in bud, white in full flower, along with **red onion** and tall chimingbells. This moist habitat pairs up complementary **subalpine larkspur** in rich purple-blue, and tall **triangleleaf** or **arrowleaf senecio** in gold. **Homely buttercup** edges a small pond, while the outlet supports sweet **pink willowherb** and sturdy spikes of little pink elephants.

The trail briefly passes through spruce and downed timber, soon emerging with a view of some more little pink elephants. **Queen's crown** presents rounded pink heads that vie with **yellow monkeyflower** for notice along a string of aging beaver dams.

Rosy pussytoes and **white pussytoes** are abundant as the circuit passes beaver slipways toward more subalpine valerian and western Jacob's ladder. Pale paintbrush crosses and shockingly brilliant **rosy paintbrush**, possibly a cross with **tall scarlet**, may attract a black and white Wiedemeyer's admiral.

The loop comes to a seep angling down to the trail. At a dip in the shaded route, check for a fabulously scented wintergreen family member, **shy wood nymph**, bowing her wavy, ivory head low over dark leaves. Rising somewhat to a tiny seep, this one crossed on stones, the trail passes spruce-shaded duff where shy wood nymph likes to hide. A sloping meadow yields yellow monkey-flower, monkshood, cow parsnip, and ferny-leaved **Porters lovage**.

The route hits a talus slope, home to piping pikas. As it curves across the rockfall, the trail rewards you with lovely clumps of **Colorado blue columbine**,

Little pink elephants

creating a nice rock garden effect. Wild rose perfumes the air, and more blue columbine heralds upcoming tall scarlet paintbrush, its bracts and modified leaves fiery red.

Travel above the lake through a rocky zone, followed by a damp place where green mitrewort thrives; bend close by a rotting log to look for the less common **sleighbells**, or **one-sided white mitrewort**. Hand lens–worthy blooms decorate one side of the straight stalk. The developing seedpods of these cousin mitreworts are as fascinating as the snowflake flowers.

A wide-skied meadow greets hikers with many wildflower species, including, in late summer, royal blue **Rocky Mountain gentian**. Pink plumes and vivid magenta **American vetch** are also visible, while littleflower penstemon borders a small stream crossed on stones, followed soon by another creek. The last waterway is spanned by a footbridge and shaded by aspens. This is Spruce Creek, which has a very short trail of its own, from the southeast corner of Big Meadows Campground.

Continue straight ahead through bunchgrass, aiming left before another footbridge; this path will take you to the east end of the dam, not far from your vehicle. On the way, a little trickle harbors **marsh marigold**, and an odd and less common member of the rose clan, **purple avens**, growing much taller and more tightly flowered than its cousin, pink plumes. Your hike nears completion as you cross the cinquefoil-dominated dam top.

Wildflower Hike 3

Hope Creek Trail

The dynamic combination of scarlet gilia and Rocky Mountain penstemon begins the Hope Creek Trail.

Trail Rating	easy to moderate
Trail Length	7 miles out and back
Location	Rio Grande National Forest/Weminuche Wilderness, west of South Fork
Elevation	9,550 to 10,300 feet
Bloom Season	mid-June to August
Peak Bloom	late June to mid-July
Directions	From South Fork, go west 11 miles on US 160. Take a right (west) on FR 410, also called Big Meadows Rd. After approximately 1.5 miles, go right again on FR 430. Follow FR 430 1.5 miles to Hope Creek Trail No. 838. Casual parking is available to the left of the roadway.

Located just up a Forest Service road from Big Meadows Reservoir to the west of South Fork, Hope Creek Trail gains elevation almost effortlessly. The trek's gentle grade, with only a few steep ascents, makes a relaxing day hike, and diverse habitats promise a variety of wildflower species. Forest dominates the route, but openings and streamside plant life keep the flora changing. At mile 3, the trail reaches 10,000 feet and enters the Weminuche Wilderness. Continue to this description's end at a view of an avalanche path. For those wishing to take a longer hike, Hope Creek Trail continues to the scenic Continental Divide at approximately 12,000 feet.

Parking is tight at best, being a shallow roadside pullout at the trailhead with room for two vehicles. Fortunately, not many hikers take advantage of Hope Creek, so parking may well be available.

On the inside of the parking curve, gritty soil supports **shrubby cinquefoil, harebell, yarrow, salsify, scorpionweed**, and **scarlet gilia**. **Twinberry honeysuckle, mountain parsley, Rocky Mountain penstemon**, and **senecio** varieties appear in the first few yards on the near side of a trail sign. Clear water and an amber-colored bed make Hope Creek look like fast-flowing honey.

Enjoying the creek's moist banks are **cow parsnip, tall chimingbells**, and **golden banner**, a yellow-gold member of the pea or legume family. Rising above the stream, the trail follows a slope featuring scarlet gilia, perfumed **wild rose**, frothy **northern bedstraw**, and medicinal yarrow. This ferny-leaved, off-white composite is a coagulant, pain reliever, and antiseptic, and the Greek hero Achilles was said to have used it on his soldiers' wounds.

Rocky Mountain penstemon's marine blue attracts tiger swallowtail butterflies on the dry embankment. Where the trail evens out, the red of scarlet gilia and the yellows of senecio and golden banner make a showy combination.

Traveling west, hikers pass **many-rayed goldenrod, pussytoes**, and **wild strawberry**.

ROCKY MOUNTAIN PENSTEMON
Penstemon strictus

Large and sturdy and growing up to 30 inches tall, this penstemon is tolerant of many soils, though it prefers mesic—one of balanced moisture and light. The showy, saturated dark blue tubes are suffused with violet and mainly arranged on one side of a straight stalk, often in clusters. Basal leaves are wider than stem leaves. This penstemon can be found mostly on the Continental Divide's western side and can spread in clumps. It makes a good garden candidate.

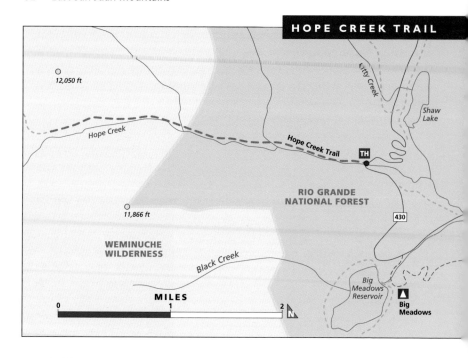

HOPE CREEK TRAIL

12,050 ft

Hope Creek

Kirty Creek

Shaw Lake

Hope Creek Trail

TH

RIO GRANDE NATIONAL FOREST

11,866 ft

430

WEMINUCHE WILDERNESS

Black Creek

Big Meadows Reservoir

Big Meadows

MILES

0   1   2

Purple-blue Rocky Mountain penstemon adds to the red and gold display on the right; on the left, willows shelter **wild geranium, heartleaf arnica**, and cinquefoil. Look carefully beneath spruce trees for **rattlesnake plantain orchid**, a modest little orchid. Its veined leaves, with a prominent whitish midrib, lie flat on the forest floor. This same area features a big trailside boulder with a death's-head shape in lichen encrusted upon it; here, you may spot a half-dozen **shy wood nymphs** guarded by a few spruces. This wintergreen, though small and bowed, exudes a heavenly perfume.

You can hear the creek along this section, though willows hide it from view until **false Solomon's seal**, with its polished, leathery leaves and thick racemes of creamy flowers, allows another glimpse. Quaking aspens cap a steep, grassy slope on the opposite side, brightened by a palette of already-noted wildflowers. On the riparian side are cow parsnip and lush tall chimingbells, a favorite food of elk.

Spruce shade accommodates white **parrot's beak lousewort**, which sports entire leaves instead of the usually ferny growth of other louseworts. **One-sided wintergreen**'s little bells dangle from an arced stalk. It is always a joy to spot **western red columbine**'s glowing lanterns, and this forest habitat is just the right place to look.

Coming upon a trailside boulder affords a look at **white violet** and wild geranium; the latter was once brewed as a birth control tea by resourceful American Indians. Later, **fireweed**, said to bloom when eaglets fledge, will add a magenta note. **Twistedstalk**, with its kink-stalked bells hiding under veined leaves, occurs here and there. **Meadowrue** is evident as well. Dainty and white, **subalpine valerian** blooms in the shade.

On an open hillside, white-barked aspens contrast with scarlet gilia, or **sky rocket**. Parrot's beak lousewort leads back to the creek. Like many pack trails, this one often has clover alongside it. In an area of downed logs, look for an island of snowy **bittercress** and tall chimingbells.

In the damp environs, twistedstalk's ivory bells will mature into orange-scarlet berries on waist-high plants. **Alpine veronica** is merely fingertip-high, but a stunning blue. **Yellow avens** is a tallish denizen, but wildflowerists must bend low to spot **bishop's cap**, or **green mitrewort**. Also thriving is **brook saxifrage**, its blooms nodding on wiry, reddish stems over clumps of evenly toothed, kidney-shaped leaves.

Travel to a willow-shaded seep on the right, home to **blue violet**, white **cowbane**, **pink willowherb**, white violet, and ubiquitous tall chimingbells. The trail is a bit muddy underfoot as it climbs to a grassy pocket meadow where **red onion** displays both flowers and bulbs. Finely flowered subalpine valerian dwells here as well. Nearby, willows shelter golden banner.

Open skies shine on shrubby cinquefoil, and rushes signal **edible valerian**, a homely cousin of the pretty subalpine valerian. **Wallflower**, a fragrant early bloomer, has soft yellow petals in cruciform configuration.

Straight ahead, a 12,000-foot mountain ridge forms the backbone of the Continental Divide. From a slightly stony, entrenched trail, look for **wild iris**, **whiplash fleabane**, cinquefoil, and **spergulastrum**, or **rock starwort**, a sandwort. Soon, the route comes upon **orange sneezeweed**, **orange agoseris**, and more shrubby cinquefoil, complementing purple-veined wild iris.

Where spreading evergreen mats of **kinnikinnick** cluster trailside, the route starts a more serious ascent, accompanied by wild rose and more scarlet gilia, sometimes called **fairy trumpets**. Below, a beaver pond displays **little pink elephants**.

The trail levels upon entering conifers. Look for **mountain candytuft**'s tiny white flowers, and eye-catching western red columbine, whose myriad yellow stamens poke out from pale yellow sepals and red petals. Subalpine valerian's small trumpets cluster in an exquisite inflorescence.

The trail continues pleasantly, coming upon **delicate Jacob's ladder**. Very early-season hikers might spot the beautiful pink **calypso**, or **fairy slipper orchid**, decorating an evergreen log so rotted, it is closer to earth than tree. The orchid's bulb is two parted, one side producing a single leaf, the other, the unforgettable flower. Picking one, however, means death for this plant.

A bunchgrass opening in the forest offers **false hellebore**, or **cornhusk lily**, a highly toxic plant. **Pink plumes** and shrubby cinquefoil represent the rose family.

A steeper ascent allows a wider perspective of the ridge noted earlier. The dry south aspect is perfect for harebell, mountain parsley, and scarlet gilia.

Hope Creek flows into view, readying hikers for another pocket meadow pairing northern bedstraw and shrubby cinquefoil bushes.

The route reaches a Weminuche Wilderness sign. Late summer brings fireweed's magenta spires. As the trail continues upward, look for **Whipple** or **dusky penstemon**'s subtle port wine–colored tubes. The route evens out and **mountain death camas** is visible, its stalks hooked like a shepherd's crook when in bud, but erect when flowering. Late summer will scatter sapphire **Rocky Mountain gentian** in forest openings.

The trail crosses two small streams. Spergulastrum, like spokes of a wheel, tends to spread its white stars in every direction. After a long forest segment, continue to an opening that reveals the ridge previously seen, now off to the south, a precursor of 12,834-foot Mount Hope. To the west, a rounded mountain shoulder brings on cowbane, wild geranium, and tall-growing **triangleleaf senecio**.

Ahead, the tread is roots and rocks. A small stream nurtures a number of **green bog orchids**. **Yellow monkeyflower** basks by the sandy-bedded waterway, along with lacy cowbane and pink willowherb. Claiming a small boulder is airy brook saxifrage and green mitrewort, with snowflake traceries masquerading as flowers. **Monkshood** joins **buttercup** for a poisonous pairing, both being extremely toxic.

The trail rises, passing **Porters lovage**, while a damp spot boasts pristine white bittercress, a peppery member of the mustard tribe and cousin to watercress. Like its produce-aisle relative, bittercress, sometimes called **brookcress**, likes wet places, often growing right by streams.

Soon, an avalanche trough coursing down a steep slope claims hikers' attention. Unstable snow conditions create these dangerous chutes. In the bunchgrass meadow here, wild iris is supplanted by orange sneezeweed as summer marches on. Keeping an eye to the sky for building thunderstorms, take your time here and enjoy the views. When you are ready, return by the same route.

Hunters Lake Loop

Wildflower Hike 4

Reflected mountains in Hunters Lake capture the beauty of high-country hiking.

moderate to difficult	***Trail Rating***
4.2-mile loop plus 0.25-mile tundra spur	***Trail Length***
Rio Grande National Forest/Weminuche Wilderness, south of Creede	***Location***
11,400 to 12,100 feet	***Elevation***
July to August	***Bloom Season***
mid-July	***Peak Bloom***
From South Fork, head west on US 160 for 11 miles, turning right (west) onto FR 410, also called Big Meadows Rd. After approximately 1.5 miles, bear right right onto FR 430. Follow this road approximately 11 miles, looking to the left (west) for the trailhead spur.	***Directions***

If solitude appeals to you, along with marvelous mountain scenery, a serene lake, and a brief climb to view tundra flora, then Hunters Lake Loop might be your perfect hike. A number of ecozones allow wildflower variety, adding up to a fair number of species. Little used except by anglers, the trail appears and disappears until it reaches the lake's far side, but is worth every adventurous step.

The 4.2-mile loop travels clockwise, heading down to the lake and along its west shore. An open area follows as the trail crosses the south side of a loaflike mountain, then continues steadily up a long traverse to a saddle. From here, a brief spur climbs steeply to an amazing view and lovely tundra flora. The loop continues from the spur's return across the level backside of the mountain before dropping down into a forest. Be on the lookout for a fork to the right, which will take you back to your vehicle. If you miss it, you will eventually come to the main road, but it is an extra mile back to the parking area.

The parking area is generous and accommodates anglers and horseback riders as well as hikers.

BRANDEGEE CLOVER
Trifolium brandegei

Unlike the rounded head of florets that characterizes most clovers, the florets of Brandegee clover dangle singly like bright, magenta-rose pendants. The few vivid, fragrant flowers are in abbreviated racemes. Found from subalpine to alpine zones in Colorado and New Mexico, Brandegee clover honors Townshend Stith Brandegee, who was a topographer, botanist, and railroad engineer with the 1875 Hayden Survey.

Though a pretty meadow is before you, the trail to Hunters Lake begins to the right in a spruce forest, by an ingress sign for the 500,000-acre Weminuche Wilderness. The winding path presents wildflowers, such as deep pink, almost burgundy **Brandegee clover** and **tall chimingbells**. **Prickly mountain currant**'s hazy salmon blossoms lead up to **cowbane** and **triangleleaf senecio**, both thriving in damp areas.

The trail then skirts a meadow featuring **false hellebore, American bistort**, pale **northern paintbrush, wild geranium**, little blue **alpine speedwell**, and rosy, round-headed **Parry clover**. **Red onion** bears the distinctive oniony aroma of its kin; some of its pointed, reddish flowers are replaced by pulpy, small bulbs.

To the south, a ridgeline mountain comes into view. More cool yellow northern paintbrush and red onion appear, along with **yarrow** and **snowball saxifrage**. In the distance, a far, flat-topped mountain is visible, while the foreground is dominated by Parry clover, **rosy paintbrush**, snowy **bittercress**, pink and blue tall chimingbells, and brassy **cinquefoil**.

With the return of spruce shade comes more Brandegee clover, each pendant floret an intense rose hue. Look upstream for big-leaved clumps of **Parry primrose** in hot pink. The trail comes upon the curvy white blossoms of **parrot's beak lousewort**, and soon Hunters Lake is glimpsed through the trees. The lake is framed by evergreens and the flat ridgeline of 12,688-foot Table Mountain.

The north side of the lake is moist, and more floristic as well. Where damp meets duff, look for **subalpine daisy**'s cool pink rays. Even more fond of wet places are **marsh marigold** and Parry primrose, both thriving along the moist margins. Keeping to the high ground above the shore still allows examination of wildflowers such as **twistedstalk**, with its telltale kinked stalks. More subalpine daisy and spongy soil announce **bog saxifrage**, a homely cousin of the snowball saxifrage seen earlier. Cross an inlet a bit upstream and head to drier footing, where **subalpine larkspur** puts on a show of deep purple-blue. Though the trail plays hide-and-seek, keep the faith; it reappears where drier ground dominates, often in spruce groves.

A rockfall to the northwest allows a view of the high ridge and cirque, while its soil pockets nurture beautiful **Colorado blue columbine**, the state flower since 1899. Nearby, **twinberry honeysuckle** bushes thrive by **old man of the mountains**, or **alpine sunflower**, reminding hikers of the lofty elevation here.

The trail, now above the lake, goes south, becoming easier to follow as it rises over a stony ridge, bringing hikers to a rock cairn. At this point, a drier aspect dominates, and **wallflower** and **red globe anemone** complement Colorado blue columbine. Listen for the squeals of pikas, a snowshoe hare relation. Along the rockfall "toe" are more elegant Colorado blue columbine and **subalpine arnica**.

A scenic combination of flowers and water at Hunters Lake

Descending now, look for a sandwort of sorts, **spergulastrum**, or **rock starwort**, appearing as a prostrate mat. The track arrives at a sign for the Rio Grande National Forest and Weminuche Wilderness. **Many-rayed goldenrod** and northern paintbrush are abundant, along with conical spruces. As the trail

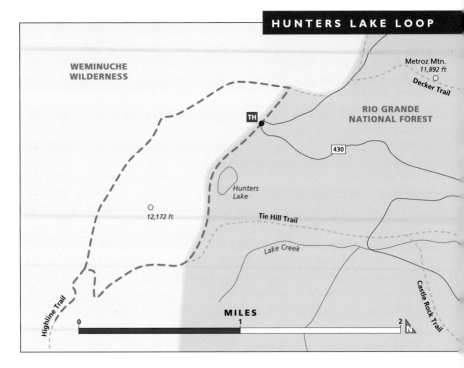

HUNTERS LAKE LOOP

WEMINUCHE
WILDERNESS

Metroz Mtn.
11,892 ft

Decker Trail

RIO GRANDE
NATIONAL FOREST

TH

430

Hunters
Lake

12,172 ft

Tie Hill Trail

Lake Creek

Highline Trail

Castle Rock Trail

MILES

0   1   2

N

ascends, look for **Rocky Mountain gentian**'s blue chalices in late summer, along with skinny **rockcress**, creamy **Parry lousewort**, **single-headed daisy**, and wine-colored **Whipple penstemon**. As it enters spruce forest, the trail offers shy **blue violet**, then angles uphill along the edge of the 12,172-foot mountain. Steep slopes and deep forest reveal sparse touches of color, such as **tall scarlet paintbrush**, Whipple penstemon, **purple fringe**, and the gold coins of **shrubby cinquefoil**. A cirque, circled by snowbanks, rises over spruces. In the foreground, a massive meadow is a good place to look for resident elk.

Table Mountain, your reward for the difficult grade, looms before you. The trail then switches from west to east, continuing its ascent to reach a wide saddle. A rock outcrop on the left signals a turn to the north. **Black-headed daisy**, with its fuzzy, dark hairs under white rays, blooms where early-season hikers would find **globeflower**.

Delicate Jacob's ladder and five-petaled **alpine avens** lead up to a sign indicating the Highline Trail. Take a left (westward) turn on this spur as it leads out of the trees and up to a marvelous vista and tundra. Be assured that the brief, if steep, climb is worthwhile.

You are rising on what is known as the Stairsteps, on the way to the Continental Divide; the upper Stairsteps are considered dangerous due to cliffs, but this description does not go that far. Watch boot placement as you ascend, noting alpine avens. Tundra is not easy to come by on day hikes in this part of the San Juans, and this example is a veritable wildflower treasure chest. **Moss campion**'s bright pink blossoms are the first gems to spill out, followed by tight mounds of **alpine sandwort** and **alpine sorrel**, with its kidney-shaped leaves and rusty red, winged seedpods. In the vicinity, look for **beetleaf** or **alpine senecio, king's crown** with its broad, brick red heads, old man of the mountains, and clumps of lovely Colorado blue columbine.

As the trail eases onto a grassy verge, look for tidy mounds of **rock** or **Fremont senecio** in its favorite lithic habitat, as well as **rockslide daisy**, succulent **alpine spring beauty**, and **frosty ball** or **Hooker thistle**, soft in appearance, but as prickly as any proper thistle.

Take in the gorgeous panorama, which sweeps in a full half circle, from lofty ridges to semicirques, and down into secluded meadows. Look here for **sky pilot**, charming with its blue-purple, trumpetlike blossoms, **alpine alum-root**, a cousin to coralbells, and **pygmy saxifrage**, with its tiny white flowers rising on thready stems. The rocky trail features fragrant **fernleaf candytuft** and **alpine phlox**. For a break, pause on the stony knob and enjoy the abbreviated cirque supporting the shoulder of Table Mountain. This connects to Sawtooth Mountain in the south.

Back on the trail, keep an eye out for **alpine chimingbells**' blue corollas, bicolored **alpine clover**, shrubby cinquefoil, diminutive **alpine cinquefoil**, and **pinnate-leaf daisy**. Watch for building thunderstorms, as you are exposed at this elevation.

Return to the main trail and head left (north), using caution while you descend. After rejoining the Hunters Lake Loop on the Highline in the forest, the next mile or so is shady and nearly flat. **Daffodil senecio**, alpine avens, **draba**, and **buttercup** perk up the spruce shade with yellow touches.

In an open area, the trail fades into a dryish meadow anchored by a rustic cairn that points to another cairn. Sassy alpine avens and waving American bistort accompany the trail toward spruces. Approaching a cairn near the meadow's end, the trail turns left into forest and encounters little pagodas of intensely pigmented Brandegee clover.

Still headed north, the trail passes a post and returns to spruce forest. The whites of bittercress and marsh marigold appear alongside tall chimingbells. As the trees thin, distant ranges appear to the east. A gentle turn along an open slope, once logged, offers beautiful views of these mountains. The gravelly slope yields **black-tipped senecio** and prone spergulastrum. Wallflower in four-petaled yellow competes with **orange sneezeweed** and **rosy pussytoes**. Looking toward the outcrops reveals tall scarlet paintbrush.

The trail continues through the forest, requiring hikers be on the alert for an obscure trail junction near the wilderness boundary, where the loop heads right (southward). Downed trees may mask the new direction, so be watching for the turn. If you should miss the turnoff, you will reach FR 430 eventually, but it means a longer hike back to your vehicle.

Wildflower Hike 5

Continental Divide Trail North from Lobo Overlook

Tundra at the beginning of the Continental Divide Trail from Lobo Overlook

Trail Rating	moderate
Trail Length	6 miles out and back
Location	San Juan National Forest/Weminuche Wilderness, southwest of South Fork
Elevation	11,750 to 11,000 feet
Bloom Season	late June to August
Peak Bloom	early July
Directions	From South Fork, take US 160 19.5 miles west. At Wolf Creek Pass, go right (north) at the signed turnoff and continue 3 miles to Lobo Overlook.

Lobo Overlook is a study in brilliant color. In July, vivid violet of Halls penstemon cascades down the rocky pitch below the overlook railing, while the panorama of the south San Juan Mountains stretches before you. From here, you can join the Continental Divide Trail—the CDT—as it heads northwest from the overlook. Once off the ridge, the trail generally continues westward, and follows a southern aspect that makes its bloom period earlier than one might expect. This description takes the CDT as far as the Weminuche Wilderness boundary.

Parking at the overlook features picnic tables and restrooms and is wide-open.

The short spur to Lobo Overlook is well trammeled, but hardy wildflowers such as vibrant, violet-blue **Halls penstemon, pinnate-leaf daisy, tonestus, alpine sunflower, alpine chimingbells,** and tenacious **alpine clover** thrive in the stony soil between the parking area and the overlook.

Walk up to the rail and peer over. The concentration of vivid Halls penstemon saturates the hillside with color. Near this high-elevation member of the snapdragon family, you might note **purple fringe, king's crown, wallflower,** and alpine sunflower along with other flowers already noted. After taking in the scenery, walk along the roadway to the tower and the signed CDT.

Between the overlook and the microwave tower is a low knoll. Almost paved with stone, it supports a collection of rock garden wildflowers such as wallflower, purple fringe, pinnate-leaf daisy, **beauty cinquefoil, fanleaf parsley,** a bit of bright rose **Brandegee clover,** and alpine sunflower, or **old man of the mountain.**

Purple fringe thrives in the disturbed lithic soil as hikers head northwest at the kiosk signs for the CDT. If a trekker were to follow all 3,200 miles of the CDT, they would pass through 25 national forests, 3 national parks, and 475 watersheds. With a few steps more, they would touch the boundaries of Canada and Mexico—or, in other words, they would travel the approximate distance from coast to coast of the United States.

Small spruces introduce king's crown, old man of the mountains, **wild candytuft, delicate Jacob's ladder, alpine speedwell, northern paintbrush,** and **alpine sandwort.** Continue the wildflower count as you prepare to enter a level stretch of tundra meadow. **Alpine violet** and **alpine parsley** are early-blooming inhabitants; late summer will boast powder-blue **Rocky Mountain gentian. Snow willow** hugs the ground with glossy leaves, gnarly gray branches, and oversized red catkins, inflorescences resembling cats' tails; "catkin" is derived from a Tudor word for kitten.

Among stunted spruce stands and tight willow carrs, look for the salmon, salverform blooms of **prickly mountain currant,** known in some circles as **red-fruited gooseberry.** Extremely thorny, these bushes may shelter **queen's crown.** As you negotiate a decline, a view of Wolf Creek Pass stretches out below. Just

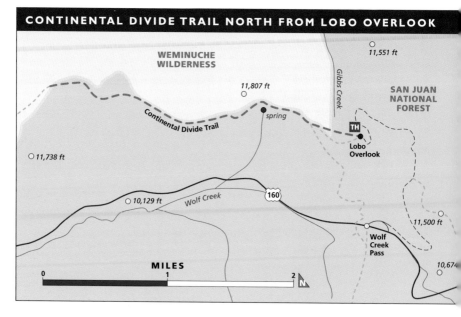

CONTINENTAL DIVIDE TRAIL NORTH FROM LOBO OVERLOOK

WEMINUCHE
WILDERNESS

11,551 ft

11,807 ft

Gibbs Creek

SAN JUAN
NATIONAL
FOREST

Continental Divide Trail

spring

TH

Lobo
Overlook

11,738 ft

10,129 ft   Wolf Creek

160

11,500 ft

Wolf
Creek
Pass

MILES

10,674

0   1   2

down from here, furry-leaved old man of the mountains faces east, ready for the rising sun.

The trail now wanders across the ridge to expose views to the left and right, and the accompanying willows may harbor cream-colored **globeflower**, or **trollius**, early in the season. At a post signed for the CDT, the ridgetop route comes to an almost sheer slope. Continue on to a meadow where sweet alpine violet is abundant and **pygmy bitterroot** cradles translucent pink starbursts within a nest of succulent, linear leaves.

The long-blooming and widespread alpine sandwort, affectionately known as **sandywinks**, joins sedges to take the trail over the willow-flanked ridge to the southwest side of the Continental Divide. On this southern aspect, spruces grow taller, with lavender delicate Jacob's ladder near their bases. A bit farther up the trail are the dainty, pink-tubed heads of **subalpine** or **hairy-fruit valerian**.

Ubiquitous **wild strawberry** leads up to king's crown, more tolerant of drier soil than his consort, queen's crown. **Tall chimingbells** indicate damper soil as the CDT continues toward flaming **tall scarlet paintbrush**. The steep downhill slope presents alpine chimingbells in blue, as well as omnipresent off-white **yarrow** and more scarlet paintbrush. Lemon-colored wallflower complements dusky purple **Whipple penstemon**. Purple fringe, with its exerted gold stamens, finds a happy roothold in the lithic soil.

Gazing across to almost 12,000-foot-high Treasure Mountain, be aware of rolling cones and stones as you continue to descend. Lichen-covered rocks signal the presence of vivid Brandegee clover, with pendant florets hanging like magenta jewels. On the angled sideslope, **black-tipped senecio**'s big, pale green, rubbery leaves look almost tropical, flourishing in the well-drained soil. The wildflower-covered slope serves as a colorful foreground for a beautiful, 180-degree panorama.

Guided by sweet-scented white **alpine phlox** cushions, round a bend into forest, which is soon followed by another slope. King's crown, **alpine sorrel**, white-umbelled **Porters lovage**, and pink **wild geranium** are visible here. In the swale below, look for a thick stand of **false hellebore**, with its pleated leaves.

As you enter the next sloped meadow, listen for the high-pitched squeaks of the pika, a rabbit relative with a ventriloquist voice. Thriving here is **Nuttalls gilia**, or **linanthastrum**, which features a loose collection of skinny, linear leaves and white flowers, resembling a small bush sprinkled with a galaxy's worth of stars. In the vicinity, minuscule blooms of **rock primrose** bounce on fine, wiry stems above tiny rosettes.

Nuttalls gilia, a member of the phlox family, is more prevalent as you approach a craggy, pale rust volcanic outcrop. In the outcrop area, watch for intense, blue-purple **subalpine larkspur** in a lush, palmate-leaved clump. Coil-headed **scorpionweed** grows nearby, as do cerise cups of **red globe anemone**.

Bushes of Nuttalls gilia lead to a rock garden on the right containing wall-flower, paintbrush, alpine chimingbells, and clingy alpine clover, draping over the rock. **Cutleaf or fernleaf fleabane** adds a lavender touch. These wildflowers tolerate and even thrive in the harsh formations, softening the sharp contours of their abode as eons of weather have not.

Traipsing through a colony of odd-smelling false hellebore introduces you to a remarkable plant found in Colorado's southwest quadrant: **Lushmoe**, or to be more formal, **Cases fitweed** or **corydalis**. In a single season, this member of the toxic fumitory family grows from the ground up to heights of 6 feet. Its lush, poppylike foliage, smooth to the touch, boasts terminal clusters of interesting, magenta-tipped ivory flowers. Also found

PRICKLY MOUNTAIN CURRANT
Ribes montigenum

The Latin species name of this member of the gooseberry clan means "mountain-born," signaling its preference for montane and subalpine dry spruce forests. Other common names, such as red-fruited gooseberry and red prickly currant, point to the wicked stem spines protecting the edible fruit, which was used by American Indians for teas, wine, and pemmican. The bristly fruits were rolled in hot ashes to remove the offending prickles. The saucer-shaped flowers, a soft pinkish-red, come in droopy racemes as does the ensuing fruit. Bushes can grow up to 3 feet high. The mapleleaf-like leaves are hairy, and the berries, granular.

in the moist conditions are tall chimingbells, subalpine valerian, and plate-sized heads of **cow parsnip**, all serving as vibrant foreground to Treasure Mountain.

Continuing through the hellebore brings hikers to a little spring, featuring tall chimingbells, rangy **triangleleaf senecio**, and more of the fascinating Cases fitweed. Subalpine larkspur makes a strong showing as well.

A grassy meadow of alpine violet, pygmy bitterroot, and alpine parsley takes hikers over a saddle, where a wooden sign announces your entry into the Weminuche Wilderness. A long view of many mountain ranges sends you back to the other side of the Divide. Find a handy log, have a snack on the spine of the United States, then retrace your steps back to Lobo Overlook.

The largest bloom on the tundra, old man of the mountains faces east to bask in the sun.

Continental Divide Trail South

*Wildflower
Hike 6*

*Interpretive signs introduce hikers to the Continental Divide
Trail, featuring many subalpine and alpine wildflowers.*

moderate to difficult	*Trail Rating*
5 miles out and back	*Trail Length*
San Juan National Forest, southwest of South Fork	*Location*
10,857 to 11,770 feet	*Elevation*
July to August	*Bloom Season*
mid-July	*Peak Bloom*
From South Fork, take US 160 19.5 miles west. Park at the kiosk on the south side of Wolf Creek Pass.	*Directions*

When visiting the popular parking area on 10,857-foot Wolf Creek Pass, most folks are content to snap their picture straddling a bronze strip that marks the Continental Divide. On one side, water flows east to the Gulf of Mexico, on the other, west to the Pacific Ocean. For the wildflowerist, the log-lined trail leading south along the Continental Divide Trail (CDT) invites further exploration. Though much of this CDT segment switchbacks its way up through conifer shade, the beginning meadow and the tundra on top feature subalpine and alpine flora. And the vistas are superb.

After crossing a well-watered meadow, the trail climbs 1,000 feet to a scenic point on the Great Divide. Flowery meadows begin the hike, a selection of tundra flowers highlight the middle, and an easy stroll along the Divide puts wildflowers and vistas at your disposal in the final section. Go in mid-July to net the widest variety of wildflowers.

Parking is generous, though in high demand, with most sightseers coming and going in short order. Conifers shade much of the way, but be aware of gathering thunderheads, especially when higher up the trail.

The world's most widespread plant success story has to be the ubiquitous **dandelion**. And here on Wolf Creek Pass, the perky golden heads begin the flower season, along with **senecio** and **marsh marigold**. At a footbridge, look for **homely buttercup**'s sparse petals and **bittercress** in clean white. Conifer shade provides a home for pale, lavender-blue **delicate Jacob's ladder**.

Crossing the entrenched waterway leads towards a confusing network of trails. While the Continental Divide Trail officially heads left, this description is going to take a brief jaunt to the right, to introduce meadow species before tackling the actual CDT.

Turning right takes you along a channeled waterway to find **bracted** or **fernleaf lousewort**, its creamy yellow helmets encircling a thick stem. While most louseworts typically sport fernlike foliage, **parrot's beak lousewort** has leaves that are uncut and smooth. Its white flowers bloom in evergreen shade, curling like an inverse **rams-horn**, another common name for this plant. As you continue on this spur, look for small, white, fragrant **mountain candytuft**.

The trail leads into a meadow splashed with white marsh marigold, **little pink elephants**, and **American bistort**. Creamy **globeflower** is finishing its seasonal appearance in the meadow in early summer. Tiny blue nosegays of **mountain violet** complement yellow buttercup. Late summer will offer rich blue **Rocky Mountain gentian**.

Before this spur starts upward, turn around. Take an immediate left after the footbridge onto the CDT, which soon makes a U-turn south and continues in this direction for the remainder of the hike. **Red-fruited gooseberry**, also called **prickly mountain currant**, opens its salverform, salmon-colored blossoms alongside **heartleaf arnica** and **few-flowered false Solomon's seal**.

The trail is soon flanked by willows, sheltering **blue violet** and palest yellow **northern paintbrush** as well as **cinquefoil**. Continue straight ahead, where a confusion of social trails crisscross the hillock. Conifers shade the way as you ascend, passing buttercup and **tall chimingbells**. **Mountain parsley** and **alpine hawksbeard** add scattered gold touches to the shade. Purple violet abounds with little competition early in the bloom season. **Sibbaldia**, also called **cloverleaf rose**, is an inconspicuous bloomer in the rose family and is most colorful in autumn when its toothed leaves become salmon colored.

The ascent steepens some, taking you by parrot's beak lousewort. Use the shaded switchbacks to climb, passing small pockets of **Porters lovage** with its whitish umbels, and plush tall chimingbells, a member of the borage family, displaying pink buds and blue tubes. A bit of **red-berried elder** accompanies the trail as its drifts from one side of the Divide to the other. Soon, grand views open up, while **poppy-leaved** or **subalpine buttercup** and **one-sided wintergreen** make an appearance.

Mount the "spine" via a trail that zigzags, keeping west of the Wolf Creek Ski Area. Enjoy the alpine vista here where the CDT runs on the north side of the pass. The view is foregrounded by globe-flower and rosy-tinted **tall scarlet paintbrush**, a hybrid, grows near chimingbells and **alpine avens**.

A wide, open zone is blanketed with prostrate **snow willow, snowball saxifrage, king's crown**, and avens. Sparscly flowered **broom huckleberry** dangles tiny bells that will turn into blue fruit. The trail is winding and narrow, skirting a rockfall. Look here for white **black-headed daisy**, so called because of the dark, woolly hairs on the phyllaries.

The reward for the ascent is a 180-degree panorama of the majestic San Juan Mountains, which run east and west, an anomaly within the Rockies' general north-south orientation. Another reward is the sunny head of the tundra's largest flowering plant, **old man of the mountains**.

OLD MAN OF THE MOUNTAINS
Rydbergia grandiflora

Also known as alpine sunflower, the oversized heads of old man of the mountains are the biggest blooms on the tundra. Aiming their toothed rays and broad, disk-flower center away from the prevailing winds, the showy flowers generally face the rising sun. Downy white hairs give the gray-green foliage a cobwebby look. The Latin genus name honors Per Axel Rydberg, a Swede who collected widely in Colorado, publishing works on Rocky Mountain flora.

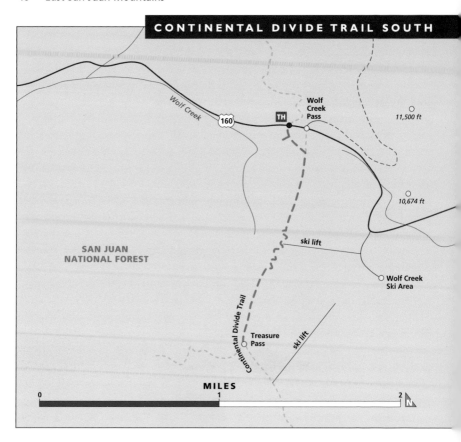

CONTINENTAL DIVIDE TRAIL SOUTH

Wolf Creek

160

Wolf Creek Pass

TH

11,500 ft

10,674 ft

ski lift

SAN JUAN
NATIONAL FOREST

Wolf Creek
Ski Area

Continental Divide Trail

Treasure
Pass

ski lift

MILES

0   1   2

The trail switchbacks to overlook a field of broken and jumbled rock. Along the precipitous edge, look for the gracefully spurred heads of **Colorado blue columbine**, framed by soft greenery. Here, lichens are at their tedious job of breaking down rock, and in doing so, creating pockets of soil that support lavender **fleabane daisy**, gold old man of the mountains, and alpine avens.

This hardscape suits the pika. At home in the lithic jumble, this little scurrying creature is a farmer, cutting "hay" for winter and storing it in his home under the rocks. Hikers may want to linger in this spot to listen and watch for the round-eared pika.

Look in the crevices and soil pockets nearby for mats of **dotted saxifrage** draping over the stone. Short specimens of **mountain death camas** may catch the eye, but it is the hot pink cushions of **moss campion** that command attention. Bits of yellow, such as **alpine parsley**, **Parry lousewort**, and the succulent-leaved **beetleaf senecio**, are also visible here.

After passing the ski lift station at 11,670 feet, stick close to a layered outcrop that features Colorado blue columbine, black-ringed **alpine pussytoes**, and alpine sorrel. This is a good spot to check the peaks for thunderheads.

Changing to the other side of the Divide, continue ahead into an area that boasts royal blue **Parry gentian** in late summer. In damp areas among spruce and willow, look for the five creamy petals of globeflower. A member of the purslane family, **pygmy bitterroot** looks like pink stars tucked into a nest of succulent, linear leaves. Snowball saxifrage is also in this area, with a shape that resembles a lollipop.

The trail continues through the forest to once again take you to the other side of the mountain. Check a dry scree area for **Whipple penstemon** and **fanleaf parsley**. Soon you arrive at another vista, this one of the south San Juans' extended escarpments and striated peaks.

Close at hand is **pinnate-leaf daisy**, a perky purple fleabane. More cinquefoil, parsley, **yellow stonecrop**, and **yarrow** serve as foreground for the grand view. Nearby, short but intense **alpine chimingbells**, **wallflower**, **alpine violet**, and **Brandegee clover**, with its intense, deep pink pendant florets, also thrive here.

King's crown leads the way to a cliff overlook, where a sign indicates Continental Divide Trail No. 813. You have officially arrived. The "spine" here is fairly flat and home to a gathering of old man of the mountains. Additionally, Parry lousewort, moss campion, **alpine sandwort**, American bistort, **purple fringe**, and other wildflowers decorate the panorama.

With the south San Juan Mountains in the background and lovely Lane Creek drainage before you, this makes a good place to turn around.

Wildflower Hike 7

West Fork San Juan Trail to West Fork Bridge

A footbridge spans the crystalline West Fork of the San Juan River.

After descending the west side of Wolf Creek Pass, you will see a Forest Service road heading north. A few miles down this road is the trailhead for West Fork Trail, sometimes referred to as the Rainbow Trail. Generally paralleling the West Fork of the San Juan River, it offers a variety of wildflowers and the chance to explore a portion of the 500,000-acre Weminuche Wilderness. With an entry elevation of 8,400 feet, this hike allows a fairly early start on the San Juan Mountains' hiking season.

The trail begins by following the West Fork Trail along an ascending road through about 1 mile of private property before entering the Weminuche

Trail Rating	easy to moderate
Trail Length	6 miles out and back to bridge
Location	San Juan National Forest/Weminuche Wilderness, southwest of South Fork and northeast of Pagosa Springs
Elevation	8,400 to 8,900 feet
Bloom Season	June to August
Peak Bloom	late June to early July
Directions	From South Fork, take US 160 west approximately 31 miles over Wolf Creek Pass to FR 648. Go right (north) on FR 648, which becomes FR 33, and proceed approximately 6 miles to the trailhead at the road's end.

Wilderness. Gaining moderate elevation, it continues up a forested drainage for about 3 miles to a sturdy footbridge. This description goes to the bridge, though for hardy hikers there is a popular hot springs area a couple miles farther on.

Wildflower species are plentiful and late June is good time to tally them with the help of a regional wildflower guide. Parking is adequate in a cleared space and restroom facilities are available near the trailhead.

As you leave the shaded parking area and pass the restroom, look for **tall coneflower**, or **goldenglow**, lifting its drooping blooms high over smooth, divided foliage. In the vicinity, check out frothy white **northern bedstraw**, a member of madder family, to which coffee also belongs. Bedstraw provided pioneers with sweet-scented mattress filling.

Wild geranium, once sought by resourceful American Indians for a spring potherb or birth control tea, blooms in pink. Tall and erect **Indian warriors**, or **fernleaf lousewort**, sports red-streaked, buff helmets on a stout stalk.

Meadowrue, or **false columbine**, shaded by Rocky mountain maple, leads up to a sign announcing private property. While the trail heads west, listen for the river to the east. Riparian habitat supports **cow parsnip**, **tall chimingbells**, and goldenglow, its prominent cones elongating with maturity.

Firs and spruces stand over colonizing **heartleaf arnica**, more leaf than sunny flower. Less showy is toxic **baneberry**, with its filmy white inflorescences. **False Solomon's seal** displays a crooked stem with leathery leaves, ending in a raceme of fine, creamy stars. **White violet** adds a demure touch as well. The roadway ascends at a fairly steep pitch as **dogbane**'s little bells ring the base of an outcrop on the left.

After a challenging start, the trail levels where perky **fleabane daisy** sports thin rays. Crossing a small tributary brings shrublike **thimbleberry**, with its few white flowers perched in a mass of big maple-shaped leaves. Signs then direct the West Fork Trail to the right. A small water hazard is crossed on stones, or a log, where you may view the less common giant ladyfern. These plush clumps boast fronds about 3 feet long; in ideal conditions, they may be up to 4 feet long.

The route takes on more of a wagon-road character as it goes left, up West Fork Canyon. **Narrowleaf paintbrush** may be skinny, but it's easily visible in scarlet, each bright calyx displaying a chartreuse, toothpicklike flower. A rocky incline, followed by a brief drop, is home to **creeping grapeholly**, or **mahonia**; early-season hikers will find it bright with fragrant yellow flower clusters that become tart, blue-black berries. Whereas most louseworts have fernlike leaves, upcoming **parrot's beak lousewort**, or **rams-horn**, has whole leaves. Also known as **coiled beak lousewort**, this forest dweller is a member of the snapdragon or figwort family, as is paintbrush.

Along another rocky pitch, look for **many-rayed goldenrod** and **aspen sunflower**. **Twinberry honeysuckle** grows near early-blooming **western red columbine** and, farther up, **harebell**. Nearby, a small pond feeds an outlet for the West Fork of the San Juan River. Narrowing to a single-track route, the trail passes electric blue damselflies that relish the lush vegetation that grows high above the river.

A sign marks the end of the mile-long private property segment. A well-watered ravine introduces **Cases fitweed**, or **corydalis**. This Amazonian-looking member of the fumitory family grows like a weed, attaining heights of 6 or 7 feet in the short high-country growth season. The poppylike, smooth foliage terminates in showy bloom clusters, looking like pyramids of bowing, ivory-gowned ballerinas in purple tiaras.

CASES FITWEED
Corydalis caseana

Related to bleeding heart, Cases fitweed grows up to 7 feet tall every year. The inflorescences are pyramidal white blossoms with purplish beaks. Abundant in southwestern Colorado's spruce-fir forests, aspen copses, and even in sodden soil in the open, this member of the fumitory family boasts blue-green, poppylike leaves. *Corydalis* is Greek for "crested lark," while the species name honors the plant's discoverer, Professor E. L. Case.

Small creeks support tall chimingbells, lanky **twistedstalk**, and lacy **cowbane**. As you get closer to the damp zone, **triangleleaf senecio** appears, with its mop of gold flowers. Forest duff highlights native **Coulter daisy**'s narrow white rays.

A lovely stand of quaking aspens leads to a mass of **false hellebore**, which is poisonous even to pollinating bees. More Cases fitweed grows above **red onion**. **Orange sneezeweed**'s gold rays appear near the palmate leaves of **beauty cinquefoil**, each yellow petal base marked with an orange beauty mark.

Continuing among bracken fern interspersed with **white peavine** and lush tall chimingbells, look for tiger swallowtail butterflies, but also keep an eye out for mosquitos. Fortunately, mosquitos are rather territorial, so hikers can outmarch them.

Soon, you reach the sign for the Weminuche Wilderness, with the West Fork pitching down between two huge boulders. A footbridge presents shade-loving **blue violet** and western red columbine. **Serviceberry** bushes—their edible blue-black fruit still green in early summer—accompany the rising and rocky trail, along with **wild rose** and **mountain parsley**.

The route eases for a short distance before ascending again into a grove of stately aspens. **Monkshood** thrives in little seeps, which also nurture cowbane and **yellow monkeyflower**. Tropical-looking, mint green clumps of **green gentian** send up stout stalks, displaying flowers the same hue as the leaves.

A rocky outcrop on the left, topped by a big spruce, is the place to spot western red columbine about mid-June. False columbine abounds in the shade, while a mossy seep is home not only to yellow monkeyflower, but **bishop's cap**, or **green mitrewort**, a saxifrage family member. A hand lens reveals the maroon tracery of the minuscule snowflake flowers.

Continue on to find baneberry, its frothy spires giving way to glossy red or occasionally white berries. Also visible are **red-berried elder**, Cases fitweed, and the graceful giant ladyfern. Uphill, near worn lumps of crude breccia, **subalpine larkspur** shows its royal purple-blue blooms.

A falls offers another chance to study bishop's cap. Nearby are the flowers of **redtwig dogwood**, which will mature into pale berries later in the season. The route then passes outcrops of volcanic breccia, then crosses a creek, where **Hornemanns willowherb** and more bishop's cap thrive in the moisture.

Four descending switchbacks bring you to the river. The trail continues downward, passing a switchback where aromatic-leaved **aletes**, a parsley, produces tight yellow umbels. Here, too, are mats of **dotted saxifrage** creeping over rough rock.

Beware of rolling stones underfoot along this part of the trail. Monkey-flower enlivens a second switchback, while in the damp soil nearby is **self-heal**, a member of the mint family. **Bittercress**' snowy, four-petaled blooms make a showing as well. As the trail nears the West Fork of the San Juan River, look for western red columbine.

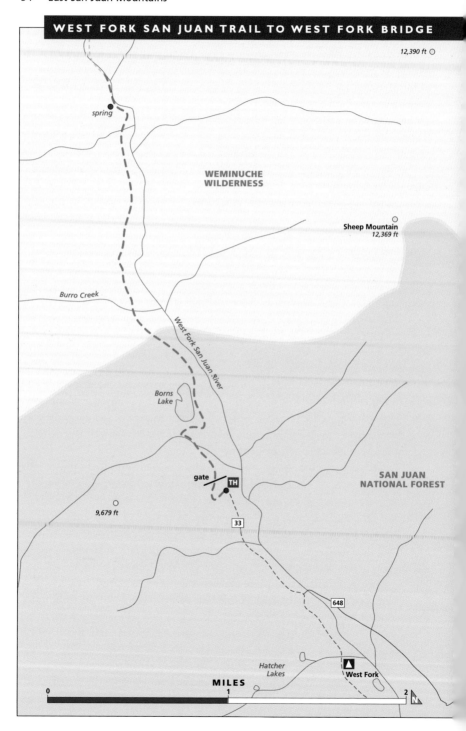

12,390 ft ○

spring

WEMINUCHE
WILDERNESS

Sheep Mountain
12,369 ft

Burro Creek

West Fork San Juan River

Borns
Lake

gate   TH

SAN JUAN
NATIONAL FOREST

9,679 ft

33

648

Hatcher
Lakes

West Fork

MILES

0   1   2

Traveling alongside the river, the route takes you past thimbleberry, heartleaf arnica, **black-tipped senecio**, **gooseberry**, and false Solomon's seal, which takes its name from the signet-ring shape of the leaf scars. A sturdy footbridge spans the West Fork of the San Juan, where dotted saxifrage drapes over outcrops above the clear river. The waterway will eventually empty into slickrock desert. There, it becomes a sediment-laden flow that ends in Lake Powell, although its waters will ultimately pass through Glen Canyon Dam and into the Colorado River.

Take a moment to enjoy the water from the bridge railing or perhaps edge down through small boulders to the river's banks. You may decide to turn around at this point. Beyond the bridge, the trail gets rougher, following the rocky streambed before arriving at a smaller footbridge.

The beginning of the West Fork Trail

Wildflower Hike 8

Upper Box Piedra River

Clear and cold, the Middle Fork of the Piedra River carves its way through a box.

Trail Rating	easy
Trail Length	3 miles out and back
Location	San Juan National Forest, northwest of Pagosa Springs
Elevation	7,650 to 7,500 feet
Bloom Season	June to August
Peak Bloom	late June
Directions	From Pagosa Springs, head west on US 160 2.5 miles to FR 631, also called Piedra Rd. Turn right (north) and continue 15 miles to the Piedra River Trailhead. The trailhead and parking area are located on the left (west) side of the road.

This hike along the upper Piedra River follows a short, easily accessed trail segment and offers riverside walking through an open-ended "box," wider than it is deep. Located about 15 miles north of Pagosa Springs, the north Piedra River Trailhead takes you down to river level, staying within sight, and certainly sound, of the rushing waters most of the way.

The trail begins easily, then gets a bit more rugged as it heads down to the box; overall, it is relatively genial, with the exception of trailside patches of poison ivy to watch out for. The wildflowers are varied as the trail passes through xeric zones, seeps, rock crevices, and conifer shade. A level parking area shared by anglers also accommodates hikers' vehicles.

Above the tops of narrowleaf cottonwoods lining the Piedra River, a view north highlights the San Juans and rolling ranchland. Heading south from the parking area, the yellow blooms of **shrubby cinquefoil** and pink **wild geranium** start off the trail.

At the trail sign, look for **pink plumes** and a contrasting patch of blue **Rocky Mountain penstemon**. On the whitish end of the spectrum, look for **yarrow**, **edible valerian**, and **fleabane daisy**, accented by a bit of **scarlet gilia**. **Wild rose** appears as the trail travels above the river in a fairly xeric zone. Rocky Mountain penstemon's violet-tinged, dark blue tubes punctuate the scene.

Not assertive and almost dainty in flowering is **redroot buckwheat**. Tiny, reddish-pink flowers delicately cluster on the ends of bare, branched stems that may be as tall as 2 feet, rising from a clump of woolly basal leaves. **Silvery cinquefoil** and **pussytoes** grow on the hillside below the prolific invader **butter and eggs**. **Many-flowered puccoon** leads up to an aspen copse, interspersed with **silvery lupine**'s pea-flowered, blue-purple spires.

Near an interpretive sign for river otters, look for **Parry** or **Rocky Mountain gentian**, typically a late-summer bloomer. Winding its bright magenta, pea-type flowers around its neighbors, **American vetch** is sometimes, for obvious reasons, called **climbing vetch**. Watch also for **red globe anemone**, and pink plumes in damper soils.

REDROOT BUCKWHEAT
Eriogonum racemosum

Tiny white flowers gather in narrow-sprayed racemes on bare stems that may rise about 2 to 3 feet. Each minute petal is pink-ribbed underneath; the flowers age to a rusty tint. Woolly-haired leaves, mostly basal, sport petioles, or leafstalks, almost as long as the oblong blades. Fond of oak and ponderosa companions, redroot buckwheat is a distant cousin to rhubarb.

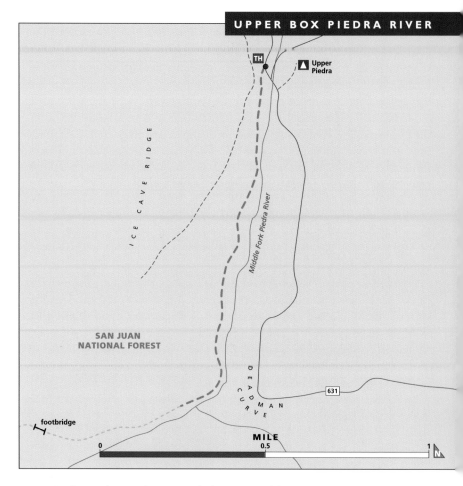

As the trail meanders toward the river, **golden aster** is visible along the edges. Also popping up in verdant patches is poison ivy: Remember the maxim "leaves of three, leave them be," and give this toxic plant a wide berth.

Wild blue flax is best viewed in the morning hours, when it blooms in sky blue. Bright red scarlet gilia and dark blue Rocky Mountain penstemon make a dynamic entry to the head of the Piedra River's upper box. The tread, uneven as it passes over rocky stretches, is enlivened by more Rocky Mountain penstemon, blooming in a blue so intense, it looks straight from the artist's tube. Forming colorful clumps, this flamboyant species adapts well to many habitats, from damp to dry, including the home flower garden.

An outcrop of shelf rock supports **wild raspberry**; the fruit is delicious— just ask the wildlife that depend upon it. A brief rocky rise introduces tiny-flowered **Indian hemp**, a lanky member of the dogbane family. Perfumed wild rose flourishes at the base of a slanted outcrop. Be sure to stop and enjoy its intoxicating scent—though don't forget to check for bees first!

The river grows louder as you enter the limestone gorge. Toward the water, note a slab of rock with petrified ripple marks from a long-gone sea. The trail forks; aim toward the Piedra River on the left fork. Be on the watch for the American dipper, or water ouzel, which likes to fly just above the waters, then dip into them for dinner.

Spruces increase as the box walls close in. Golden silt softens the trail, and frothy white **northern bedstraw** indicates a damper habitat that also nurtures **tall chimingbells**. **Slender-flowered gooseberry**, with its tiny bristles, likes canyon walls such as those rising beside you. Carved over the eons, the crevices of the gorge support wildflower species such as **king's crown**, which survives despite the harsh conditions. A small ascent takes hikers up into scrub oak punctuated by the lemon-yellow blossoms of **common evening primrose**.

Giants blocks of limestone, levered from the walls, show vestiges of dark desert varnish. A gnarled old spruce along the river's edge shelters **meadowrue**. **Stinging nettle** appears as the gorge tightens. **Twinberry honeysuckle** bushes lead to **alumroot**. While not showy, the light yellowish-green inflorescence rises on a bare stem over a rosette of scalloped leaves. Once, alumroot juices were used to make an invisible ink that could only be read under running water. **Red-berried elder** and white-headed **cow parsnip** are also visible here.

Continuing on, look for **few-flowered false Solomon's seal**, also known as **star Solomon's seal**. Growing under overhanging cliffs, wonderful pink wild rose sends its aroma wafting. Mineralized precipitates on a trailside cliff produce a white deposit on the sheer walls. Among the loose rocks, keep an eye out for bright **fireweed**.

Continuing higher above the Piedra now, the trail meets a lush glade of tall chimingbells and meadowrue, overhung with wild raspberry. Very early-blooming **yellow wintercress**, a mustard clan member, hangs on in the cool depths. The composition of the rock changes to more of a sandstone character.

The canyon box opens to a bunchgrass slope that supports **harebell** and hot pink wild geranium. Keep a poison ivy lookout as you descend a bit alongside vertical walls. When you look down toward the river, check the slope for the occasional **sego** or **mariposa lily**, spreading its showy petals over grasslike foliage. Underground, the small bulb spent three to five years maturing before it sent up the bloom you now see. The pinkish blossoms of **four o'clock** look over snowy **mouse-ears**, each petal notched to resemble the namesake rodent.

Heading gently downhill, the trail finds **thimbleberry**, a member of the rose family with lots of big leaves but few white blossoms. At river level, the grade is flat through a meadow sporting scarlet gilia and lots of edible valerian.

Parallel the Piedra River in the company of more oleander-related Indian hemp and **candle anemone**. The name of the latter refers to the seedhead, which elongates upon maturity. A brief stint above the river takes you to a grassy meadow, with a sandy trail underfoot. If the river calls to you, plan to pause for a snack before returning the way you came.

Wildflower Hike 9

Williams Creek Trail

An aerobic start to the Williams Creek Trail takes hikers to quiet meadows.

Trail Rating	moderate to difficult
Trail Length	6 miles out and back
Location	San Juan National Forest/Weminuche Wilderness, north of Pagosa Springs
Elevation	8,400 to 9,300 feet
Bloom Season	June to August
Peak Bloom	early to mid-July
Directions	From Pagosa Springs, travel west on US 160 approximately 2.5 miles, taking a right (north) onto FR 631, also called Piedra Rd. Follow FR 631 22 miles to Williams Lake Rd./FR 640 and go right (north). The trailhead is located at the end of the road, just under 5 miles from the turnoff.

Beginning in a level forest, it doesn't take Williams Creek Trail No. 587 long to increase in grade. Then it's a steady climb above the stream for about 1 mile before the trail eases again. Waist-high bunchgrass interspersed with wildflowers fills the meadows. Creek crossings, each spanned by huge logs, require both good boots and good balance. The creek fills Williams Creek Reservoir, the scenic lake you passed on the way to the trailhead. Wildflowers vary with the amount of sun and moisture available, and habitats range from dry, lithic soil, to verdant meadows, to riparian environments and sparse forest understory.

Sign the trail register before beginning Williams Creek Trail, initially shaded by mixed conifers and aspens and decorated with **mountain parsley**'s yellow blossoms and the fine rays of **fleabane daisy**. Look for **wild geranium**'s five pink petals near the signs stating trail mileage and designating entrance into the Weminuche Wilderness.

The trail starts out rocky and slightly uphill, but soon levels out before beginning a much more serious climb, which soon changes to an easygoing tread. Enjoy the impressive views of volcanic peaks.

On the left, a steep scree slope supports **umbrellawort**, but it takes a keen eye to spot it before its lucent pink flowers open in the afternoon. A member of the four o'clock family, this spindly, spare-leaved wildflower may be easier to spot on the return hike. **Spotted coralroot orchid**, devoid of chlorophyll but sporting exquisite miniature blooms with speckled lips, occasionally pops up under evergreens.

The incline continues, showcasing occasional **orange sneezeweed**. Kitten-paw-soft when new, **pussytoes** likes the lithic soil and grows in mats of evergreen leaves. When you top out out at last, at about the 1-mile mark, take a moment to relax and rehydrate. When you are ready start again, be sure to look for **cinquefoil** and **buckthorn**, a low, spiky relative

TALL CHIMINGBELLS
Mertensia ciliata

Smooth, blue-green leaves line stems that grow up to 4 feet tall, each sporting pendant clusters of pink buds that morph into blue corollas, although some specimens remain all pink. Also called mountain blue-bells, this lush wildflower favors wet places, especially streamsides in the montane, subalpine, and lower alpine zones. Popular elk forage, this member of the borage family was named for F. K. Mertens, a botanist from Germany.

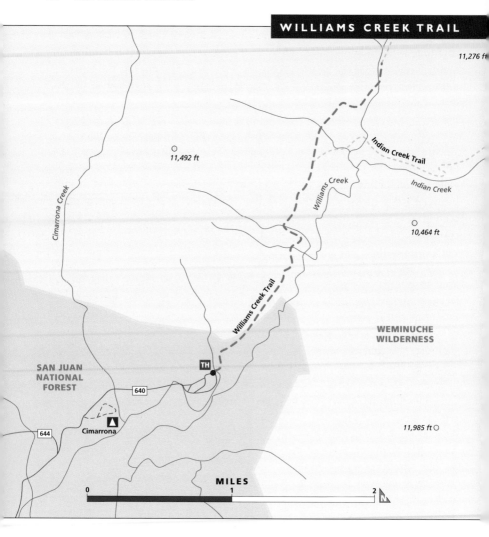

WILLIAMS CREEK TRAIL

11,276 ft

○
11,492 ft

Indian Creek Trail

Williams Creek

Indian Creek

○
10,464 ft

Williams Creek Trail

WEMINUCHE
WILDERNESS

Cimarrona Creek

TH

SAN JUAN
NATIONAL
FOREST

640

644

Cimarrona

11,985 ft ○

MILES

0   1   2

of the lilac defined by sharp branchlets and myriad minuscule flowers gathered into aromatic clusters.

Continue along on the south aspect, which suits **many-flowered puccoon**, one of the borage bunch; this one dangles golden tubes. Early-season hikers see **creeping grapeholly**'s vibrant yellow blooms, which mature into tart, bluish-black berries. Its bright yellow root was once used medicinally and may be again, as research confirms it works as a treatment for malaria.

Evergreens provide shade; **scarlet gilia** provides color. Also known as **sky rocket**, this biennial flowers high over a snowflake rosette, attractive but skunky-smelling when its foliage is rubbed. Aspens shade **early fleabane**'s pale lavender rays and the charming **Colorado blue columbine**, the state flower, with sweet, honeysuckle-scented blossoms.

Climbing gently on a steady rise, the trail shelters **meadowrue**, or **false columbine**, whose leaf shape resembles true columbines. **Many-rayed goldenrod** lends a gold hue. At this point, the river passes through a canyon of breccia—crude, welded ash—far below. The San Juan Mountains are visible in the distance. At a switchback comes an opportunity to view the carved canyon, but be extremely cautious as the edge is dangerously abrupt.

After heading east, the trail switches to a westerly direction. Dropping into a ravine over loose stones brings you to a welcome zone of moisture, supporting **tall chimingbells**, **cow parsnip**, and **white geranium**. A small rivulet nurtures **yellow monkeyflower**, whose emerald leaves were once used to soothe rope burns. A ledgy rockface draped with moss sustains mats of **dotted saxifrage**, each little white star flecked with red specks. Look in the damp soil for lacy **cowbane** and snowy **bittercress**. **Wild raspberry** doesn't offer showy blooms, but its ripe fruit is delicious.

Cross the small creek on convenient stones to begin the next climb and keep an eye out for many-flowered puccoon on the embankment. Drift down to encounter fragrant **wild rose**. Perking up the scene are the bright-colored rays of **heartleaf arnica**.

Progressing more easily now, the trail curves into another ravine, this one slighter larger and populated by wild geranium, wild rose, and more arnica. This a good place to look for **western red columbine**'s hanging lanterns, or perhaps a specimen or two of spotted coralroot orchid.

Hugging the stream is **thimbleberry**, with its oversized maplelike leaves. Cow parsnip's umbels, wide and flat as saucers, are made up of countless tiny flowers. Tall chimingbells present pink buds opening to blue bells. As the trail follows the streambed for a stretch, look for cheerful yellow monkeyflower and the blue flowers of **alpine veronica**.

By a rock face, prepare to ascend again. Alders and Rocky Mountain maples throw shade on **tall coneflower**, or **goldenglow**. **Sweet cicely**'s helicopter seedheads lead to a switchback. **Wild strawberry** is ubiquitous, and Williams Creek Trail features two varieties—the blue-green or glaucous-leaved wild strawberry and the plain green **woodland strawberry**. **American vetch** appears after the switchbacks, as does **Indian warriors**, a sturdy lousewort with helmet-like blossoms.

Easing, the route encounters **mountain death camas** before leveling off entirely. A downhill segment takes you past **twinflower**, a member of the honey-suckle family. Each set of pale pink, paired bells hangs above a creeping evergreen mat of tiny, lime-colored leaves.

Rising again, the trail comes across **green-flowered wintergreen**, featuring small but broad bells the color and shape of pattypan squash, as well as cow parsnip, goldenglow, and deep purple-blue **subalpine larkspur**. Hot pink wild rose wafts an intoxicating perfume, while yellow monkeyflower, cowbane, **twistedstalk**, and **pink willowherb** thrive along the streambank.

The route heads into a sunny expanse, where American vetch and orange sneezeweed grow among thick grasses. This trail segment is flat as it passes grass-covered slopes. Look for **alumroot, white violet,** and subalpine larkspur. Meadow bunchgrass is accented by more orange sneezeweed and **red onion.**

At approximately mile 2, the meadow lengthens. Look for a junction sign where the Indian Creek Trail goes right (east); the Williams Creek Trail described here continues ahead on the left fork. Pleated leaves of poisonous **false hellebore,** or **cornhusk lily,** serve as background for **orange agoseris, yarrow,** and fragrant **northern bedstraw.** Related to coffee, its white frothy flowers define a plant that, in dire circumstances, might be roasted as a coffee substitute.

As you enter mixed woods, look for more larkspur, as well as the moisture-loving **monkshood, triangleleaf senecio,** cowbane, and bittercress. Horsetails herald the appearance of delicately flowered **bishop's cap,** or **green mitrewort.** If you have a lens with you, look at the snowflake tracery of this saxifrage family member. **Green bog orchid** shows up in the wet moss, as does **yellow avens.**

The trail opens into a grand meadow where aspens overlook **leafy Jacob's ladder.** Look also for **wild iris, shrubby cinquefoil,** red onion, and yellow-tinted **paintbrush.** At the meadow's end, the path ascends to a saddle in a forested spot, brightened by heartleaf arnica and western red columbine.

From here, the trail descends to meet Williams Creek. Look for **twin-berry honeysuckle** and **Porters lovage,** a medicinal plant used by American Indians. Deep in conifer shade on a bank, you might find the heavily veined leaves of an unusual wintergreen, **spotted shinleaf.**

And then you arrive at the river. Head right to find a hefty log spanning the noisy torrent. If you choose to cross, don't hesitate to scoot across instead of walking on the log's rounded top. On the north bank, watch for western red columbine and Colorado blue columbine near an eroded rock. Farther on, a stream to the right is flanked by the same combination.

Views soon open up on the left as the trail crosses loose rock. Along the way, **tall scarlet paintbrush, alpine chimingbells,** and a bit of **mountain** or **wild candytuft** may be in bloom. Look also for the less common **one-sided white mitrewort,** also known as **side-flowered mitrewort** or, affectionately, **sleighbells.**

Prickly mountain currant opens the way to a bunchgrass meadow with horizontally striated cliffs rising behind. Here, you encounter another stream crossing. The horse ford is obvious; less apparent is a log span a little farther on. If you choose not to cross here, this makes a good turnaround point. On the stream's near side, up a bit from the horse ford, look for **Cases fitweed,** or **corydalis,** sometimes locally called **lushmoe.** It rises up to 6 feet here, present-ing a packed spire of purple-tongued, ivory flowers.

Weminuche Trail via Poison Park Trailhead

A wide meadow dotted with orange sneezeweed showcases rugged peaks.

easy to moderate	**Trail Rating**
5 miles out and back	**Trail Length**
San Juan National Forest/Weminuche Wilderness, northwest of Pagosa Springs	**Location**
9,210 to 8,500 feet	**Elevation**
late June to August	**Bloom Season**
early to mid-July	**Peak Bloom**
From Pagosa Springs, travel west 2.5 miles on US 160 to Piedra Rd., also called FR 631. Turn right (north) and continue 22 miles. Take a right (north) onto Williams Lake Rd./FR 640 and go 3.5 miles to FR 644, which branches off to the left (west). Follow this road for about 3 miles to the Poison Park Trailhead.	**Directions**

With a name like Poison Park for a trailhead, it is a wonder anyone goes there. But not only is this trailhead used by hikers, it's even more popular with horseback riders. Located a little over 30 miles northwest of Pagosa Springs via a wonderfully scenic route, the Weminuche Trail No. 592 from Poison Park is a favorite of local wildflower enthusiasts. Big aspens and mixed conifer forest shade much of the trail on the way to an open meadow, where, in the northeast, Cimarrona Peak summits at 12,577 feet.

The trail descends from the start, eases through the Hossick Creek area, and dips into a pretty meadow surrounded by primeval-looking forest. Over about 2.5 miles, the route loses close to 800 vertical feet, regained on the return via gentle switchbacks.

Plush pockets of wildflowers flank the trail. Expect different species in the well-watered, aspen-shaded places than in drier conifer areas or sunny meadows.

Parking, possibly shared by some good-sized horse trailers, is generous. Restrooms are a welcome addition. Afternoon thunderstorms are the norm in the summer, so aim for an early start.

After enjoying the rainbow of wildflowers on the spur road to the trailhead, be ready for more along the parking area's east boundary. Thriving here are **orange sneezeweed**, **tall chimingbells**, **yarrow**, **wild geranium**, **tall western larkspur**, and **leafy Jacob's ladder**. **Wild rose** adds its perfumed blossoms to this mix as well.

On the way to the trailhead sign, check for parsley family members **cow parsnip** and **Porters lovage**, a rangy white umbellate native that bears close resemblance to import poison hemlock.

Near the trail register are the yellow, snowflakelike umbels of **mountain parsley**. After the sign-in, the trail passes through a gently sloping meadow sporting **red onion**, **false hellebore**, wild geranium, and **Rocky Mountain gentian**, with its electric blue blossoms at their peak in late summer.

Grasses abound, framing **tall coneflower**, or **goldenglow**, as well as subalpine larkspur's regal, blue-purple spurred blooms. Nearby, **shrubby cinquefoil** and **senecio** display yellow petals. **American vetch** winds itself among them with its violet-magenta pea flowers.

Note **northern bedstraw's** frothy inflorescence; it is related to the coffee plant. White **Coulter daisy** appears as well. Early-season hikers enjoy showy **wild iris**. Ubiquitous **fleabane daisy** dots the ground.

Heading downhill, the trail re-enters a mixed wood of mature aspens and conifers. Loose stones, dislodged by numerous horseshoes, cover the route as it passes **orange agoseris**. Here a coppery color, in lower elevations it is often brighter and known as **tall burnt orange false dandelion**. **White peavine** likes the quaking aspen shade, which also covers subalpine larkspur and tall chimingbells, with its pink bud and blue corolla. The damp ground is also the place to spot **meadowrue**, or **false columbine**, so called because of its leaf shape.

Watch carefully for **Colorado blue columbine**. Showy and slightly scented, it overshadows drab **waterleaf**. A stand of intense blue-purple subalpine larkspur rises en masse, complemented by tall coneflower. Cow parsnip and tall chiming-bells thrive near a tiny trickle from the right.

Still meandering among giant aspens, the trail showcases **Indian warriors**, or **fernleaf lousewort**, populating the understory. These strapping members of the snapdragon family put forth buff-colored, reddish-streaked helmets on a sturdy stalk. As the route curves into a shallow ravine, early-season hikers should also look for paper-white **bittercress**.

Be on the watch for a somewhat bushy plant that produces opaque, glassy berries; **baneberry** produces red or white berries, both of which are poisonous. Nearby, terminal clusters of leafy Jacob's ladder add lavender hues, but beware of crushing the foliage, which gives off a distinctive, skunky smell. The understory supports tall western larkspur, much rangier than its subalpine cousin, and more tolerant of drier conditions as well. Delphinium family members such as larkspur are toxic.

Small forest openings reveal glimpses of the Weminuche Valley, named after a band of Ute Indians. **Heartleaf arnica** lightens the shadows with showy blossoms. Big-leaved **thimbleberry** is parsimonious with its white blossoms, while vivid pink wild rose generously perfumes the air.

Spruces dominate a section of trail where frivolous-looking **tansy mustard** displays a yellow profusion of minuscule, four-petaled flowers so small, the observer might need a magnifying lens. Almost as tiny are the blooms of **rock primrose**, held up by fine stems.

A downward curve offers a view of volcanic peaks to the north. At a switch-back, look for the hanging blossoms of **western red columbine**, each red-spurred bloom enclosing soft yellow sepals.

False Solomon's seal greets early-season hikers on a slope that is filled with

TALL CONEFLOWER
Rudbeckia ampla

More lyrically called goldenglow, this tall sunflower family member may grow up to 7 feet high. Surrounded by 2-inch lax rays, the prominent cone of disk flowers elongates with age. Smooth, divided leaves emerge from sturdy stems. Found in foothills and montane elevations from Montana to New Mexico, it is reportedly poisonous to domestic livestock such as sheep, pigs, and cattle. Partial to streamsides, tall coneflower honors Olaf Rudbeck and his son, also Olaf Rudbeck, both 18th-century Swedish botanists.

heartleaf arnica and **mountain death camas**, its purplish-green buds clinging to a shepherd's crook stalk that will straighten as the buds open. Underground is a darkly netted bulb responsible for the plant's name. Early American Indians called it **poison onion**.

By this time, the name Poison Park sounds plausible, given the list of toxic inhabitants. And you can add one more: Blush-colored **dogbane** also appears in the vicinity.

As the trail continues its descent, look for **Canada violet** and western red columbine. Aiming northwest now, enjoy the occasional views of the mountain crests. Switching back again, your heading is momentarily south, passing more baneberry before continuing north once more. On the upside of the trail, **pink-headed daisy**, with its fuzzy, angora-like buds, puts in an appearance. Damper conditions also support tall coneflower and subalpine larkspur, which make a complementary pairing.

The sound of running water sends hikers down a truncated path to the sound's source, where you find **cowbane**, western red columbine, **sweet cicely**, and **twinberry honeysuckle**. Alders, maples, and **redtwig dogwood** shade wild geranium and tall chimingbells. Lined with logs now, the trail exposes **monkshood**, sometimes called **friar's cap**, and its locally prolific cousin, larkspur, both poisonous members of the delphinium family. By this point, the hike could be labeled the "Larkspur Trail," so abundant is the flamboyant flower.

The trail is alternately rocky and muddy as it moves through mixed conifer woods. As aspens increase, head-high bracken ferns accompany substantial clumps of richly hued larkspur and orange sneezeweed. Early-season hikers enjoy the elegance of wild iris.

To the east, the trail offers a glimpse of a ridged mountain through an aspen copse. Box elder trees signal an upcoming view of the upper Weminuche Valley. To the west is Weminuche Creek, which sustains this ranching valley.

At a pasture fence, the volcanic ridges that you have caught only partial glimpses of are now plainly visible. Morning sun encourages the azure petals of **wild blue flax** to open. The stems of these sparsely foliaged plants enclose tough fibers utilized by American Indians for cordage, nets, and snares.

At mile 2, the trail comes to the junction with the Hossick Creek Trail. Turn toward an irrigation ditch to find graceful wild iris near the fence; cattle do not like this tough plant with its toxic roots. The offshoot of Hossick Creek presents a challenge to cross at the horse ford; hikers might want to check upstream for a convenient fallen tree trunk to span the stream, or brave souls can wade through the cold flow.

Once this obstacle is crossed, Weminuche Trail passes through an aspen copse, then forest as it approaches Hossick Creek proper. A shallow ford, bedded by colorful stones, takes hikers to the sign for the Weminuche Wilderness, 500,000 acres set aside in perpetuity.

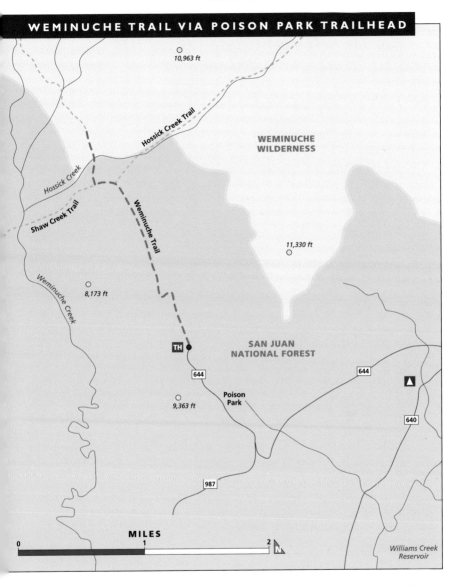

After navigating a stretch of rough, rocky tread, you are rewarded by entry into a vast meadow, with ragged mountains rising as high as 12,605 feet to the north. To the east is 12,577-foot Cimarrona Peak. The grassy slopes are home to **harebell**, American vetch, and orange sneezeweed, as well as **red-berried elder** bushes and patches of wild iris.

Whether in the sun or in conifer shade, find a place to rest and enjoy the scenic site. This is also a good spot to turn around for the uphill hike back to the Poison Park Trailhead.

*Wildflower
Hike 11*

Squaw Creek Trail

*Sweetvetch appears often along Squaw Creek Trail,
which accommodates both hikers and riders.*

Trail Rating	moderate
Trail Length	8 miles out and back
Location	Rio Grande National Forest/Weminuche Wilderness, southwest of Creede
Elevation	9,400 to 10,000 feet
Bloom Season	June to August
Peak Bloom	early to mid-July
Directions	From Creede, take CO 149 west approximately 20 miles to FR 520, also called Rio Grande Rd. Bear left (west) onto FR 520 and follow it 12 miles to Thirtymile Campground. Go left over the bridge to the parking area on the right.

The Creede area boasts a plethora of hiking possibilities. Many are long backcountry trails, sections of which are ideal for day hikes. Squaw Creek Trail makes a fine day's outing, ending at a beaver pond marsh. With a trailhead at Thirtymile Campground just east of the Rio Grande Reservoir, the hike follows Squaw Creek into the Weminuche Wilderness and is popular with hikers, backpackers, and equestrians. Most of the route is above Squaw Creek, though you can hear it much of the way. The drainage that holds Squaw Creek rises to the Continental Divide on the west.

The 4-mile segment of the Squaw Creek Trail to the beaver pond marsh ascends fairly steadily but gently, gaining a mere 600 feet in elevation in those miles. Signed also as Squaw Creek Stock Driveway, those on foot should expect horse traffic and be prepared to give way to the horses and riders on the narrow trail.

Diverse habitats support a wide variety of wildflower species—marshlands nurture western Jacob's ladder and purple avens, while dry aspen slopes sustain carrotroot chimingbells and sweetvetch.

Parking is generous on the north side of Thirtymile Campground in a large, maintained gravel space.

Head south, crossing the campground to reach a sign-in trail register. The trailhead is a shared one and Squaw Creek Trail No. 814 starts beyond it. While at the register, look across the way for a patch of **wild iris**.

Rising south in mixed spruce-aspen woods, the trail passes **scarlet gilia**, **cinquefoil**, and the substantial, dark-blue tubes of **Rocky Mountain penstemon. Shrubby cinquefoil, wild strawberry**, and lavender **fleabane daisy** lead into the forest. **Twinflower** appears in conifer shade with patches of glossy leaves, each the size of a little fingernail, and wiry stems forking to dangle paired bells. **Heartleaf arnica**'s cheery blossoms share this area with the five-petaled pink flowers of **wild geranium**.

CARROTROOT CHIMINGBELLS
Mertensia brevistyla

Known also as dwarf chimingbells or Utah chimingbells, this member of the borage family is an early bloomer and practically disappears with the heat of high summer. Terminal clusters of blue, matte tubes hang to one side, each ready to mature into a quartet of nutlets. The tuberous root, shaped like a drop spindle, tapers at the top and bottom, while stiff hairs point to the leaf margins. A 10-inch native of western Colorado and Utah's montane and subalpine life zones, the genus name honors German botanist F. K. Mertens.

More dainty twinflower drapes itself gracefully over cutbanks. This honey-suckle family member was reportedly the favorite of Linnaeus, the father of the Latin binomial system used for flora and fauna. Rounding an exposed rock exposes **spergulastrum**, or **rock starwort**, a sandwort with delicate star-shaped blossoms on sprawling, prostrate foliage. The lithic soil suits fleabane daisy's fine-rayed pastel heads, as well as **golden aster**'s wider rays and **narrowleaf paintbrush**'s thin bracts and modified leaves.

Well-drained soil is perfect for **sweetvetch**, or **chainpod**, its mature seed vessels resembling linked sequins. Soon, you'll see aspens scarred by the lower incisors of elk, where you can look for **many-rayed goldenrod**. Flattening, the route presents more sweetvetch and the five-sectioned seed capsules of **western red columbine**, an early-season bloomer. The trail meets **meadowrue** before coming upon wonderfully perfumed **wild rose**. Shortly after is rubbery **black-tipped senecio**, its big leaf clump looking like mint green mule deer ears.

As the trail descends toward the creek, added moisture nurtures **one-sided wintergreen** and **white violet**. Tall scarlet paintbrush livens up the scene. The fresh green foliage of **Parry goldenweed** sets off the vermilion and pale yellow glow of western red columbine, thriving in the company of mosses and lichens.

A sturdy footbridge takes hikers across a creek, where, on the upstream side, **shy wood nymph** clusters, resembling a society of white-wimpled nuns demurely bowing their heads. **Tall chimingbells** and snowy **bittercress** grace the banks as well.

Once across the bridge, you soon will reach a sign for the Weminuche Wilderness/Rio Grande National Forest. Look here also for shy wood nymph. The trail turns a corner marked by pink-budded tall chimingbells and **wild raspberry**. The turn sends the route uphill, encountering **purple fringe** and mats of needle-leaved **dotted saxifrage**, each suspended white star freckled with minute red dots.

Farther along is **twinberry honeysuckle**, with its paired, dull gold tubes framed by rich red bracts that mature into shiny black berries. Late-season hikers find magenta **fireweed** where wild geranium blooms earlier in the summer. An outcrop on the left is softened by wild rose. Where two outcrops flank a gravel slope, look for scarlet gilia and Rocky Mountain penstemon.

For a close look at dark purple **sticky gilia**, check the next gravelly slope. Near the creek, **cow parsnip** thrives thanks to adequate moisture. Growing on the steep east bank slope and preferring more xeric conditions are **harebell**'s dangling thimbles, scarlet gilia's flared trumpets, and the yellow blossoms of **mountain parsley**. Wild rose is interspersed with powder blue clumps of **carrotroot chimingbells**, whose hidden taproot is spindle shaped.

The trail soon edges between sheer cliffs and the creek. Tinted by the salmon-colored blossoms of **prickly mountain currant**, it takes hikers down to a riparian zone full of willows. From here, the route lifts, passing dark, pocked volcanic rocks where tiny but tough ferns cling. The ascent presents another

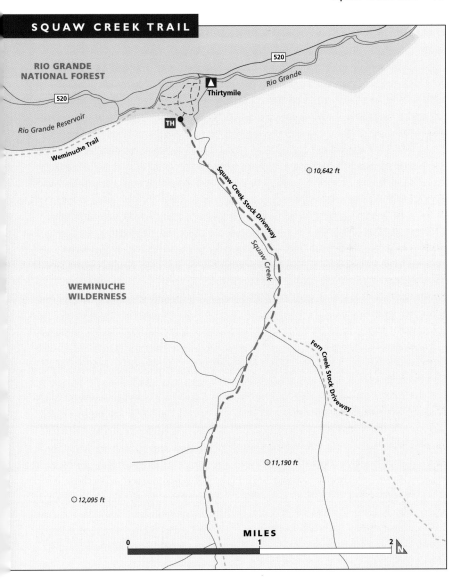

SQUAW CREEK TRAIL

RIO GRANDE
NATIONAL FOREST

520

Thirtymile

Rio Grande

Rio Grande Reservoir

520

TH

Weminuche Trail

○ 10,642 ft

Squaw Creek Stock Driveway

Squaw Creek

WEMINUCHE
WILDERNESS

Fern Creek Stock Driveway

○ 11,190 ft

○ 12,095 ft

MILES

0   1   2

chance to examine dotted saxifrage's spotted petals. An aspen copse is home to stately **Indian warriors**, each helmet streaked with red. Patches of **pussytoes** and **red globe anemone** decorate the lithic soil.

Note the damp spot on the left that sustains **green bog orchid**. Now undulating, the trail passes more Indian warriors, sometimes called **giant** or **fernleaf lousewort**, as well as pink sweetvetch, Engelmann spruce, **alpine milkvetch**, and **drop-pod locoweed**.

Willows reappear along with **hairy fruit** or **subalpine valerian**. Its homely cousin, **edible valerian**, sometimes called **ladies' tobacco**, is nearby. Ascending through willows and aspens, the trail passes deep purple **monkshood**, along with some specimens that show a dusky burgundy.

Another rise takes you through aspens littered with volcanic outcroppings. Look for **mountain death camas**, with its white stars and greenish glands. The trail continues uphill until, at last, a sidehill reveals the distant mountains that form the Continental Divide. At a small seep, monkshood has the height advantage over perky **yellow monkeyflower** and **alpine speedwell**'s little blue petals. Near a muddy spot, look for golden **triangleleaf senecio**, its tall, leafy stalks supporting a head of unkempt flowers. Out in the open, morning-loving **wild blue flax** offers vivid petals complementing buttery **wallflower** and shrubby cinquefoil. Scarlet gilia adds a sharp accent.

The next seep brings **little pink elephants** and yellow monkeyflower. Continuing on brings you to less common **western Jacob's ladder**. Its pretty, light purple, flared funnels and extruded gold stamens belie its skunky-smelling foliage. Crushing it will cause fellow hikers to avoid you. Under open skies, little white **whiplash fleabane** thrives.

The long meadow ahead passes through a parkland where you might spot **pink plumes**' dusty tint. Mostly level now, the trail features coppery **orange agoseris**, more cinquefoil, lanky **orange sneezeweed**, **Coulter daisy**, and **littleflower penstemon**.

As it passes close to Squaw Creek, the trail features pale pink subalpine valerian heads as well as swabs of cool, pale **northern paintbrush**. At a stand of tall **yellow avens**, bear up and left. A breached beaver dam and lodge hosts little pink elephants. The trail here is mucky, but before turning around, look for a cluster of monkshood pointing to an unusual cousin of pink plumes, **purple avens**, sometimes referred to as **chocolateflower**. Reportedly, its roots were once used to make a cocoa-flavored beverage. The nodding heads of this rose relation are a dull, reddish-brown with purple overtones. Surrounding them is a profusion of colorful wildflowers, drawing this hike to a close. Many of these flowers are probably by now familiar friends.

WESTERN JACOB'S LADDER

Polemonium caeruleum ssp. *amygdalinum*

Found on both sides of the Bering Strait, western Jacob's ladder is fond of mossy bogs, especially willow-birch bogs. Growing erectly to 3 feet, its upward-facing, flaring corollas are soft lavender-blue. Slim rhizomes send up sticky, slender stalks of skunky-smelling foliage, which is typical of polemoniums. Mostly subalpine, but occasionally upper montane, this lovely wildflower appears infrequently. The species nomenclature *caeruleum* means "blue," while that of the subspecies means "almond-scented," which refers to the flowers, not the ladder leaves.

Ivy Creek Trail

*Wildflower
Hike 12*

Ivy Creek flows quietly through gentle meadows.

easy to moderate	*Trail Rating*
5 miles out and back	*Trail Length*
Rio Grande National Forest/Weminuche Wilderness, south of Creede	*Location*
9,200 to 10,000 feet	*Elevation*
June to August	*Bloom Season*
mid-July	*Peak Bloom*

Directions

From Creede, go west on CO 149 6.2 miles, turning left (south) on Middle Creek Rd., which is also known as FR 523. Continue 4 miles on FR 523, then take a left (southeast) onto FR 528. After 3.5 miles, turn right on FR 526 and proceed 2 miles to the trailhead at Ivy Creek Campground (the last stretch is rough).

Situated in the mountains southwest of Creede, Ivy Creek Trail No. 805 follows a lively brook through long, wildflower-dotted meadows and wanders off to finish at the base of a deeply forested slope. Ivy Creek makes a good beginner's hike, especially in midsummer when the water is lower at crossings. Keeping boots dry is tricky but usually doable. Although the first part of Ivy Creek Trail is a bit rough, the majority saunters through meadows with hardly a perceptible rise.

Parking is at the small, little-used campground where the ground is rather uneven. Keep an eye out for building thunderheads in summer afternoons.

COMMON HAREBELL
Campanula rotundifolia

Though the species name refers to round leaves, it is the narrow, linear leaves that are evident. Dangling like amethyst thimbles from wiry stems, harebells grow from foothills to alpine life zones. Long blooming, these members of the bellflower family are more widely known as the Bluebells of Scotland, and are found throughout the northern hemisphere. The genus name, *campanula*, means "little bell."

To the right of the trail register where hikers sign in, take a moment to peruse the wildflowers along the banks of Ivy Creek. Look for frilly white **northern bedstraw** and **beauty cinquefoil**, defined by palmate leaves that are dark green above and white underneath. Near the water, you may find lacy **cowbane** and a bit of **yellow monkeyflower**.

Take time to cross the stream on the footbridge. On the far side, check under spruces on the left for the paired, dainty bells of **twinflower**, a scented member of the honeysuckle family. Then retrace your steps back across the bridge.

Back at the trail register, a sign welcomes hikers and equestrians who are traveling into the Weminuche Wilderness. The nearby lithic soil supports an array of wildflowers. **Silvery cinquefoil**, **New Mexico senecio**, and **many-rayed goldenrod** represent the yellows. **Yarrow**, **wild strawberry**, **pussytoes**, and northern bedstraw display white blooms. Reds come in the form of **scarlet gilia** and **narrowleaf paintbrush**, with its thin scarlet bracts and green, toothpick-like flowers.

A carved post lets you know you are officially on Ivy Creek Trail.

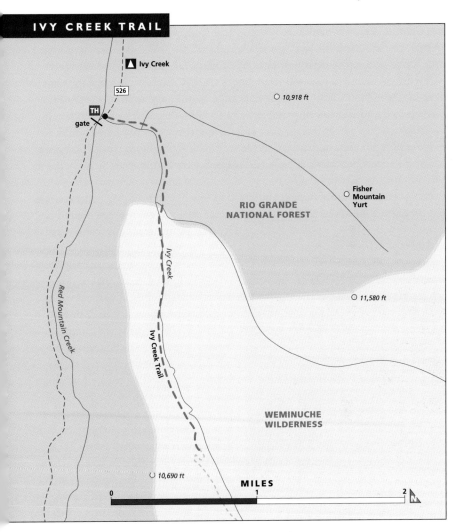

Nodding onion, shell pink in color with stamens protruding, grows in mixed aspen-spruce shade. At a tributary of Ivy Creek, note the whites of cowbane and **bittercress**, a watercress cousin with peppery, vitamin C–charged leaves.

An aspen slope brings drier conditions, along with scarlet gilia and **wild rose**. Appreciating the same mesic soil—one balanced of moisture and light—are *Campanula* cousins **Parry harebell**, with its upturned, purple corolla, and **common harebell**, which dangles cool purple bells.

At a seep, yellow monkeyflower flourishes. Its leaves were once used not only for food, but as a treatment for rope and other burns. A more xeric zone follows, suiting nodding onion, **fleabane daisy**, and **wild geranium**.

Creekside flora include **tall chimingbells**, which is a favorite food of elk, and **twistedstalk**, with its bells dangling from kinked pedicels, bearing out its common name. When mature, the whitish bells will become smooth, scarlet-orange berries, a wildlife food source.

The trail rises, offering views of boulder islands rising from the creek. Growing between willows, tall **triangleleaf senecio** displays more foliage than flowers. As the track levels, **meadowrue** appears, followed soon by rangy **orange sneezeweed** and short **orange agoseris**. At low elevations, orange agoseris may be known as **tall burnt orange false dandelion**; it is, in fact, a native, unlike the ubiquitous common dandelion. Once, the milky sap from snapped agoseris stems was dried into rubbery balls and chewed to clean the teeth. Early peoples also ate the raw flowers and leaves.

As the creek grows louder and the trail touches an overhang to view white water, look for **western red columbine**; its yellow and vermilion colors are unmistakable. Close examination will reveal yellow stamens protruding from pearly yellow lobes. A small stand of rather scraggly spruces harbors rosettes of **rattlesnake plantain orchid**, a little orchid so retiring as to go unnoticed, if not for its vein-mottled leaves. The whitish midveins braid into a vague image of the rattles on a rattlesnake's tail.

Continuing on, observant hikers might note minuscule blossoms of **rock primrose** rising on wiry stems. Tucked into damp spruce shade where lichen and moss thrive is **shy wood nymph**, a perfumed member of the wintergreen clan. A few steps up the trail reveals **one-sided wintergreen**, the charming nymph's plainer cousin.

At a posted point, trekkers enter the 500,000-acre Weminuche Wilderness, a name that honors a band of Ute Indians. Nearby grow **twinberry honeysuckle** shrubs, whose paired, dull gold tubes mature into inky, inedible twin berries protected by crimson bracts.

Fine-rayed, snowy **Coulter daisy** and **white geranium** grow close to a small trickle, where pristine bittercress

PARRY HAREBELL
Campanula parryi

Purple bellflower is another common name for this pretty, upfacing hare-bell whose pointed corolla lobes are split at least halfway. Like a small, startled tulip, this wildflower has a trilobed stigma and a sticky pistil. It prefers moist meadows and aspen copses, as well as its own company. American Indians dried and powdered the plants to sprinkle on sores; the chewed roots were applied for treatment of bruises. It is named for Iowa physician Charles C. Parry, who carried out botanical studies in Colorado in the last half of the 1800s.

and royal purple **monkshood** also thrive. Monkshood and **mountain death camas**, which appears next, are both poisonous. Death camas' foliage resembles the lily, but the black-netted bulb is a dead giveaway to its toxicity.

Stones allow passage across the next seep area, after which early-season hikers find western red columbine. Keeping a low profile in a mass of ladder leaflets, **alpine milkvetch** sends out petite, purple-tipped, pea-type flowers.

A pretty, open meadow finds swallowtail and fritillary butterflies fluttering along an entrenched trail. Butterflies, who sample nectar with their feet, favor wide-headed flowers as landing platforms. In the meadow grasses, orange sneezeweed and **shrubby cinquefoil** accompany triple-headed **pink plumes**. The latter two are members of the rose family.

A little uptick brings you into aspen territory where you may spot gray, ladder-leaved **drop-pod locoweed**, which lives up to its name when seedpods form, though the dingy purple terminal flowers are not showy.

This brings you to a creek crossing. Horseback riders can charge right across, but hikers may want to proceed upstream to search in the willows spanning Ivy Creek. Having crossed, hikers follow the trail to another meadow where **Indian warriors** are visible, with their red-streaked heads.

Off to the side in the damp areas, **little pink elephants** thrives. **Rayless senecio** grows in the grasses in both barrel-shaped and fluted varieties, one chartreuse and the other burgundy. Prepare for another makeshift bridge of logs, with yellow monkeyflower, cool **northern paintbrush**, and starry white **stitchwort** nearby.

Horsetails, an ancient plant, point the trail to a drier aspect where the route is again entrenched. Lush bunchgrass thrives, and you will have to search for purple Parry harebell, along with the hanging thimble heads of its common harebell cousin.

Petals of **wild blue flax** grace the meadow grasses, most notably in the cool hours of morning; warm afternoons see the silken petals fall. Though flax petals are delicate, their stems are tough and American Indians wove the fibers into snares, cordage, and nets. More Indian warriors, or **giant lousewort** as it's also known, is chest-high here. Black and white Wiedemeyer's admirals flutter over **red globe anemone**'s cerise cups.

A far view materializes of the Continental Divide at 13,000 feet. Small but widespread, alpine milkvetch crawls along close to the harebell cousins, Parry and common. In the direction of Ivy Creek, a patch of northern paintbrush appears in cool yellow. Closer to the trail, coppery-rayed orange agoseris, the same color as fluttering fritillaries, displays its bright heads.

The trail weaves through the lengthy meadow until it passes into a conifer forest. Traveling in evergreen shade, hikers eventually come to the base of a steep slope. For this description, the spot where the route switchbacks up marks the turnaround point.

Wildflower Hike 13

Creede Trail to San Luis Pass

Fiery red paintbrush is your company on the Creede Trail to San Luis Pass.

The drive to Creede Trail features some of the most picturesque mining structures anywhere as it winds through the steep, tight gorge carved by West Willow Creek. With a competent driver and a vehicle with decent clearance, the road—part of the fascinating Bachelor Loop—accommodates passenger cars when winter conditions are past. The hike begins across from Equity Mine on the west side of West Willow Creek. Colorful flowers begin here as well.

Unmarked, the 3.1-mile trail starts out up a small berm just left of the interpretive sign for the Equity Mine. It follows an abandoned roadway until meeting a four-wheel-drive road, which crosses a creek. That road comes to a post indicating hikers continue north toward San Luis Pass.

Trail Rating	easy to moderate
Trail Length	6.2 miles out and back
Location	Rio Grande National Forest, north of Creede
Elevation	11,200 to 11,940 feet
Bloom Season	late June to August
Peak Bloom	July
Directions	From Main St. in Creede, head north on FR 503, also known as W. Willow Creek Rd., for a steep 7.5 miles to the Equity Mine. Stay right at the fork and park to the left by the interpretive sign.

Neon-colored paintbrush and myriad other subalpine wildflowers line the route from its beginning to its end at nearly 12,000 feet. The trail travels under open skies its entire length. All around are high-country views, including 14,014-foot San Luis Peak at the pass. Parking is generous.

To the west of the interpretive sign for the Equity Mine, climb the small berm to an overgrown, abandoned roadway just inside the Forest Service boundary. Right off, **orange agoseris** and creamy whorls of **Parry lousewort** join **New Mexico senecio**, **orange sneezeweed**, and flaming red **paintbrush** clumps.

Progress is slow if you pause to inspect every blooming thing, such as **mouse-ears**, **yarrow**, unobtrusive **alpine bistort**, and starburst **stitchwort**—all in white. A mustard family member, **yellow draba** has tiny, four-petaled flowers that contrast with purple **monkshood**.

Coming into a mossy zone, look for spikes of **little pink elephants**, the rounded pink heads of **queen's crown**, and **cowbane**. A rivulet, easily crossed on stones, presents **brook saxifrage**, with dainty white flowers held high above massed emerald leaves, each evenly toothed. On a sunny bank, orange sneezeweed opens wide heads of droopy petals and tight disk-flower centers. Though the old roadbed is often obscured by grasses, **tall chimingbells** and **Porters lovage** rise above it, as do the chartreuse drums of **rayless senecio**. **Red onion** blooms in pointy pink tubes, some of which are replaced by red bulblets.

Continuing along, look uphill in an open area to see stately **wild iris** complemented by gold coins of **shrubby cinquefoil**. Paintbrush accompanies an ascent on a rocky tread. Check out the wine-colored tubes of **Whipple penstemon** and the pink embroidery knots of **mountain sheep sorrel**. Skinny white **arabis**, in the mustard family, appears near rosy **Parry clover**.

A rocky stretch arrives before a wet spot offering little pink elephants. Thoroughly poisonous monkshood stands in the company of red paintbrush,

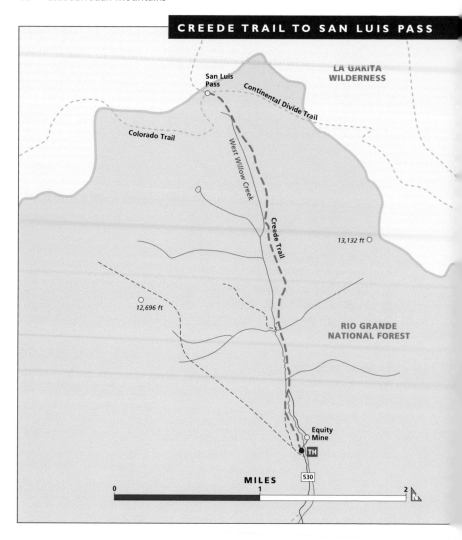

CREEDE TRAIL TO SAN LUIS PASS

LA GARITA WILDERNESS

San Luis Pass

Continental Divide Trail

Colorado Trail

West Willow Creek

Creede Trail

13,132 ft ○

12,696 ft

RIO GRANDE NATIONAL FOREST

Equity Mine

TH

MILES

530

0   1   2

while **rock primrose** and five-petaled **white geranium** lead up to a nice garden of purple-blue **subalpine larkspur**. Look also for tall chimingbells, in the borage family, and the lanky, off-white umbels of Porters lovage, a parsley relative.

Many-rayed goldenrod's bright inflorescences lead toward cutbank seeps that nurture troops of **yellow monkeyflower**, with their red-freckled throats. Nearby, native **subalpine dock** produces substantial leaves to support cones of reddish-pink flowers that become a mass of winged seeds. A slender cousin in the knotweed family is mountain sheep sorrel, with tight wads of pinkish flowers.

The roadway soon passes **Coulter daisy**, **pink-headed daisy**, and prolific rayless senecio. As the route descends, a steeply angled, lithic cutbank supports early-blooming **purple fringe**, its bright stamens poking from amethyst trumpets. **Tall scarlet paintbrush** and more pink-headed daisy also add color.

Flattening, the track passes a well-watered zone, featuring **pink willow-herb** and **bittercress**, before easing upward again to join the Forest Service road, which soon dips to rejoin the abandoned road from Equity Mine. As this road peters out, look for later-blooming **star gentian** in dusky purple, and **fringed gentian** unwinding showy amethyst petals.

The maintained road is now flanked by the golds of cinquefoil, primarily **beauty cinquefoil**, with its palmate leaves, and **silvery cinquefoil**, with grayish-white, pinnate-style leaves. These two hybridize freely.

Where the roadbed dips to cross West Willow Creek, watch for queen's crown, yellow monkeyflower, and **subalpine daisy**. Tall chimingbells anchor midstream islands. Once across, look for Whipple penstemon, red onion, and stately monkshood.

The road parallels West Willow Creek, with a rivulet on the right lined with pastel blossoms. A cutbank supports a **harebell** population where early-season hikers can see purple fringe. A mix of cool pink subalpine and snowy Coulter daisy represents two of the taller fleabanes. Late-summer trekkers find the rich blue chalices of **Rocky Mountain gentian** sprinkled along the meadowed slopes. **Pink plumes**, deep purple-blue subalpine larkspur, and monkshood put in appearances as well.

Prepare for a swing in the trail as a bare summit juts straight ahead and the route encounters a stream crossing. Stones help negotiate the crossing. On the right bank, compressed volcanic ash highlights subalpine dock, or **marsh dock**, with its burnt red seedpod flanges, little pink elephants, brook saxifrage, and **golden draba**. The second part of the crossing is accompanied by pink queen's crown and beautiful **Parry primrose**. An incline displays **mountain parsley** and many-rayed goldenrod, complemented a bit farther on by **littleflower penstemon**'s intense blue tubes and the whorls of **creamy lousewort**.

At a bend in the trail, early-August hikers enjoy a grand display of fringed gentian, with **little rose gentian** in the same area. Look also for pink plumes, **American bistort**, and **rosy paintbrush**.

BEETLEAF SENECIO
Ligularia holmii

Found at higher elevations, beetleaf or Holm senecio resembles a dwarf version of daffodil senecio. This Colorado endemic has light yellow, outfacing flowers, looking like golden daisies bowing their rays. Each rounded, oval leaf emanating from the base has an often beet-colored leafstalk, or petiole. The species name honors the Danish botanist Herman Theodor Holm, who collected plants in Colorado from 1896 to 1899.

The Creede Trail to San Luis Pass begins at a post that bars motorized vehicles and continues straight ahead. The four-wheel-drive road that goes left up a serious incline is not for the uninitiated driver. The Creede Trail generally parallels the creek from here. Wildflowers include little pink elephants, rosy paintbrush, pink willowherb, queen's crown, **subalpine arnica**, white paintbrush, and cowbane.

At the sign permitting foot and horse traffic, look for Whipple penstemon. This elevation supports **alpine chimingbells** and **sibbaldia**, or **cloverleaf rose**. **Blueleaf cinquefoil** and **alpine avens** indicate an alpine influence.

A stream crossing turns hikers up a drier aspect that features **sawtooth** or **sawleaf senecio** and cinquefoil. Be cautious as you drop fairly steeply back to another creek crossing. To the left, framed by dove gray rock, are violet-pink **Halls penstemon**, subtle **alumroot**, and Parry clover.

At last, the trail levels, offering views of **snowball saxifrage**, **subalpine valerian**, rosy and red paintbrush, monkshood, and alpine and American bistort. The creek disappears from sight where the trail features **alpine sandwort's** white flowers clinging to a dark mound. Tundra dominates where lavender rays of **single-headed daisy** stand solitary on short stems. Almost imperceptibly rising, the route nears the creek again, accompanied by vibrant tall scarlet paintbrush.

As the ascent increases, note **Colorado blue columbine** and subalpine larkspur. Along the way are **old man of the mountains** and **yellow stonecrop**. Where the track bends in a bit, look downslope for vivid Halls penstemon, short but showy. Well-drained soil supports **beetleaf** or **Holm senecio**, whose heads might be likened to a smaller version of a daffodil senecio.

A little tributary brings more Colorado blue columbine, as well as sawleaf senecio, alpine chimingbells, alpine avens, and perky white mouse-ears. Continue the easygoing ascent to a dense colony of native subalpine or marsh dock with its coral-red spikes of winged seedpods. Note also **homely buttercup** in this segment.

The trail continues up a rocky slope featuring both **daffodil** and **black-tipped senecio**. At a rock cairn, enjoy the views of the mountain.

Just above the creek now, Creede Trail comes upon the source of West Willow Creek, a lush bowl just this side of the Continental Divide. Little pink elephants thrive here, as well as yellow monkeyflower, cinquefoil, arnica, parsley, clear blue alpine chimingbells, and a bit of Colorado blue columbine. The gritty soil uptrail suits the translucent pink starbursts of **pygmy bitterroot**.

You arrive at the Continental Divide at 11,940 feet, on a flat. The views extend from distant, blue-toned ranges to the rocky high country, including, to the northeast, 14,014-foot San Luis Peak. Using your imagination, straddle the Divide at the line that sends waters to the Gulf of Mexico and the Pacific Ocean. A quartet of signs mark a junction for thru-hikers. One announces La Garita Wilderness. In the vicinity of the signage, **Arctic gentian**, a harbinger of coming snows, sends up white flutes decorated with dark purple streaks. When you have finished enjoying the views, return the way you came.

Table Mountain Saddle via Crystal Lake Road

Wildflower Hike 14

A colorful expanse of high-country wildflowers at Ouray Park

moderate (short but steep elevation gain)	*Trail Rating*
0.75-mile keyhole loop	*Trail Length*
Rio Grande National Forest, west of Creede	*Location*
11,500 to 11,750 feet	*Elevation*
July to August	*Bloom Season*
mid- to late July	*Peak Bloom*
From Creede, take CO 149 west just over 27 miles. Turn right (east) onto Bristol Head Rd./FR 532, soon fording a creek (a high-clearance vehicle is suggested). Follow FR 532 to Crystal Lake Rd./FR 532.2A. The hike begins here. Park off the road carefully.	*Directions*

For adventure-prone wildflowerists, this floriferous, nontraditional trail, called for the purposes of this book Table Mountain Saddle, offers a number of surprises, beginning with crossing Spring Creek en route to the "trailhead." In midsummer, it is typically about 6 to 8 inches deep, requiring a high-clearance vehicle. This crossing takes place not far before Spring Creek joins North Clear Creek, together soon pitching over a 60-foot waterfall.

The Bristol Head access road is sometimes rough but not difficult, climbing from 10,000 to 11,500 feet. Enjoy the colorful expanse of Ouray Park, named after Ute Chief Ouray, which offers a wonderful array of high-elevation wildflowers.

The "trail" is really the start of Crystal Lake Road, which soon deteriorates into a four-wheel-drive track. But the 0.25 mile described for this hike is quite gentle, rising a few hundred feet to a broad, scenic saddle ideal for spotting wildflowers. Long mountain vistas stretch both east and west. Treeline is deceptively high here at an elevation of roughly 12,000 feet.

Parking requires pulling over to the east side of the Bristol Head/Crystal Lake Road junction so other traffic can pass.

Few hikes offer such a glorious place to begin as this one, starting in Ouray Park. Meadows stretch for thousands of acres as your vehicle clears the trees. Drive slowly—not that there is much of a choice—to savor the gold and lavender tones.

Park at the "trailhead" intersection and feel free to roam. To the west is the 13,821-foot Rio Grande Pyramid. In the foreground, a profusion of **pink plumes** nod their triple heads, each bloom maturing into feathery tops. Stepping carefully

COLORADO THISTLE
Cirsium scariosum

This widespread member of the sunflower family is often stemless, lying flat on the ground, though in some circumstances it is a rangy plant. In the case of ground-hugging specimens, a broad, prickly rosette harbors a level bouquet of pale purple to eggshell white disk flowers, packed like the bristles of an old-fashioned shaving brush. The edible roots are nutritious, as are the peeled stems of this spiny thistle. Also called elk thistle, both elk and bear relish it. The Greek word *cirsos* means "swollen vein."

between wildflowers takes you to **littleflower penstemon**. Its rich blue to violet tubes whorl in thick clusters on a short stalk, making the penstemon, sometimes called **clustered penstemon**, look like an ultramarine exclamation point among meadow forbs and grasses.

Native **tall burnt orange false dandelion** also goes by the shorter name of **orange agoseris**. In Greek, *aix* means "goat" and *seris* means "chickory." Coppery and short at this elevation, orange agoseris holds up its rayed head, while nearby grows **dandelion**, a nonnative that has conquered every corner of Colorado, and most of the world.

Staying with the yellows, **beauty cinquefoil** sprays rise above palmate leaves, with each petal base boasting an orange spot. **Mountain parsley** lifts umbels resembling gilded snowflakes, while brassy, five-petaled **alpine avens** contrasts with cool **northern paintbrush**. The hottest yellow of the bunch belongs to less common **one-flowered** or **plantain-leaved goldenweed**, a low-growing dandelion relation.

Also in the vicinity are **sky pilot**, with its fragrant, flared trumpets rising over infamously skunky foliage, and **alpine chimingbells**, its matte blue corollas dangling. **Alpine speedwell**, a widespread veronica, requires a hand lens to look at its soft sapphire petals.

Mouse-ears, **yarrow**, **wild strawberry**, tiny-blossomed **rock primrose**, and quiet **pussytoes** tame the vivid colors with white spatters. Shyest of all is **Drummond cockle**, with its sticky, inflated, striped calyx barely revealing bits of pale pink petal.

Head to the east side of Bristol Head Road and walk up Crystal Lake Road. The colors are less exuberant here as lush grasses dominate. As you start up the road, you are accompanied by many of the flowers already encountered, such as alpine chimingbells, alpine avens, sky pilot, and cinquefoil. Over these wave the blossoms of **American bistort**, looking like plush cotton swabs.

Glancing up to the north reveals a flat, mesalike geoscape aptly called Table Mountain. A stone base rings the south contours, as does a band of residual snow, not unexpected at this 12,500-foot elevation. Back at ground level, **Colorado thistle**, quite prolific here, spreads its prickly rosettes, each overlapping leaf laid flat to frame a huddled bouquet resembling a tight bunch of artichoke blooms. The flowers, as well as the central veins of the leaves, may be pale lavender or off-white.

Standing on a bare stem over a rosette of thick, rhomboidal or diamond-shaped leaves, **snowball saxifrage** looks like a lollipop rolled in lint when fresh; it elongates as it matures. A late-summer visitor will encounter the royal blue chalices of **Rocky Mountain gentian**. The whole scene is abuzz with pollinators trying to get a big job done in a very short summer season.

Rising steadily east, the main road branches off from an overgrown route to the left. Turn here to enjoy a less-traveled path. Grasses give native Colorado

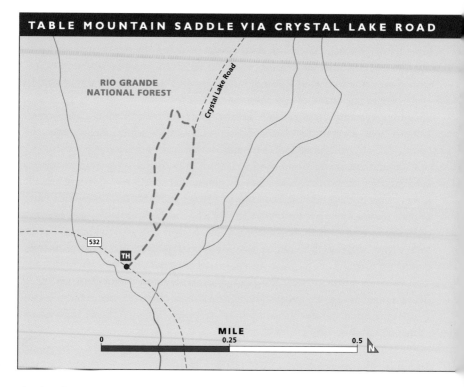

TABLE MOUNTAIN SADDLE VIA CRYSTAL LAKE ROAD

RIO GRANDE
NATIONAL FOREST

Crystal Lake Road

532

TH

MILE
0   0.25   0.5

thistle, abundant on this gentle slope, a wide berth. Nearby are the bright heads of plantain-leaved goldenweed. Alpine chimingbells' charming pink buds and blue bells add a delicate touch of color.

All clovers are fragrant, and the oversized globes of **Parry clover** are exceptionally so. **Alumroot**, related to cultivated coralbells, is a cool ivory color while **Parry lousewort**'s creamy, beaked blossoms swirl in pinwheel fashion.

A bit of lanky **orange sneezeweed** leads you up to a thick, short willow stand. Walk around the edges to the left, where it shelters pretty **subalpine valerian**. Its demure head of tiny, light pink tubes doesn't suggest the other common name for this plant, **hairy-fruit valerian**.

Neither dainty nor demure, **rosy paintbrush** stands out with vibrant, bracted swabs. Paintbrush is known for its range of hues, from pastels to primary colors. In between the willows, bright garden patches thrive, thanks, in part, to nature's rototiller, the gopher. In the rodent's upturned earth, small plants such as **mountain** or **wild candytuft** and **golden draba** gain a roothold.

At this point, the roadway is obscure. Make your way through a narrow path in the short willows to reach the far side, where a seasonal creek has carved a shallow ravine. **Alpine sandwort**'s dark mats hug the ground, whereas **rockcress** grows tall in the company of **Whipple penstemon**'s dusky, wine-colored tubes. Lined with rosy Parry clover, the route leads you right (south) to the road, crossing where the sandy-soiled seasonal waterway resumes. Within a few feet of the road, look for vibrant clumps of **purple wallflower**, a perfumed member of the mustard family. Right beside the road shoulder, look for **slender-tipped clover**. Also enjoying the loose, sandy soil is **purple fringe**, with its exerted gold stamens.

Returning eastward, look for the minute, star-shaped blossoms of **rock starwort**, or **spergulastrum**, the latter deriving from its Latin name. For a contrast in size, **old man of the mountains**, or **alpine sunflower**, offers the tundra's largest blossom, but only after years of storing energy to bloom grandly, then perish. Thinking small again, check under the white-rayed heads of **black-headed daisy** for woolly, purple-black hairs. Smaller yet are **alpine mouse-ears**' snowy, notched petals. Like unformed snowflakes, **alpine parsley**'s tight yellow umbels deserve a search. A rose family member, alpine avens stands high over fernlike foliage. Its nearby cousin **blueleaf cinquefoil** displays bright gold as well, drawing attention to its five-petaled flowers.

Arriving at the wide saddle south of Table Mountain, you may be greeted by the chirping of a white-crowned sparrow. Look west and east to take in the full panorama of the San Juan Range of the majestic Rocky Mountains before following the jeep road back down to your vehicle.

Colorful flowers at Table Mountain Saddle

Wildflower Hike 15

North Clear Creek Falls Loop

North Clear Creek Falls plunges into a volcanic gorge.

A serene stream for most of its length, North Clear Creek harbors an impressive surprise, plunging over 60 feet in a stunning waterfall. A lot of film and pixels attempt to capture this spectacle, but wildflowerists can also enjoy an easygoing, 0.5-mile loop that showcases a good selection of wildflowers, including a couple of unusual and showy species. One, the Colorado tansy aster, is locally abundant here.

Though a trail begins and wraps up this impromptu loop, the middle section is undefined. But the area is open and makes for simple navigation through a variety of landforms and wildflowers. This is an easy walk with little elevation gain.

Trail Rating	easy
Trail Length	0.5-mile loop
Location	Rio Grande National Forest, west of Creede
Elevation	10,030 feet
Bloom Season	June to August
Peak Bloom	mid-July
Directions	From Creede, take CO 149 approximately 27.5 miles west to milepost 49. Turn right (east) onto FR 510, a paved access road. Limited parking is available at the falls overlook.

North Clear Creek Falls is popular, and the short entry road, located about halfway between Creede and Lake City, is paved, as is the parking area. Most visitors depart soon after seeing the falls, opening up parking spaces. Restrooms are on-site.

Just yards west of the highway, North Clear Creek Falls is an unexpectedly beautiful waterfall set in gorgeous scenery. Most people make a beeline for the view, hardly pausing to peruse interpretive signs. But these are well worth your time, offering the fascinating history of North Clear Creek Falls during the gold rush of the 1870s.

After enjoying the waterfall's sound and fury, begin noting the blooming things around you. Following the trail near the rim downstream leads you to soft violet-pink **Colorado tansy aster** spreading its showy rays on a low plant. The daisylike blooms on short stems are set off by gray-green leaves, each tooth drawn out to a spinelike point. Though fairly abundant locally, it is partial only to southwestern and central Colorado's open parks. **Silvery cinquefoil**, prolific throughout the state, complements the tansy aster.

The chasm's volcanic character can be seen in the exposed, fissured rock between the trail and the rim. **Wild raspberry** and **shrubby cinquefoil** set off mats of **dotted saxifrage** and tufts of **alumroot** tucked in the dark rock's crevices. Like a spiky grass, the skinny-leaved clumps of **Fendler sandwort** surround wiry stems ending in delicate stars. The great jumble of rocks below may turn up a yellow-bellied marmot soaking up high-country sun. On the inside of the path, **pink plumes** nods its trio of heads before turning them into wispy, dusty pink seedheads. Other common names include **old man's beard** and **three-flowered avens**.

A slight grade takes you to spruces, where **mountain death camas'** off-white flowers enjoy the neighborly blues of **carrotroot chimingbells**. Although sometimes called **Utah chimingbells**, this member of the borage bunch is at

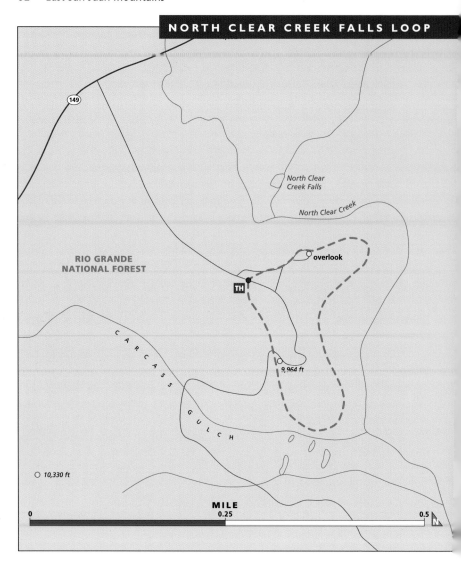

NORTH CLEAR CREEK FALLS LOOP

149

North Clear
Creek Falls

North Clear Creek

RIO GRANDE
NATIONAL FOREST

overlook

TH

9,964 ft

C A R C A S S

G U L C H

○ 10,330 ft

MILE
0.25

0   0.5

N

home in western Colorado as well. A tapering taproot supports a mounding fan of periwinkle flowers. Purple **harebell** accompanies barely-there blooms of **edible valerian**, and **many-rayed goldenrod** joins **New Mexico senecio** in yellow. Rising on a rocky hillside, the trail passes **squaw** or **wax currant** bushes. Take a moment to enjoy another view of the falls. Sporadic mats of dotted saxifrage drape over convenient rocks. **Red globe** or **cliff anemone** stands straight, its seedheads resembling cotton swabs.

The rocky knob reveals the first of a number of **mat penstemon** specimens. Despite its name, this member of the snapdragon family often forms loose mounds of linear leaves and displays blue to lavender tubes. Coming around a corner offers another look into the gorge and its broken columns of volcanic rock, and beyond to a grand panorama of peaks. A pile of pancaked rock on the right is a repository for early-blooming **wild iris**.

A short spur heads down to a rather precipitous overlook point. Instead, head up right through rocks and reach a gravel area where scented **alpine phlox** clusters among mat penstemon mounds and deep purple **sticky gilia**, each treelike inflorescence rising from a teal-tinted snowflake rosette. Almost desertlike in its vegetation distribution and coarse gravel pavement, the flat surface is the place to search for a faint trail headed west, dipping and slightly rising on a knoll. Along here, check the golden stamens of more mat penstemon and the tufts of rose-colored Colorado tansy aster. In the same area, look for spindly-leaved Fendler sandwort lifting its tiny white stars. **Wild blue flax** likes cool temperatures to open its pointy buds into silky petals.

Lavender **early fleabane, rosy pussytoes,** and red globe anemone signal a pause to look down into a bunchgrass meadow. More moisture in this area supports **clustered** or **littleflower penstemon** and **buttercup. Mouse-ears** get its common name from its white, cleft petals. As you regain the gravelly ridge in sight of the parking area, watch in another bunchgrass meadow for morning-loving wild blue flax.

Pass a white, silty depression on your left to arrive in a bunchgrass bowl where richly pigmented littleflower penstemon, shrubby cinquefoil, **silky lupine,** and **showy locoweed** with its magenta blooms, thrive. **Yarrow** and many-rayed goldenrod, both members of the sunflower or aster family, enjoy the mesic soil in this drier zone. Gophers have helped make seed germination easier, bringing on a colorful collection of many of the wildflowers you've encountered so far, with the additions of **scarlet gilia** and **orange sneezeweed.**

Round the foot of the hillock and look over aspen stands to 12,700-foot Bristol Head with its palisaded pewter

COLORADO TANSY ASTER
Machaeranthera coloradoensis

Very discriminating in soil and site selection, the violet-pink Colorado tansy aster is a find. The 2- to 4-inch plants have gray-green, toothed leaves tipped with flexible spines, and prefer open areas. The wide daisylike heads sport golden centers of disk flowers. The pointed phyllaries are recurved on this gravel-loving aster (in Greek, *aster* means "star"). With one head to a stem, this showy, low-growing native is a long bloomer.

face. Check nearby for **leafy aster**'s red stems and purple rays, and listen for broad-tailed hummingbirds whizzing in to visit scarlet gilia, also known as **fairy trumpets** or **sky rocket**.

As the path approaches a hairpin turn on FR 510, staying east of the roadway, look for the light blue-purple flowers of later-blooming **dusty penstemon**, open over a tuft of basal leaves paired on an upright stalk. Both scarlet **narrowleaf** and orangy **broad-bracted paintbrush** appear.

A very low-growing, miniaturized species of lupine takes a keen eye to spot. It likes lithic soil or gravel and goes by the descriptive moniker of **littlebunch** or **dwarf lupine**. Only a few seem to survive, but this height-challenged member of the pea clan is a find, so keep your eye out for a cluster of palmate leaves with a short spike of light purple, pea-type flowers.

Red onion also appears, its pointy blossoms sharing space with fleshy red bulblets. **Tall pale agoseris**, a native dandelion, likes this lumpy soil. More of the erect, purplish dusty penstemon provides a foil for magenta **Colorado locoweed**.

At this point, the impromptu loop crosses the dirt road not far from the edge of an aspen stand, swinging to the north. Pale blue **stickseed** leads into a draw of rushes—look for a faint trail to the right of where shrubby cinquefoil's gold complements the dense blues of littleflower penstemon, part of a genus that has more than 260 species and counting. Rising upward along a path, note carrotroot chimingbells, also known as **dwarf chimingbells**, perhaps in reference to their short, smaller corollas. A weedy and prolific mustard family member, **western pepperweed** likes disturbed soil; its minutely petaled, whitish heads look like a loose gathering of tiny, dirty snowballs.

Continue steadily up the wildflower-filled slope. The last uptick puts you on a dry ridgetop inhabited by powder blue carrotroot chimingbells and vermilion **paintbrush**. Head west and meet the road at the North Clear Creek Falls Observation Area sign, following the pavement back to the circle fronting the restrooms and parking area.

Rito Hondo Reservoir Loop

Wildflower Hike 16

From a serene lake to a running creek, and a marsh to a verdant seep, the landscape at Rito Hondo Reservoir surprises.

easy	**Trail Rating**
2-mile loop	**Trail Length**
Rio Grande National Forest, west of Creede	**Location**
10,120 feet	**Elevation**
late June to August	**Bloom Season**
early to mid-July	**Peak Bloom**
From Creede, go west on CO 149 just over 27 miles to the turnoff for Continental Reservoir. At the sign, take a left (west) on FR 513 and continue 4 miles to Rito Hondo Reservoir. Park at the restrooms.	**Directions**

Sitting off by itself in a wide swale, Rito Hondo Reservoir is a state wildlife area appealing mainly to anglers. However, a 2-mile loop around the lake makes it a great destination for the wildflower enthusiast. Located in a draw opening onto rolling ranchland, Rito Hondo's treeless shoreline means a sunny wildflower walk at about 10,000 feet elevation. With little elevation change, encircling the lake is easy except for crossing a somewhat boggy inlet area.

Located off the main highway that travels between Creede and Lake City, Rito Hondo provides a glimpse into traditional ranching in a wide valley called North Clear Creek Park. The North Clear Creek Falls walk (p. 90) could be combined with Rito Hondo, as both are short loops.

Wildflowering at Rito Hondo Reservoir covers several ecozones, from seep to bog to shoreline to dry slopes. The trail presents an interesting array of flora, including a couple of flowering plants that are locally plentiful but generally uncommon—Colorado tansy aster and plantain-leaved goldenweed.

Plenty of parking can be had most anywhere, but for this description, leave your vehicle by the restrooms. Be sure to watch, as always, for afternoon thunderstorms.

PLANTAIN-LEAVED GOLDENWEED
Pyrrocoma uniflora

One-flowered goldenweed is another name for this plant, which features neon gold–rayed heads sitting on reddish stems. Preferring somewhat moist, alkaline soil in dryish sub-alpine meadows, the 8- to 12-inch flowering stems rise from woody rootstocks. The stems and bracts sport white hairs, and the elongated leaves have long-petioled, three-nerved leaf blades. Its Latin genus name has Greek origins; *pyrrhos* means "tawny" while *coma* means "mane."

Head north, down from the day-use parking area toward the boat ramp. Right off, **clustered** or **little-flower penstemon** garners attention with its whorls of inky blue tubes. **Shrubby cinquefoil** sets itself up to complement the penstemon. **Mouse-ears'** white, cleft petals contrast with the stocky heads of **pink plumes**, its blooms dangling in triplicate.

As it curves down, the trail passes a garden of sun-loving wildflowers, including butter yellow **wallflower**, with its cruciform petal arrange-ment, **New Mexico senecio**, **wild blue flax**, and low-lying, daisylike **Colorado tansy aster**. The flowers thrive in the loose soil tilled by gophers, Mother Nature's underground engineers.

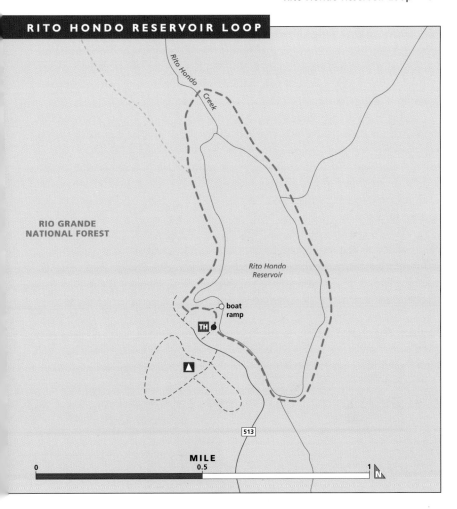

Rito Hondo Creek

RIO GRANDE
NATIONAL FOREST

*Rito Hondo
Reservoir*

boat
ramp

TH

513

MILE
0   0.5   1

    At the boat ramp, begin looping around the lake by heading left, along
an arm sporting bright blue damselflies. **Alpine milkvetch** is recognized by its
small, purple-tipped, pea-type flowers. Enjoying the moist soil lakeside are **pink
willowherb** and lanky **yellow avens**, a member of the rose clan with a tripartite
end leaf. Blue **alpine speedwell** and **red onion** cling to the shoreline where lush
grasses prosper in a narrow band; the verges get drier quickly.
    Wind your way through the gold, white, and blue of cinquefoil, **dandelion**,
mouse-ears, **yarrow**, and **Rocky Mountain penstemon**. Pink plumes throws
in the occasional accent. As the lake finger points west, damper soil nurtures
northern paintbrush's pale yellow bracts and modified leaves.
    At this point, a dirt road turns the trail toward distant, flat-topped Snow
Mesa to the east. Here is a promising place to look for a dandelion-like native
denizen, the rare and somewhat prosaicly named **plantain-leaved goldenweed**,
or **one-flowered goldenweed**. Upon examination, these brilliantly gold-rayed

heads have an equally gold center of disk florets, making them appear lit from within. They like the limelight and tend to appear singly. The flowers perch on whiskery, reddish stems rising from long, stiff basal leaves. Keeping the dandelion theme going is **tall pale false dandelion**, better known as **tall pale agoseris**, a native as well.

As the road ends, find your way cautiously along a sidehill abutting the water. Or you can choose to walk more easily above it. Blue damselflies hover as you travel the shore among cinquefoil and penstemon, where early-season visitors find **wild iris**. At water's edge is, appropriately, **water spring beauty**, a delicate member of the purslane family. Where it's a bit drier along the abrupt embankment, **scarlet gilia** takes over. This section of the trail is tricky, so step carefully.

Make your way cautiously, looking for **silverweed**, a cinquefoil cousin once valued by native peoples for its nutritional rootstock. The handsome, ladderlike leaves are comprised of toothed leaflets with smaller leaflets in the interstices. The five-petaled flowers are bright yellow, and slim red stolons snake out to claim new territory at the nodes.

Drifting inland makes walking easier as **orange agoseris**, also called **tall burnt orange false dandelion**, rises. As you approach the north end inlet area, keep an eye out for waterfowl. The marshy inlet zone supports **marsh marigold** along a trail obscured by verdant grasses. Passing by boulders, look to the right

Shoreline grasses at Rito Hondo Reservoir

of the smaller one to find **monkshood** and **little pink elephants**, both thriving in damp areas.

Hummocky grass makes for challenging hiking. Shrubby cinquefoil bushes shelter alpine speedwell's tiny blue blossoms, and red onion displays onion-scented foliage. A lichen-encrusted volcanic rock signals a turn upstream to an oxbow, where you can cross the inlet at a narrow place. Lavender-blue **western Jacob's ladder** and little pink elephants watch your progress. Not all that common, this member of the phlox family likes bogs. Along the clear waterway, a bit of **queen's crown** forms rounded pink heads. In the water itself, **white water crowfoot**, a floating buttercup family member, flourishes. Its foliage looks much like the sinuous plant that waves in home aquariums.

The next watercourse makes the ground you are on a semi-island. **Purple avens**, a less common cousin of pink plumes, **bittercress**, a few shy **violets**, and several bold little pink elephants have taken to island life. Heading upstream of this eastside inlet makes clear that this is not quite an island, as seeps, brightened by knee-deep **yellow monkeyflower**, issue from the dry slope above. Bright green moss encourages **American speedwell**, or **brooklime**, to show off its dainty, soft blue blossoms.

Return creekside, following the path until you spot a trail traveling along the flank of a xeric slope. Stony and dry, the soil supports **showy locoweed**, with its bright, rose-colored beaks enclosed in fuzzy foliage. Tall pale agoseris rises, and so may a killdeer, warning you away from her nearly-impossible-to-locate nest. Fleabane species, including **whiplash fleabane**, grow amidst bunchgrass on a sere gradient where the occasional **lupine** or scarlet gilia offer color.

A little incline sends hikers through more shrubby cinquefoil, alpine milkvetch, and cool and pale northern paintbrush. Here, spread like a many-armed starfish clinging to terra firma, is **Colorado thistle**, the stalkless version. Its blooms huddle like a bunch of miniature artichokes flowers centered in a prickly rosette.

The stone dam rises above a little cove surrounded by sedges, rushes, and grasses. If you're not sure which is which, remember this easy rhyme: "Sedges have edges, rushes are round, grasses have nodes, from the blades to the ground."

Littleflower penstemon, plantain-leaved goldenweed, and wallflower end this sector on the east side of Rito Hondo Reservoir. Wild blue flax and **silky lupine** grow in the gritty soil that leads to the dam. Crossing the level dam top allows you to enjoy the wide Colorado sky. Lots of **golden aster**, cinquefoil, and more showy Colorado tansy aster make an impressive finish to the loop hike of Rito Hondo Reservoir. Your vehicle is only a short distance ahead through more western Colorado wildflowers.

Wildflower Hike 17

Tumble Creek via Skyline Trail

Expansive vistas along the Tumble Creek segment of the Skyline Trail

Trail Rating	easy to moderate
Trail Length	6 miles out and back
Location	Gunnison National Forest/La Garita Wilderness, northwest of Creede and southeast of Lake City
Elevation	10,280 to 11,200 feet
Bloom Season	June to September
Peak Bloom	early to mid-July
Directions	Head west from Creede or east from Lake City on CO 149 to milepost 56. Turn north onto Gardner Ridge Rd./FR 729, continuing approximately 2 miles to the trailhead on the right (east).

The Tumble Creek section of the Skyline Trail makes for an easygoing to moderate hike offering a rewarding array of wildflowers. Beginning in a ranching valley about midway between Lake City and Creede just north of Spring Creek Pass, Tumble Creek via the Skyline Trail crosses a number of ecozones, from riparian habitat to montane forest, and dry south slope to subalpine meadow. Several stream crossings make sturdy boots essential. You may be sharing the first part of the trail with grazing cattle, but soon should have the path—and the flowers—to yourself.

The trail is apparently little used, promising some solitude especially on weekdays, but it's well defined despite the lack of traffic. For the first 2 miles, the gentle gradient alongside Tumble Creek allows hikers to adjust to the altitude. Crossing the creek starts a climb through spruce forest to arrive at the base of a rockfall, featuring blue columbine.

Adequate parking is available at a signed trailhead shared with the Cebolla Creek Trail. Get an early start to avoid late-afternoon storms.

Having signed the trail register, proceed downhill toward a gate. The broad valley, complete with buck and rail fence, lends this portion of the hike an Old West ambiance. Looking east at the skyline, note peaks such as 13,383-foot Baldy Cinco on the Continental Divide.

Silvery cinquefoil, together with **yarrow** and lavender **fleabane daisy**, start off the wildflower count. **Littleflower penstemon**'s intense, blue-violet clustered tubes spatter the grazed meadowland. **Beauty cinquefoil**, a defining orange beauty mark on each petal base, easily hybridizes with prolific silvery cinquefoil.

Meadow grasses hide **showy** or **whorled locoweed**, whose fuzzy silver foliage hides bright magenta blooms. In the same area, **pink plumes**' triple heads nod in dusty rose-pink; each matures into similarly-tinted feathery plumes. Like potentilla, pink plumes claims membership in the rose family.

The trail drifts down toward the stream, where a few erect specimens of **western Jacob's ladder**, less common than most polemonium species, bring hikers to Cebolla Creek. Across the waterway is **little pink elephants**. Crossing the creek is best done slightly upstream of a sign, on conveniently placed rocks.

On the far side, check streambank edges for the rounded pink heads and succulent leaves of **queen's crown**. Hugging the ground nearby, **silverweed**, a potentilla, sends out red runners. Its frond-shaped ladder leaves once were used as a medicinal tea; its starchy rootstock served as a food source.

The trail eases upward as it approaches an old beaver pond. Another opportunity arrives to view showy locoweed, of pea or legume lineage, as well as **Parry lousewort**, with its creamy blooms situated over ferny leaves like those found in little pink elephants, its cousin in the snapdragon or figwort family.

A second gate is preceded by **northern paintbrush**'s cool yellow swabs. Whenever you encounter a gate while hiking, remember to leave it as you found it. After the gate is Tumble Creek. Head upstream to cross where it narrows.

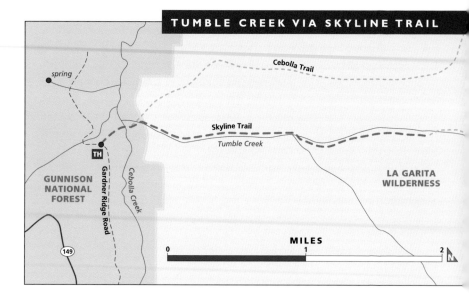

A junction soon arrives where the Cebolla Trail goes left, while Tumble Creek via Skyline Trail forges straight ahead. As you continue, check the grasses for **alpine milkvetch** with its purple-tinged tips. Willow-lined Tumble Creek creates a riparian zone; on the drier side of the track, bunchgrass and fringed sage grow alongside scattered clumps of **wild iris**. Waving grasses flank the route and pink plumes, sometimes called **old man's beard**, show sepaled heads with the petals tucked up inside.

A lichen-covered boulder presents **meadowrue** and **gooseberry**. As you approach another trailside outcrop supporting magenta **fireweed**, watch for a breached beaver dam. Nearby are gangly **yellow avens** and **red onion**.

A north-facing slope accommodates a thick spruce forest. **Harebell**'s dangling, cool purple thimbles appear trailside. A mossy seep is home to another member of the bellflower family, **Parry harebell**, whose warm purple, pointed petals open wide.

A post with a rock cairn base keeps hikers headed east as the trail offers sightings of **tall pale false dandelion** or **tall pale agoseris**, a native with long, blue-green leaves. Native **wavy-leaved dandelion** pops up next, its showy, shaggy rays much brighter than those of agoseris.

Willowherb and silverweed decorate the next seep, making way for **sego lily**, which blooms here about mid-July. Also known as **mariposa lily**—derived from the Spanish word for butterfly—the three-petaled white cup, painted with a dark maroon band that rings the pistil and stamens, looks like a graceful tulip. **Leafy aster**'s violet rays slip into the wildflower parade.

A quaking aspen copse introduces **Colorado rubberweed**, a plant shooting out sprays of rayed gold flowers from bouncing stems; its gray-green leaves are shaped like a bird's foot. The slope above, crowned by a long line of aspens, is lit by **scarlet gilia**'s narrow trumpets. Trailside, **mat penstemon** presents a low profile, mounded loosely with gray-green linear leaves and small, blue-edged, lavender-violet tubes.

Where willows grow close to the trail, look for **subalpine** or **hairy-fruit valerian**. The common names do not convey the daintiness of the pink tubes that form the head of this flower. Soon, a volcanic rockflow slides down from a cantilevered rusty red outcrop. Look here for bright blue spires of **mountain** or **branched larkspur**, with its slender, wavy, palmate leaves. A bit of bright pink **sweetvetch** dwells here as well.

The trail's grade increases, but the climb is sweetened by the perfumed scent of **wild rose**. Rocky now and still rising, the track passes more mountain larkspur and sweet-vetch, a pretty blue and pink duo, accenting **shrubby cinquefoil**'s gold, coinlike blossoms. Adding more vivid color is **Rocky Mountain penstemon**. Its diminutive relative, mat penstemon, spreads nearby.

At this point, an overgrown beaver dam appears below the trail, with **Colorado thistle** in view. Little pink elephants populates a seep where **yellow monkeyflower**, **pink willowherb**, and **miser milkvetch** gain a damp roothold. Climbing steadily, the route passes harebell cinquefoil, and fleabane daisy. **Orange sneezeweed** adds a snappy hue. Flanked by waist-deep vegeta-tion, the track arrives at a moist area nurturing **triangleleaf senecio**, which complements western Jacob's ladder. A willow draw by an old beaver lodge and dam brings on spires of deep purple **monks-hood**. You might even see a moose amid the willows and beaver dams.

SILVERWEED
Argentina anserina

Sluggish streams and moist meadows are favored homes of silverweed. The leaflets, adding up to as many as 31, form a leaf that resembles a coarse green feather, bright on top and silvery-white underneath. Long red stolons or runners root at the nodes, creating new plants. Tannic compounds produce an astringent that once served as a tea for indigestion and as a skin treatment. The rhizomatous roots, best collected in the cold months, offered nutrition; they were eaten raw or else cooked and dried, then powdered as a starchy food. The first part of the scientific name, *Argentina,* comes from the Latin word *argentum,* for "silver," while *anserina* means "of geese."

Open skies see the tread get rockier as it continues to pass rock cairns. Yarrow, typically off-white, shows in pink. Check for the violet-blue, pea-type flowers and pendant seed vessels of **drop-pod locoweed**. Look uphill to note warm orange **paintbrush**.

White geranium appears streamside, along with rangy orange sneezeweed and the occasional **orange agoseris**. Narrowing, the drainage sees the grade increase. Where aspens come close, look for wild iris and its tripartite seed capsules, as well as scented, lemon yellow **wallflower**.

As it enters conifer forest, the trail begins a more serious ascent. Along the way are brilliant **rosy paintbrush**, cool yellow northern paintbrush, and sunny flares of **heartleaf arnica**. Spruce shade is a favored habitat for **delicate Jacob's ladder**. Keen eyes might spot **least wintergreen**'s light-colored bells hanging from a straight stalk, or dusky purple **star gentian** thriving in damp places.

Whipple penstemon grows near **red-berried elder** bushes, showcasing a great fall of lichen-encrusted rock. As unforgiving as the hardscape looks, it is flush with elegant **Colorado blue columbine**. Finding pockets of soil among the rocks are mats of **dotted saxifrage** and mounds of fragrant **alpine phlox**.

Pinched between the gigantic rockfall and the tight willows, the equally rocky trail finds both **black-tipped** and **rock senecio**. Still rising and rocky through a sparse understory, the route meets a log-lined causeway where **nodding** or **daffodil senecio** teams with **snowball saxifrage**. Delicate-headed subalpine valerian and coarse **Grays angelica** call this spot home as well.

Another creek crossing looms, but instead, enjoy the view of the triangle-crested peak that rises above the trees of the creek drainage. This is a good turnaround point, especially if the weather looks ominous. If you choose to cross Tumble Creek, the route changes to a steep, entrenched trail section on the way up to a saddle, gaining about another 1,000 feet in elevation.

Brush Creek Trail

*Growing tall and straight, Indian warriors
line easygoing Brush Creek Trail.*

easy	***Trail Rating***
4 miles out and back	***Trail Length***
Gunnison National Forest, south of Lake City	***Location***
10,200 to 10,400 feet	***Elevation***
June to August	***Bloom Season***
July	***Peak Bloom***
From Lake City, take CO 149 south just under 15 miles to Los Piños–Cebolla Rd./FR 788. Turn left (north) onto FR 788 and continue approximately 6 miles to the trailhead. Park in the area to the left (east) of Brush Creek. Coming from Creede, take CO 149 west approximately 35 miles to FR 788.	***Directions***

Short and sweet, the 2-mile hike along Brush Creek Trail parallels the Powder-horn Wilderness boundary, just on the other side of the stream, and finally crosses into the wilderness near the turnaround point. The trail runs on the west side of the creek and formally meets Brush Creek only at the beginning and end of this description. As the route passes in and out of evergreen shade, a lovely variety of wildflowers line the route.

Gaining little elevation, the trail follows the Brush Creek drainage for 2 miles to the junction with the Cañon Infierno Trail. For a longer, more strenuous hike, continue up the latter route, where you will eventually arrive at Devils Lake, situated between Calf Creek and Cannibal Plateaus.

Wildflower species are diverse, reflecting riparian, grassland, forest, and scrubland habitats. Parking is casual in a spot east of the Brush Creek culvert under FR 788.

Before you head up Brush Creek's west bank, take a moment to walk a few paces east on the Los Piños–Cebolla Road you drove in on. You'll be rewarded with a slope of interesting wildflowers.

Adjacent to the road, a sandy cutbank on the left supports a thriving population of **wild cosmos**, with finely cut gray-green leaves supporting showy, white-rayed heads with yellow-brown, disk-flower centers. Sharing the loose slope and equally showy is **tufted evening primrose**, which is notably fragrant, particularly when the four huge light petals open in late afternoon; they wilt into a warm pink the following day. Pink **wild geranium** clumps are lush here. **Mat penstemon**'s pretty lilac-blue tubes emerge from fine, needlelike foliage and form loose mounds on the angled cutbank. **Dusty maiden**, or **pincushion**, brings up the rear, its pallid disk set atop pale, sparse foliage.

Retrace your steps, heading west back up the road and passing the Brush Creek sign. Check the sheltering willows for **white geranium**, **shrubby cinquefoil**, and **Parry harebell**. A little farther, look streamside

INDIAN WARRIORS
Pedicularis procera

Often mistaken for a fern before the bloomstalk emerges, this member of the snapdragon or figwort family also bears the name fernleaf lousewort. The red-streaked, yellow-helmeted flowers, called galeas, line the top of a sturdy stalk that may rise to 3 to 4 feet, giving credence to yet another common name, giant lousewort. Indian warriors thrives in a bit of moisture in montane and subalpine shade. The species name, *procera*, means "tall."

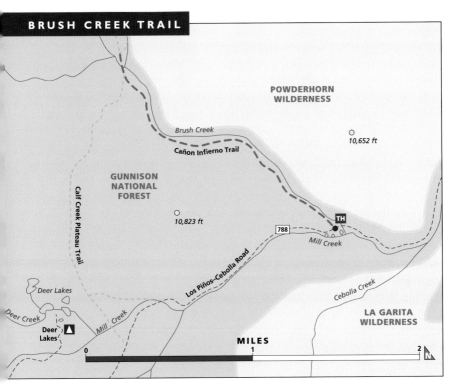

for **yellow monkeyflower** and **tall chimingbells**. A drier spot near the clear creek may offer **wild rose**'s hot pink blossoms, each imbued with an intoxicating and sensual fragrance.

As you continue, note where recent beaver activity has flooded a sedge area, nearly touching the road. This little pond is covered with **floating buttercup**. Lightly riding the water's surface, the yellow petals rise among leaves resembling shamrocks. Equally sunny is **yellow avens**, happy at the pond's periphery.

On the west side of Brush Creek, a trail register greets hikers coming north off the roadway. Sign in here. Then look for **scarlet gilia** and upturned faces of Parry harebell, which looks a bit like a startled purple tulip hiding in the grasses. Rising over the harebell is **tall pale agoseris**, a native with shaggy, dandelion-type heads. An outcropping of lava rock to the left may expose the electric blue of **branched** or **mountain larkspur** peering from behind a wild rose.

This easy jaunt lets hikers see the floral differences between the riparian habitat on the right, where Brush Creek flows, and the more xeric left side, where lithic soil drains quickly. Patches of shade allow glimpses of flowers that prefer shelter from the direct sun, while open spaces show a variety of sun lovers.

A healthy bunchgrass meadow boasts bright swaths of **wild blue flax**, especially vibrant in morning hours or on cloudy days. The delicate petals fall each day to be replaced by a seemingly endless supply of pointy buds. Lavender **fleabane daisy**, sometimes called **mountain daisy**, keeps company with buttery

wallflower, a scented member of the mustard tribe. Also growing here are the ubiquitous shrubby cinquefoil and showy blue branched larkspur.

The meadow ends with a Y intersection—go straight ahead along the right fork to continue this hike. The willows indicate more available moisture, which suits such plants as tall chimingbells and yellow avens. Under arching willows, a trickling seep supports snowy **bittercress**, a mountain cousin of watercress. The willow arch ends in **wild iris** clumps and a view of a small canyon carved by the creek. Widespread and wonderfully perfumed, wild rose is happy in many habitats. Its adaptibility might account for its age: The rose has been around for 40 million—yes, million—years, according its fossil record.

Rising above the stream, the trail approaches **leafy aster**, with warm purple rays, and **Rocky Mountain penstemon**, with intense blue-purple tubes; this pairing is complemented by the "McDonald's bush," shrubby cinquefoil. Many a burger is served in sight of the tough, bright yellow bush synonymous with durable landscaping.

Rocky and still rising, the next segment offers more fragrant wallflower as wide skies shine on the narrow leaf divisions of branched larkspur. Early Californians called spurred delphinium family members *espuela del caballero*, meaning "cavalier's spur." Sky blue wild blue flax's ephemeral petals juxtapose the larkspur's sturdy flowers. **Orange sneezeweed** leads the trail west, approaching quaking aspens, whose leaf petioles act as swivels.

Walking is easier now as **Indian warriors** rises about waist- to chest-high in the shadow of a small conifer stand; **fernleaf lousewort** is another name for this red-streaked, buff-colored member of the snapdragon or figwort family. Early-blooming and drought tolerant, **lanceleaf chimingbells** enjoys open areas, each delicate pink bud ready to morph into a blue bell. **Orange agoseris'** coppery dandelion heads lead to a sign announcing you have hiked 2 miles.

Hardy hikers may want to push on, taking the Cañon Infierno Trail up to Devils Lake. For this description, taking the right fork toward Brush Creek means the turnaround point is almost in sight. While at the trail junction, look for **Colorado blue columbine** sheltered under spruces on the left.

At long last, Brush Creek Trail heads down to its namesake, promising a riparian finale to the hike. Note wild iris along the way. The route banks down to meet a rocky floodplain, and the trail vanishes in lush growth. Yellow monkeyflower thrives at the water's edge. Willow islands created by braiding waters bend over grasses. At creekside, soft **pink willowherb**, **alpine speedwell**, and bittercress share the grassy environs with **western Jacob's ladder**. Low growing is **alpine milkvetch**, each small, ivory, pea-type flower tipped in purple.

The willows also attract moose. A favorite of this largest member of the deer family, the trees may be mangled, indicating a local moose. Tall chimingbells grows here, a favorite food of elk. Hikers wading the creek will find a sign up the hill on the far side welcoming them into the Powderhorn Wilderness. For those happy with a hike of 4 miles out and back, turn around here.

Grizzly Gulch Trail

Wildflower Hike 19

Flower-lined Grizzly Creek is an appropriate foreground for Handies Peak, a fourteener.

moderate to difficult	*Trail Rating*
5.4 miles out and back	*Trail Length*
Uncompahgre National Forest, west of Lake City	*Location*
10,425 to 11,900 feet	*Elevation*
late June to August	*Bloom Season*
mid- to late July	*Peak Bloom*
From Lake City, follow CO 149 south 2.5 miles and turn right (south) onto Lake San Cristobal Rd./CR 30. After 4 miles, the road is no longer paved. At 12.3 miles from CO 149, the road forks. Bear right, continuing 4.2 miles (along a shelf road at times) to the trailhead. Park to the left.	*Directions*

The Grizzly Gulch drainage is on the south side of Whitecross Mountain, the peak that overlooks beautiful American Basin to the north (see p. 114). Offering a stunning array of wildflowers, Grizzly Gulch serves as an alternate, if longer, route to 14,048-foot Handies Peak.

Sharing a trailhead, a trio of fourteeners routes lead up and away from a quiet stream valley, once a townsite for hopeful miners. The trail to the south heads up Grizzly Gulch, entering the floristic basin below Handies Peak. A steady 2.7-mile ascent takes you to the base of Handies Peak, with wildflower-lined Grizzly Creek to accompany you along the way.

Grizzly Gulch turns out more than 100 species, liberally rewarding wild-flower lovers. Though the access road is part of the famous Alpine Loop, the access to the trailhead requires only a competent driver and decent clearance. The parking areas are anchored by a restroom. Peak-baggers usually get a very early start. Even casual hikers in fourteener country are wise to follow their lead, in order to beat the infamous summer afternoon storms.

Grizzly Gulch Trailhead points hikers south, through willow clumps and over an arched footbridge that spans the Lake Fork of the Gunnison River. On the far side, willows harbor **tall chimingbells**, **meadowrue**, **yarrow**, **wallflower**, and, for keen eyes, tiny **yellow draba**, a wallflower cousin in the mustard clan.

Looking back reveals a fine view of Sunshine Peak. Continuing on brings **shrubby cinquefoil** as well as long-blooming **harebell**, droopy-rayed **orange sneezeweed**, and crisp-rayed **aspen sunflower**. Lower to the earth, **yellow stonecrop** adds a starry touch.

Yellow predominates in the meadow where hikers sign a trail register. Maroon barrels of **rayless senecio** lead the way through varied grasses, with **alpine milkvetch** and **beauty cinquefoil** trailside. As the trail ascends, look for **tall pale agoseris**, **heartleaf arnica**, and hairy-foliaged **golden aster**.

Entering conifer forest, the trail continues uphill over roots and rocks, within sound but not sight of Grizzly Creek. Look for **Parry goldenweed's** bright green foliage and sparse yellow heads, as well as **wild geranium**, with its perky pink blossoms. At a log waterbar, **mountain death camas**, **New Mexico senecio**, and **western red columbine** are visible.

Ubiquitous **wild strawberry** and **Indian warriors** accompany an outside curve in the trail. Quaking aspens shelter **tall scarlet paintbrush** and **narrowleaf paintbrush**, their linear bracts cradling toothpick-thin green flowers.

Perfumed **wild rose**, **rosy pussytoes**, dangling harebell, **mountain parsley**, and purple-rayed **aspen daisy** line the next segment. Open skies bring a view of cascading Grizzly Creek.

Kinnikinnick, with its smooth red bark and leathery leaves, forms ever-green mats to hold back lithic soil on the steep slope. Aspen daisy keeps light purple company with harebell. Golden aster—not an aster at all—is trailside as well.

Rockier and rising, Grizzly Gulch Trail leaves the open sky for mixed woods, a favored habitat for wild geranium, **delicate Jacob's ladder**, columbine, and heartleaf arnica.

Entering an aspen copse affords a chance to see Indian warriors and **edible valerian**. Along a flat trail segment, check in moist areas for the late bloomers **little rose gentian** and muted purple **star gentian**, both with satiny petals. **Subalpine valerian**'s dainty, blushed inflorescences contrast the dull green umbels of **Grays angelica**.

Ascend again into forest, continuing along to a stony bench graced by **Colorado blue columbine** and buttery wallflower. At the base of a rockfall, a favored home for pika, are yellow stonecrop, **alumroot**, and **elderberry** bushes. Dwarf **alpine golden buckwheat** thrives among the rocks, creating mats of silvery leaves. **Single-headed daisy** and mounds of **bear daisy** flourish here as well.

Rocky but meandering pleasantly now, the trail leads into a meadow where late summer displays deep blue chalices of **Rocky Mountain** or **Parry gentian**. In this lithic area, sweet-scented **alpine phlox** greets hikers early in the season.

Leaving the meadow affords easier tread for a brief stretch, as elderberry shrubs appear along with **Whipple penstemon**'s muted, wine-colored tubes. Look under a pair of uprooted spruces for columbine, tall chimingbells, **fireweed**, and **wild raspberry**.

At the base of a large rockfall is **twinberry honeysuckle**. Carefully threading your way across the jumble lets you observe sturdy rockbrake fern, clumps of Colorado blue columbine, and bear daisy patches among the lichen-spackled boulders. Hiking slightly above the creek takes you by meadowrue, tall chimingbells, and mountain parsley. Narrowing, Grizzly Creek drainage showcases **wolf currant**'s smooth twigs.

The two rockfalls frame Handies Peak. Look in this area for specimens of grass-green

ALPINE GOLDEN BUCKWHEAT
Eriogonum flavum ssp. *chloranthum*

This dwarf high-country umbellate wildflower is sometimes simply called yellow buckwheat. Its single umbels are subtended or ringed underneath by leafy bracts. The bright flowers sport long, soft hairs, and the silver, woolly leaves are almost velvety. Patches of this member of the buckwheat family hug gravelly or rocky ground, often in tundra terrain near the Continental Divide. The genus name comes from the Greek *erion*, for "wool," and *gonu*, for "knee," referring to the swollen joints. Cattle with white hides are prone to lethal sunburn if they eat buckwheat species.

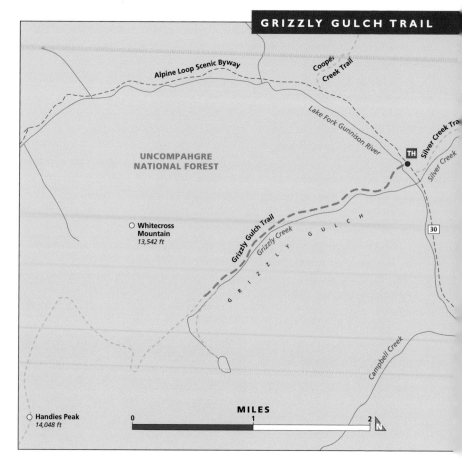

GRIZZLY GULCH TRAIL

Alpine Loop Scenic Byway

Cooper Creek Trail

Lake Fork Gunnison River

Silver Creek Trail

TH Silver Creek

UNCOMPAHGRE
NATIONAL FOREST

○ Whitecross
Mountain
13,542 ft

Grizzly Gulch Trail

Grizzly Creek

G R I Z Z L Y   G U L C H

30

Campbell Creek

○ Handies Peak
14,048 ft

MILES
0   1   2   N

greenleaf sage, as well as **drop-pod locoweed**, with fuzzy foliage and purplish flower clusters.

The ascent steepens as the trail reenters conifers and prepares to mount another rocky segment. Soon, soft duff underfoot welcomes showy mountain parsley's golden snowflakes. Demure in spruce shade, **shy wood nymph** features a five-petaled, nodding head. The spruces also shelter western red columbine, while moister conditions nurture **white geranium**, tall chimingbells, and wild strawberry.

A fall of rock fans out on the right, offering open skies. Look here for **subalpine larkspur, pink-headed daisy**, and **purple fringe**. Lovely Handies Peak rises in front of you, while behind you are two other fourteeners: 14,034-foot Redcloud Peak on the left and 14,001-foot Sunshine Peak on the right. Crossing the slope takes you to a drainage where subalpine larkspur, **subalpine arnica**, and, later in summer, magenta fireweed flourish. Continuing along brings hikers harebell, low and long-blooming **alpine chimingbells**, and white-rayed **Coulter daisy**.

Crossing another ravine, the damper trail features the usual golds, but with accents of brilliant **rosy paintbrush**, tall scarlet paintbrush, **little pink elephants**, midnight larkspur, geranium, Coulter daisy, and **cowbane**.

Pause in your uphill progress to admire the views and then enter conifer shade to tackle a steep ascent. Look for **bittercress** and tall chimingbells, and a bit farther on, aspen sunflower and **broadleaf arnica**. **Triangleleaf senecio** grows lankily, accompanied by **bracted lousewort** and subalpine larkspur.

The last big spruces signal an easier-going ascent, leading to a meadow featuring **monkshood, American bistort**, and Grays angelica flanking a seasonal waterway. Coming upon another seasonal waterway treats summer hikers to lavender-pink **subalpine daisy** and rosy paintbrush.

The views and flowers are magnificent. Barrel-headed rayless senecio, beauty cinquefoil, subalpine daisy, and **alpine arnica** foreground soaring mountains. A bit farther, **false hellebore**, or **cornhusk lily**, thrives, accented by **king's**

Subalpine daisies

crown. Sticky and inflated, the striped calyxes of **Drummond campion** keep the pale petals nearly hidden.

Hikers in columbine season are treated to clumps of elegant blue columbine, Colorado's state flower. As color complements, the yellows of senecio, orange sneezeweed, and arnica and the pinks of **queen's crown**, subalpine daisy, and rosy paintbrush flourish.

A rock cairn announces Grizzly Creek. Lining the stream are king's crown, queen's crown, cowbane, bittercress, and **yellow monkey-flower**. Mossy banks nurture **brook saxifrage**, with its wiry red stem and dainty white blooms.

Rocky tread takes you up to the last spruces and, in late July and early August, the royal blue chalices of Parry or Rocky Mountain gentian. Continuing on brings easier tread and, perhaps, shocking pink **Parry primrose** rising from a mass of big emerald leaves.

Iron-colored seeps harbor star gentian. Continue up, passing a small stream on approach to a knoll, resplendent in violet-pink **Halls penstemon**. Look north toward 13,542-foot Whitecross Mountain to catch a concentrated bunch of little pink elephants. All around you are mountains exceeding 13,000 feet, centered by soaring Handies Peak. The creek crossing highlights a pretty rock garden of queen's and king's crown accented by sunny cinquefoil. For those who wish to continue, a small alpine lake can be reached by hiking south across a talus slope.

Wildflower Hike 20

American Basin

A magnificent array of wildflowers flood beautiful American Basin.

Trail Rating	easy to moderate
Trail Length	2 miles out and back
Location	Uncompahgre National Forest, southwest of Lake City
Elevation	11,300 to 11,600 feet
Bloom Season	July to August
Peak Bloom	mid- to late July
Directions	From Lake City, go 2.5 miles south on CO 149 to the Lake San Cristobal sign. Turn right (south) on CR 30 and continue for 12.5 miles, bearing right at the fork (after 4 miles, the road is unpaved). Continue for another 8 miles, driving cautiously along the shelf road until you reach a fork and a sign indicating American Basin to the left. A four-wheel-drive vehicle is suggested. Park prior to the creek crossing if needed, or ford the creek and park in one of the soonest available casual roadside pullouts.

Located west of Lake City up the Cinnamon Pass Road, American Basin presents a panoramic, high-elevation stroll with a seemingly endless supply of wildflowers to enjoy. Take your time enjoying the vivid colors along the 2-mile round-trip hike.

The access road from Lake City is mostly a jeep road. If you don't wish to take your own vehicle, rent a jeep in Lake City. A surprising number of regular vehicles, however, do manage to crawl over miles of rough road, determined to enter American Basin. Some drivers with high-clearance vehicles choose to ford the creek that cuts across the road and park just on other side.

Part jeep road, part abandoned roadway, the "trail" only becomes such at the Handies Peak Trailhead parking area. The first 0.75 mile of this hike follows an easy ascent up to that parking area. Another 0.25 mile continues on the trail to Handies Peak, reaching the turnaround point at an outcrop featuring tundra plants.

Parking on the basin side of the creek is catch-as-catch-can; just across the stream, parking is readily available. The most splendid flower viewing is between the creek and the Handies Peak Trailhead and is best enjoyed by foot. With fourteener Handies Peak forming the basin's south wall and thirteener Whitecross Mountain on the north, weather awareness is imperative. All of American Basin is above treeline, leaving you highly vulnerable to summer afternoon storms.

This description begins on the basin side of the stream crossing of the Lake Fork of the Gunnison River. The stream is most easily forded by vehicle, but not too difficult to cross by foot using rocks. The meadow, open to the sky, is a veritable alpine treasure box, revealing **little pink elephants**, early-blooming **marsh marigold**, lacy-headed **cowbane**, and **queen's crown**. **Yarrow** and **triangleleaf senecio**, also known as **arrowleaf senecio**, add white and gold accents.

Thick willows grow on the right, but **orange sneezeweed** and triangleleaf senecio manage to push through. **Yellow monkeyflower**, tiny-flowered blue **alpine veronica**, and both **pink** and **white willowherb** grow in damp moss.

Looking on the left side of the roadway, find soft-leaved **subalpine arnica** and ivory **paintbrush**, its bract bases daubed with burgundy. Both **king's crown** and queen's crown shelter under willows. Back on the right, masses of snowy **bittercress** and **tall chimingbells** accompany **rosy paintbrush**'s bright swabs. Dark purple **monkshood** rises among the blue and white tones. Note fine-rayed **Coulter daisy** close to the road's edge.

Joining tall chimingbells and stately monkshood are lavish clumps of **subalpine larkspur** in rich blue-purple. Toward the creek, pink **Parry primrose** sends up bare stems of showy blossoms from big basal leaf clumps.

A little creek on the left supports golden orange sneezeweed and senecio, blue subalpine larkspur and tall chimingbells, and the eye-catching pink of rosy paintbrush. The rocky road continues up, passing **tall pale agoseris**, a native sometimes referred to as **tall pale false dandelion**.

Look for the subtle watercolor tints of **Colorado blue columbine**, complemented by the yellows of **beauty cinquefoil** and **alpine avens**. Down to the right, white bittercress contrasts with the deep red of king's crown. Roadside, a grassy meadow is home to **meadowrue** and **Colorado thistle**, its lilac disk flowers packed like old-fashioned shaving brushes. Lots of alpine avens lift brassy petals as white **American bistort** waves over yarrow and Coulter daisy.

A sign on the right directs you to an abandoned roadway, allowing you to leave the rocky jeep road. As you pass the sign, note **rayless senecio**, in chartreuse, contrasting golden avens, cinquefoil, and orange sneezeweed. **Sibbaldia** dots the track, as do Colorado blue columbine and wine-colored **Whipple penstemon**. Late bloomer **Parry goldenweed** leads to rosy paintbrush, **white geranium**, and soft-leaved subalpine arnica.

The route grows more grassy as it passes pink-budded, blue-belled tall chimingbells. The rocky bank along the abandoned roadway supports the shapely pink florets of queen's crown, each centered in soft rose-red. To the left, a trickling seep nourishes Colorado blue columbine, bistort, little pink elephants, marsh marigold, and **brook saxifrage**. A bit of bittercress and, for early-season hikers, Parry primrose also thrive here. **Different-leaved senecio** displays little gold heads and dual leaf shapes.

On the damper side of the meadow, look for **old man of the mountains**, Parry primrose, and king's and queen's crown. **Alpine sorrel**'s kidney-shaped leaves

COTTONSEDGE
Eriophorum altaicum var. *neogaeum*

Known as cottonsedge, cottongrass, or bogwool, this member of the sedge family blooms late, presenting a single snowy mop on the top of each stem. A patch of cottonsedge looks like a convention of cottonballs. This particular species is found in alpine areas, such as the high mountains of the San Juans, where there is sufficient moisture; there may be permafrost underneath. The bristled white heads account for another common name, Arctic wool. The Latin genus name comes from the Greek *erion*, meaning "wool," and *phoros*, meaning "bearing." The variety name, *neogaeum*, means "New World race."

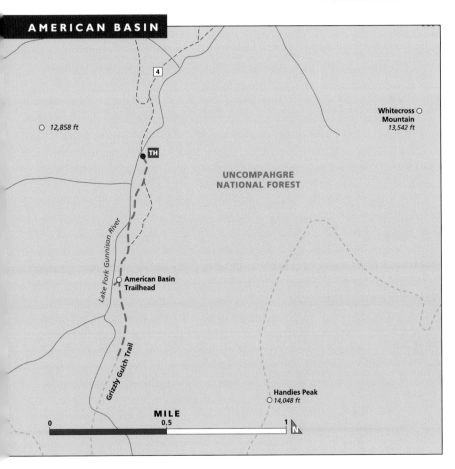

AMERICAN BASIN

4

○ 12,858 ft

Whitecross ○
Mountain
13,542 ft

TH

Lake Fork Gunnison River

UNCOMPAHGRE
NATIONAL FOREST

○ American Basin
   Trailhead

Grizzly Gulch Trail

Handies Peak
○ 14,048 ft

MILE
0   0.5   1   N

form clumps with hanging red-rimmed seed clusters. Marsh marigold, subalpine arnica, and orange sneezeweed foreground the impressive mountains above. On the right, a broken outcrop offers **blue fleabane, pussytoes, yellow stonecrop,** while both lavender **cutleaf daisy** and light purple **pinnate-leaf daisy** are in the company of **shrubby cinquefoil.**

Handies Peak dominates the view to the southeast. The face of a granitic outcrop on the left frames Whipple penstemon, king's crown, and little pink elephants, sometimes called **elephantella.** A seep presents brook saxifrage, pink willowherb, and more queen's crown. As the route crosses a few steps of bedrock, observe the range of rosy paintbrush hues, from blushed white to neon rose. Brook saxifrage's proximity affords an opportunity to note its pristine white, starlike blooms. Back on the right, a mass of monkshood and senecio grow near a nice patch of king's crown.

Merge now with the jeep road, which divides a showy display of Colorado blue columbine and larkspur. Both chartreuse and maroon rayless senecio make a statement, accompanied by orange sneezeweed and pink paintbrush. Less overwhelming is the discovery, on the right, of yellow **nodding** or **daffodil senecio**, a Colorado endemic.

Competing with brighter neighbors is Colorado thistle, its pale lavender disk flowers staying close to the ground. Alpine avens, looking like its rose family relation cinquefoil, thrives. Here, you are at the parking area for the Grizzly Gulch Trail to Handies Peak. Down to the right is the outlet creek from Sloan Lake. The water courses through a natural tunnel in front of a tailings pile. By carefully crossing the rough rock bridge to the right, you might catch sight of pure white **cottonsedge**, more colorfully referred to as **bogwool**, each blowsy head looking like a wispy hairdo.

Pass the tailings pile and go upstream on the right, where **false hellebore** grows alongside **red onion**, some of its flowers replaced by red bulblets. This is backed by masses of bittercress, marsh marigold, and wild geranium, as well as cool **northern paintbrush**. Hybridization with its partner rosy paintbrush contributes to the many bract tints around you. When the path fades, recross the unique lithic bridge to the Grizzly Gulch Trail.

Colorado blue columbine

Continuing 0.25 mile along the trail completes this hike description. Follow it up toward the head of American Basin by passing daffodil senecio, wild geranium, and Colorado thistle. The trail ascends rockily, highlighting small clumps of alpine sorrel with larkspur and tall chimingbells.

The grade steepens as you approach the trail register box. On the drier left, find **purple fringe** and dainty alpine **rock primrose**. Then push on to a slope of primary colors. Steepening, the grade reaches homely, drab green **Grays angelica**. Trailside, mounded **rock senecio** and cleft-petaled **mouse-ears** add to the wildflower list.

As the trail evens out, look for elegant Colorado blue columbine upslope; downslope, larkspur and bittercress dominate. Continuing on, note **sky pilot** and Parry primrose, appearing just before you reach a rock outcrop on the right marked by spruce krummholz patches. Old man of the mountains displays big sunflower heads, only blooming after seasons of gathering energy. Smaller plants adorning the worn rock are **dwarf clover**, **snow cinquefoil**, **alpine sandwort**, and a bit of **wallflower**. This outcrop is a favorite sunning place for marmots as well.

Travel up to a rockslide, home to pika as well as **rockslide daisy** and **moss campion**. A careful search in the thick tundra vegetation might reveal blue **moss gentian**, sometimes called **compass gentian**, each diminutive flower configured like a compass rose. With its beautiful array of tundra wildflowers, this makes a good turnaround point.

Upper Henson Creek from the Thoreau Cabin

Wildflower Hike 21

A brilliant array of wildflowers beckons hikers toward Henson Creek.

easy	**Trail Rating**
2 miles out and back	**Trail Length**
Uncompahgre Wilderness, west of Lake City	**Location**
11,200 to 11,400 feet	**Elevation**
July to August	**Bloom Season**
mid-July to early August	**Peak Bloom**
From Lake City, travel west on Henson Creek–Engineer Pass Rd./CR20, bearing left at the Capitol City site. (Drive cautiously along the shelf road.) Pull off the road and park above the Thoreau Cabin in the parking area to the right.	**Directions**

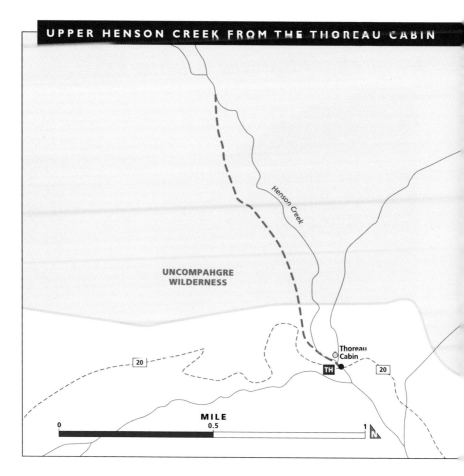

UPPER HENSON CREEK FROM THE THOREAU CABIN

UNCOMPAHGRE
WILDERNESS

Henson Creek

Thoreau
Cabin

20

TH

20

MILE
0   0.5   1

Getting to the upper Henson Creek hike from Lake City is historically interesting, as you pass by the private Ute-Ulay Mine 4 miles up Henson Creek Road and, 7 miles later, the 1877 mining town site of Capitol City, whose founder had ambitious hopes of making the town Colorado's state capital. Traveling another 1.5 miles offers a short walk to overlook Whitmore Falls. Another 2.5 miles beyond the falls brings you to Rose's Cabin site, a mining-era stagecoach overnight stop. Soon, the two-wheel-drive portion of Henson Creek Road ends, beginning the four-wheel-drive road to Engineer Pass.

At this hairpin curve is the marvelously crafted Thoreau Cabin. Just a few yards up from the private cabin's parking area is a wide spot on the right; park alongside the road on the right, just before a wilderness etiquette sign. The upper Henson Creek hike takes you northwest from this point.

Upper Henson Creek is one of those serendipitous hikes that leaves wildflower lovers exhilarated but not winded. Paintbrush is the true highlight of this gently ascending trail.

Start your wildflower walk just west of the private parking for Thoreau Cabin, a superb example of log cabin construction with an innovative bridge spanning Henson Creek.

Begin by surveying wildflowers near the bridge, such as rich purple **silvery lupine** across the road and amethyst-veined **wild iris**, both complemented by yellow **orange sneezeweed**, **triangleleaf senecio**, and **northern paintbrush**.

Back at the cabin's parking area, note **oxeye daisy** together with **Coulter daisy**, a refined native, populating the meadow as you approach an interpretive sign for alpine tundra. The elevation here is about 11,200 feet, placing it in the subalpine life zone; alpine tundra is typically above 11,500 feet. For those continuing up the four-wheel-drive section of Engineer Pass Road, the alpine life zone is just a few miles ahead.

Behind the sign, a vaguely defined route takes you through thick grasses toward an outcrop boulder. Hikers enter the Uncompahgre Wilderness, open only to foot and horse traffic. Bear in mind that sheep are frequent grazers here. Wildflower seekers in this part of the San Juan Mountains might consider an early-season outing, before flocks arrive to "mow" the meadows. Brassy **subalpine arnica**'s soft leaves lead the way up the gently rising old track.

A hidden trickle is revealed by the flora it nurtures, such as **alpine speedwell**, a veronica, and lacy white **cowbane**, along with pink-tubed clusters of **red onion**. For over 6,000 years, American Indians have found the allium or onion family a source of both food and medicine. Keep going, passing **wild strawberry** and more Coulter daisy.

The damp soil near Henson Creek supports the rounded pink heads of **queen's crown** as well as **subalpine daisy**'s cool pink rays. This late-blooming fleabane's ray flowers are wider than is typical of the *Erigeron* genus. **Marsh marigold**, with its thick sepals and leathery leaves, appreciates a cold, wet habitat. The moisture also suits both white and **rosy paintbrush**, the first of many paintbrush varieties to come.

COULTER DAISY
Erigeron coulteri

Coulter daisy is characterized by a golden disk-flower center, a plethora of fine rays on a tall stalk, and black hairs on the phyllaries. A native, it is found mainly on the Western Slope in montane and subalpine zones. At 20 years of age, John Merle Coulter spent 1871 to 1873 as a botanist with the Hayden Expedition, exploring the Rocky Mountains for the U.S. Geological Survey. The first Western botanical manual, describing 2,733 species and written in 1885, was his work.

And they do come, in the crimson, bright rose, and pale pastel hues of the *Castilleja* clan—a genus in the snapdragon or figwort family. **Orange agoseris** offers accents near a flaking rock, where **purple fringe** meets early-season hikers. **Yarrow** adds subtlety. Once called woundwort, it was the plant Achilles used to stanch bleeding and prevent infection in the wounds of his soldiers. Yarrow also served as a mild pain reliever and even a rudimentary insect repellant.

Aiming to the right of twin spruces, hikers pass even more paintbrush, with the modified leaf and bract outshining the actual flower, green and tooth-picklike as it pokes out of a showy bract. The paintbrush is complemented by the yellows of **beauty cinquefoil**, subalpine arnica, and **subalpine senecio**. **Fendler sandwort** adds a touch of white, as does **snowball saxifrage**. Low to the ground, **Colorado thistle** blooms quietly in ivory or palest lavender.

Golds are prominent thanks to **alpine avens** and **blueleaf cinquefoil**, both in the rose family. It is the changing foliage of alpine avens that turns slopes red in the fall. Above them wave the bottlebrush heads of **American bistort**, a favorite food of ptarmigans.

Myriad shades of paintbrush along the trail to upper Henson Creek

Obscured by low vegetation underfoot, the route levels. Off to the right, Henson Creek falls away and continues down a small gorge. Along the trail, paintbrush specimens increase in color and number, brightening the landscape with white, pink, bright rose, and the occasional crimson example.

Enjoy the views here: Cresting on the right is the 12,932-foot summit of Dolly Varden Mountain. Flowing from American Flats, the outlet stream from American Lake courses down from the north. Continuing along, look for **different-leaved senecio**, with two leaf shapes, and marsh marigold, whose thick white sepals generally sport a steel blue reverse. As elsewhere, paintbrush abounds.

The trail continues as a double track, probably the remnant of an old wagon road, passing **little pink elephants**. A damp spot nourishes early-blooming **globeflower**, whose seedheads resemble miniature artichokes, as well as **king's crown** and queen's crown. The king's flat inflorescence is burnt red and made up of myriad tubular florets; the queen's rounded head is a soft pink, the florets centered in muted red. Both heads perch on the terminal ends of thick stems lined with succulent leaves, typical of sedums. The plump leaves turn a glowing pink-red or coral in autumn.

The route rises above little pink elephants before coming down to a seasonal waterway, which displays the red, white, and gold combination of paintbrush, American bistort, alpine avens, and subalpine arnica.

Ascending slightly, the trail winds past dusky purple **Whipple penstemon** before reaching a brook displaying rosy paintbrush. Queen's crown, pristine white **bittercress**, and fragile-looking **brook saxifrage**, along with both **pink** and **white willowherb**, drape the waterway's front banks.

The trail changes direction slightly, edging down to meet Henson Creek itself. Small clumps of vivid **Parry primrose**, an early bloomer with huge leaves, catches your attention as you look left upon reaching the water. Search under sheltering willows for the uncommon **alpine lousewort**. Its rosy, beaked blossoms rise above fernlike foliage not unlike that of its pink elephant cousin. The pinwheel effect of this unusual flower makes a lovely finale to the upper Henson Creek hike.

This idyllic spot, surrounded by majestic scenery, is a good place to turn around and retrace your steps.

Horsethief Trail via American Flats

Brooks are lined with Parry primrose and queen's crown on the Horsethief Trail.

Trail Rating	easy
Trail Length	4 miles out and back
Location	Uncompahgre Wilderness, west of Lake City
Elevation	12,300 to 12,500 feet
Bloom Season	July to August
Peak Bloom	mid-July
Directions	From Lake City, head west on the Henson Creek–Engineer Pass Rd./CR 20, bearing left at the Capitol City site. (Be sure to drive cautiously along the shelf road.) A high-clearance, four-wheel-drive vehicle is necessary above the Thoreau Cabin. Continue up to the trailhead, located on the right near milepost 17.

If American Flats is not quite at the top of the world, then it sure feels close. Scenic expanses are pierced by mountain summits, making American Flats seem like an artist's rendition of an intriguing, just-discovered planet. The ridge of rocks to the west is 13,260-foot Darley Mountain. To the south is 13,218-foot Engineer Mountain. Evidence of past mining activity, including the Hough Mine, is all around you. Best of all, the Horsethief Trail takes you across tundra flower fields that are relatively flat, and that is important at this immoderate elevation. At this altitude, there is 40 percent less available oxygen.

After getting to the Horsethief Trailhead, the hard work is over. The trail initially rises a bit but then follows a fairly level grade for the 4-mile round-trip. The track is sometimes obscured by tundra grasses, but follow the contours, cairn posts, and vestiges of an old wagon road. If time and weather permit, hikers may want to continue on to shallow American Lake.

The Horsethief Trail supports a wide array of alpine wildflower species and pockets of tundra flora. One caveat, however: Wildflower displays may be splendid or, if flocks of sheep have gotten there first, more sporadic. Try mid-July. Regardless, the mild-mannered trail is rewarding, if for nothing else than the otherworldly scenery.

Parking is just a matter of pulling off the road. American Flats, though, is completely open to the vagaries of weather. Be sure to watch for storms and try for an early start.

Geology takes center stage as you step onto the Horsethief Trail and head northwest. Like a fleet of ships, impressive peaks define the horizon: 12,266-foot Wildhorse Peak, 13,656-foot Coxcomb Peak, 14,015-foot Wetterhorn Peak, Matterhorn Peak at 13,590 feet, and the regional centerpiece, 14,309-foot Uncompahgre Peak. Off to the side is 12,923-foot Crystal Peak.

Behind the Horsethief sign stretches an abandoned road headed

PARRY PRIMROSE
Primula parryi

A showy inhabitant of well-watered places in the high country, Parry primrose sports five hot pink, slightly cleft petals surrounding a yellow eye. Clumps of big basal leaves, said to have a grape odor, support sturdy, bare stems up to 16 inches high. The flowers emit a skunky scent, at least to some noses. Dr. Charles Parry, a 19th-century physician and botanist, is honored by the species name.

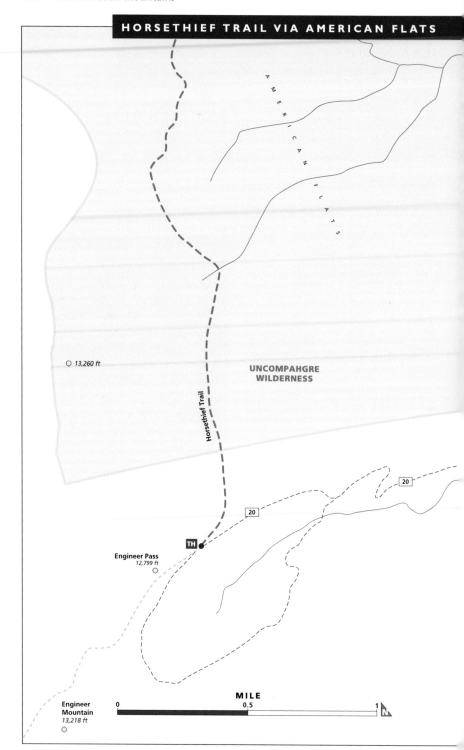

HORSETHIEF TRAIL VIA AMERICAN FLATS

A M E R I C A N   F L A T S

○ 13,260 ft

UNCOMPAHGRE WILDERNESS

Horsethief Trail

20

TH

Engineer Pass
12,799 ft
○

20

MILE

0   0.5   1

Engineer Mountain
13,218 ft
○

N

across tundra grasses. Survey the wildflowers at your feet, starting with **alpine avens**, its gold heads rising above fernlike foliage, and the smaller **blueleaf cinquefoil**, both members of the rose family. Nearby are **alpine bistort** and tiny **stitchwort**. **American bistort** waves above them, while widespread **alpine speedwell** adds a sapphire touch. A few rosy balls of fragrant **Parry clover** round out these first offerings.

Following are ground-hugging **pygmy bitterroot** displaying translucent pink stars cupped in succulent leaves, and **spergulastrum**, or **rock starwort**, whose white stars practically need a magnifying lens to examine; what they lack in size, they make up for in numbers. **Single-headed daisy** offers its amethyst rays. Another fleabane with typically fine rays is **black-headed daisy**, the most common of its kind in the alpine ecozone and characterized by a tangle of soft purple-black hairs under its white head.

A sign tells hikers it is 2.3 miles to the Bear Creek National Recreation Trail. You then enter the Uncompahgre Wilderness, open only to foot traffic, equestrians, and sheep, those efficient mowing machines.

A clear trickle supports some **marsh marigold** as the track leads across a gold-dominated landscape, accented with the blues of **alpine chimingbells** and flaring **sky pilot**. While its lavender-blue blossoms are redolent of honey, the latter's foliage, typical of the polemoniums, is skunky. Be careful not to crush the tightly laddered leaves.

A small rocky mound to the right is decorated with sweet-scented **alpine phlox**, which keeps its white to lavender-blue blooms close to its tight

Hikers will enjoy the area's magnificent views.

cushions. Long-blooming **alpine sandwort**, sometimes affectionately called sandywinks, clusters on the stony rise, as does **snow cinquefoil**.

It is impossible to miss the startling panorama that arises before you. Underfoot, the tundra is carpeted in bits of yellow, lavender, and pink. To the west, tumbled stone, resembling a ruined wall, shelters **alpine spring beauty**. This member of the purslane clan is at home in the crannies, as is **alpine violet**, pygmy bitterroot, and **alpine pussytoes**, each soft, bracted "paw" ringed with dark halos. Brick red **king's crown** appears as well.

The fallen rock is a likely place to find marmots sunning or stuffing themselves. In order to hibernate for eight months, these stout rodents must gain fat while they can.

Returning to the trail, pass between a pair of wilderness signs; the one on the left also serves as a rock cairn indicating you are on the right track. Drifting down, look for **alpine parsley's** yellow snowflakes. **Yellow draba's** tiny, four-petaled flowers cluster atop a rosetted stem, requiring a hand lens to get a good look. **Different-leaved senecio** is a bit more bold.

The old track, vague at times, is defined by posts set in rock cairns. Continue along it, past sheltered pockets of matte blue alpine chimingbells and sky pilot, complemented by ubiquitous alpine avens.

Parry primrose's hot pink calls attention to the rivulets that wet the gray rocks. Snow-white **bittercress** balances the primrose's vivid petals as does marsh marigold, its tepals sporting steel blue reverses. Another streamside species, **brook saxifrage**, lifts small blossoms high on wiry, reddish stems. Its clumps of smooth green leaves have even teeth.

Moist areas nourish **little pink elephants**. Soon another trickle, this one over a sandy bed, brings you up to a marker post guiding hikers across the treeless plain. Beyond it rises Wildhorse Peak. At a wide post, look for shining American Lake, set across the valley like a small mirror.

Horsethief Trail curves pleasantly, highlighting Parry clover on its way to a small cascade lined on one side by an eroding outcrop. A patch of marsh marigold encourages the hiker to look along the outcrop for both **rosy** and yellow **western paintbrush**. Picturesquely tucked into the crumbling crevices are the red inflorescences of king's crown. Nearby, the fuzzy leaves of **alpine arnica** contrast with the smooth ones of sour **alpine sorrel**.

Another post stands near a mossy brook whose ash gray stones support Parry primrose. Demure brook saxifrage and little pink elephants tell us this is really a seep, and more seeps soon follow. The next seeps, set dramatically against the mountain backdrop, present more showy Parry primrose.

If the weather is good, hikers may wish to continue up to the shallow waters of American Lake. If not, then exploration in the rocky areas to the west may turn up that tundra flora icon, **moss campion**. With pink flowers decorating dense mounds, this alpine dweller is related to carnations. Make your way back along the same trail when you are ready.

Placer Gulch

Wildflower Hike 23

Once a mining site, Placer Gulch now yields fields of golden arnica.

easy	*Trail Rating*
2 miles out and back	*Trail Length*
north of Silverton	*Location*
11,720 to 11,940 feet	*Elevation*
July to August	*Bloom Season*
late July to early August	*Peak Bloom*
From Silverton, head east on CO 110. The road is very rough the last 3 miles to the Animas Forks ghost town, so drive cautiously. Bear left at the far end of Animas Forks toward California Gulch. Turn left at Placer Gulch/CR 9 and park. A four-wheel-drive, high-clearance vehicle is suggested.	*Directions*

Placer gold, compared to hardrock-mined gold, is relatively easy to recover, even by late-1880s methods. In the town of Animas Forks, silver and gold were extracted mainly the hardrock way. Placer Gulch mines included both the Silver Queen and the Gold Prince with the mills that served them nearby. Today, those mines are abandoned, but gold can still be found in the form of brilliant wildflowers, which decorate the length of 12,800-foot Treasure Mountain to the east and 13,148-foot California Mountain to the west.

Old mining sites still remain in upper Placer Gulch. Nonetheless, on your way to the trailhead, be sure to stop in the ghost town of Animas Forks, which features the 1879 Bay Window House and a wealth of interpretive signage. Down by the Animas River are the concrete remains of what, for 10 years, was Colorado's largest ore-crushing mill, the Gold Prince. Around the corner on the way to Placer Gulch, a fairly intact and impressive mill still stands, with 13,052-foot Houghton Mountain behind it.

The road-cum-trail up Placer Gulch ascends steadily but gently, making it an easy route. Yes, the road is driveable, but using your own two feet is always the best way to discover wildflowers species.

Parking is casual, but try to avoid mashing the wildflowers by keeping to the side of the road, if possible.

It's not hard to discern Placer Gulch, with its sweeping slopes blanketed in golden yellow. Park immediately after your turn to the left, as the description begins at the creek culvert for the West Fork of the Animas River.

Be sure to notice the stark white mineralized coating on stones in the creek; it matches nearby **Coulter daisy**, **marsh marigold**, and **yarrow**. The willow-lined riparian area to the left displays powder blue **tall chimingbells**, **orange sneezeweed**, **subalpine daisy**, **queen's crown**, and **tall scarlet paintbrush**, joined by **triangleleaf senecio** and some **monkshood**, with its cowled sepals of rich purple. **Fireweed** and **beauty cinquefoil** put in their color bid as well.

The right side drainage yields **subalpine arnica**, **rosy paintbrush**, **pearly everlasting**, and **American bistort**. Abundant moisture suits **little pink elephants** and queen's crown, as lichen-covered boulders overlook a gilded pool accented with dark, brick red **king's crown**, drumlike heads of **rayless senecio**, and more vivid rosy paintbrush.

The roadway passes sunny arnica, tall chimingbells, and white Coulter daisy. Spruces dot the landscape. Glance left to a cropped meadow anchored by a boulder to find, in late summer, electric blue chalices of **Rocky Mountain gentian**. The gold hues here are accented by cool lavender subalpine daisy, wine-colored **Whipple penstemon**, and clumps of **yellow paintbrush**.

Still looking east, a rock-studded swale harbors **Porters lovage**, with its umbels of tiny white flowers, **white geranium**, tall chimingbells, tiny-flowered blue **alpine veronica**, cool pink **wild onion**, and show-stealing rosy paintbrush.

Placer Gulch presents a brilliant beginning. Both subalpine arnica and **thickbract senecio** display bright golden blooms, while intensely pigmented **subalpine larkspur** thrives in royal purple. The cutbank to the right harbors **white willowherb, stitchwort,** and **pussytoes.** The right competes for attention with rangy orange sneezeweed and prolific rosy paintbrush. Cooling the golden tones are the whites of Coulter daisy and yarrow. Gold fever was the stimulus for the line of huge, ore-transporting tram towers you see along Treasure Mountain to the east.

Complementing the golds, larkspur shows its purple-blue blossoms as the valley view stretches south. As the path rises gently, hikers should check for **Parry goldenweed** and **meadowrue** on the left. Switching attention right, note a patch of pearly everlasting anchoring the soil. Grasses dominate on the left and white geranium dots the hillside on the right, along with brassy **alpine avens** and a bit of late-blooming **sky pilot.** Purply-pink wild onion decorates both sides of the road.

Leveling, the route sends you left, where added moisture supports spikes of little pink elephants and rounded, pink heads of queen's crown. Though this route is only 1 mile long, the hiker gets twice the exercise just weaving from side to side. On the right side, American bistort waves oversized, Q-Tiplike heads over gilded avens, senecio, and arnica. As the terrain dips to the left, look for a swale dominated by little pink elephants. Placer Creek runs in the background.

A culvert signals a slight increase in grade. As the route levels, **Colorado blue columbine** appears on both sides. The area's mining past is evident from the tailings that pock California Mountain to the west. Wild onion's pointy tepals form legions of hemispheric heads. Indigenous peoples have utilized the distinctive onion for over six millennia for food and medicinal purposes.

A seasonal waterway curves into a culvert as you approach a damp cliff face

WHITE GERANIUM
Geranium richardsonii

White geranium has five white or barely blushed petals surrounding a pillar of unified stamens and colored anthers. Reddish-purple nectar guidelines aim pollinators toward the central column; the resulting seedpods, spring-loaded to split and coil when ripe, have been likened to a crane's bill, another common name for the plant. This widespread native is found from Canada to New Mexico. The potted bloomer popularly called geranium is actually a *Pelargonium* from Africa.

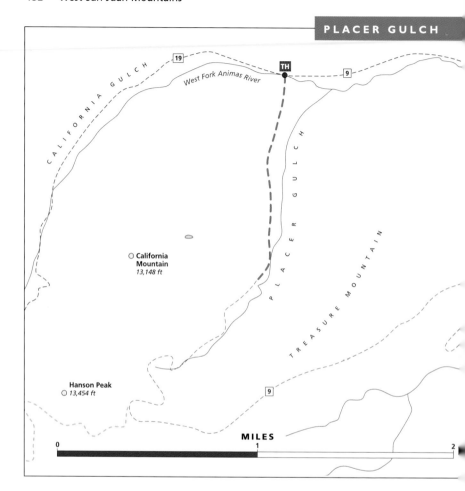

California Mountain
13,148 ft

Hanson Peak
13,454 ft

West Fork Animas River

CALIFORNIA GULCH

PLACER GULCH

TREASURE MOUNTAIN

MILES
0   1   2

on the right, with **pink willowherb** in residence. As the grade increases gently, look down the Placer Creek valley to ponds surrounded by little pink elephants. In rocky spaces along the roadway, **black-tipped senecio** dominates.

Though the **false hellebore**–colonized slopes are steep, the route levels so you might note **pink-headed daisy** and larkspur among the big, pleated hellebore leaves. More visually noteworthy are tall scarlet paintbrush, plush rosy paintbrush, and the spurred blossoms of Colorado blue columbine, each spur ending in a nectar-filled knob. Note also subalpine daisy, a lavender-pink fleabane with rays wide enough to be mistaken for an aster's.

The quiet creek below gently spills over a small lip. Broken rock on the right might harbor a marmot. Here, too, at road's edge, check out **homely buttercup** and **yellow monkeyflower**. In the valley, the Gold Prince's Sound Democrat Mill, well equipped and ready for restoration, makes a statement; king's crown, beauty cinquefoil, orange sneezeweed, and Whipple penstemon populate the vicinity.

Covered with brilliant orange lichen, an outcrop on the right shelters pink willowherb and yellow monkeyflower, its throat red speckled. **Alumroot's** bare wands of yellow-green flowers rise from basal leaves tucked into crevices, as does fireweed. This lithic pile also supports king's crown, **purple fringe,** and **rock senecio.** Early hikers will see **snowball saxifrage** and slim, erect **rockcress** in bloom.

Continue strolling up between the ridges to arrive at the wood skeleton of a mining structure, its slow decay juxtaposed with fresh blooms of Colorado blue columbine. Take time to explore a small cascade plunging down from California Mountain, surrounded by white geranium, Porters lovage, arnica, monkshood, and little pink elephants. Subalpine daisy adds to the flowers lining the lively waterway.

No matter the colors encountered, it is gold that dominates the slopes. Scattered nearby are the remains of mining operations. Some of the wooden relics are bleached as white as whalebones. Others are aged to a rich patina by years under the strong, high-country sun. Imagine how noisy now-silent Placer Gulch was in its turn-of-the-century heyday.

Crossing another culvert, the roadway rises rockily. The rough, gray-green leaves of **golden aster** and smooth, almost succulent, bright green leaves of yellow rock senecio decorate the roadside. Push on toward the head of Placer Gulch in the company of late bloomer Parry goldenweed.

To the south more grasses, in lime and chartreuse, form large hummocks. This view is at about the 1-mile point where the roadway narrows and grows more rocky. More golden blossoms claim the slopes now, punctuated by rosy paintbrush and richly pigmented larkspur. If you have had your fill, this is a good spot to turn and retrace your steps.

Wildflower Hike 24

Boulder Gulch/ South Fork Animas River

Wading through subalpine flora adds adventure to the Boulder Gulch hike.

Trail Rating	easy to moderate
Trail Length	3.4 miles out and back
Location	north of Silverton
Elevation	10,600 to 11,200 feet
Bloom Season	July to late August
Peak Bloom	late July to mid-August
Directions	From Silverton, go east on CO 110 approximately 8 miles. After crossing a bridge, take the first sharp left (west) onto CR 25. After approximately 1 mile, veer left again toward the Boulder Gulch Trailhead. High-clearance, four-wheel-drive vehicles may cross the creek and park at mile 1.8 near the old mine structure. For those who cannot clear the large boulder in the middle, park on the near side of the creek.

The Boulder Gulch Trail along the lively South Fork of the Animas River offers solitude not far from Silverton. The trail begins with crossing the South Fork—best done in late summer—and follows a well-defined route up to a meadow. From here, it's a level hike through meadow and forest to an interesting small waterfall. For those without high-clearance vehicles to ford the river, the trail will be slightly longer since you will need to park where you can before the stream.

The hike begins on an old mining road, then briefly heads upstream on the right (north). Boulder Gulch Trail branches off to the southwest, leading to the South Fork of the Animas River. After crossing, climb up steadily via switchbacks through forest and come out in a flowery meadow. From this point, elevation is gently gained.

Subalpine wildflowers flourish in meadows and along tributaries, offering the hiker pools of color. Late-season hikers will find a pond-sized pocket of cottonsedge, or bogwool, where this description ends, with a pretty creek on the left and a waterfall on the right.

Little used, this is a primitive area for those who like a bit of adventure. As ever, high-country mountains make their own weather, so always be alert to thunderstorm clouds building, especially on summer afternoons.

Having negotiated the creek crossing, either by appropriate vehicle or by foot, start your trek up the road fronting the old mine structure—which is listing and is not safe. To the east, Crown Mountain rises to 13,569 feet. An old jeep track sends hikers southwest, where **western golden ragwort**, with its dark stems and pinnate-type leaves, thrives alongside **many-rayed goldenrod** and the bright magenta spires of **fireweed**.

Pink **wild geranium** and white **yarrow** are overwhelmed by a solid phalanx of **elderberry** bushes flanking the route. **Beauty cinquefoil** and tidy **golden aster** accent graceful grasses and rushes. **Harebell** adds purple, while **Colorado thistle** is nearly neutral. Lots of **pink-headed daisies** accompany **subalpine daisy**'s wider, cooler rays, with **aspen sunflower** nearby.

DAFFODIL SENECIO
Ligularia amplectens

Also known as nodding senecio for its coy head, this groundsel is an endemic found solely in an area of Colorado mountains in the subalpine zone. It is partial to forest openings and meadows and displays outfacing, slightly rumpled, light yellow rays. The basal leaves wizen by bloom time, while its clasping stem leaves remain. The genus name comes from the Latin *ligula*, meaning "strap."

Moist areas support **triangleleaf senecio** and dark purple **monkshood**, as well as **white geranium** and finely rayed white **Coulter daisy**. Early-season visitors see **tall chimingbells** where parsley family members **Porters lovage** and **hemlock parsley** grow, the latter more delicately flowered and sparser leaved than the former.

Where the jeep trail switchbacks, angle up and keep a sharp eye out for Boulder Gulch Trail, which soon bears left as a faint path across scree. At this juncture, it's clear that Boulder Gulch is not a well-trammeled route until it crosses the creek. Ahead is a scenic basin where Tower Mountain crests at some 13,500 feet. Head southwest above the South Fork of the Animas, a creek at this point, which descends on your left. **Mountain parsley** grows near alien **butter and eggs**, an invasive species.

To the right, look for aspen copses cutting into a rockfall, where you might glimpse **tall scarlet paintbrush**. A whole passel of **tasselflower** is nearby. The trail pulls up where early bloomer **purple fringe** gives over to western golden ragwort and **black-tipped senecio**, only to level near **goldenweed**, many-rayed goldenrod, and **goldeneye**.

Another brief rise on rough tread takes hikers alongside stony mounds, where **pearly everlasting** presents its papery white bracts among young spruces. The route drops down to the creek shortly, to find **cow parsnip** and hemlock parsley.

Yellow monkeyflower accompanies delicate **pink willowherb**, as a seep supports tall chimingbells and **rosy paintbrush**. Streamside, look for pink **river-beauty**, or **broadleaf fireweed**, with its blue-green foliage and shorter stature.

Looking across the creek just west of the monkeyflower, note an established trail rising from the far side. Crossing the creek is an adventure, whether you take a sharp left through the willows and find a fallen tree or simply wade through to the south side bank.

Once across the South Fork, the trail goes up, passing triangleleaf senecio, **subalpine arnica**, and the lavender-pink heads of subalpine daisy. **Broadleaf arnica** shines over **alpine veronica**'s tiny blue flowers and pink-headed daisy's soft buds.

The trail rises steeply, but hikers are diverted by **larkspur**, **king's crown**, rosy paintbrush, and tall fireweed. As the summer season progresses, **little rose gentian** pushes its corollas up, the pointy-lobed flowers graced with delicate fringe.

Pass a slope of tall chimingbells and **orange sneezeweed**, where lilac **showy daisy** is accented by rosy paintbrush. Dainty-headed **subalpine valerian** leads into spruces shading **parrot's beak lousewort**, its coiled flowers accounting for another name, **rams-horn**.

Small steps will save energy as you continue. Mountain parsley's yellow snowflakelike blooms accompany **nodding** or **daffodil senecio**. The moister,

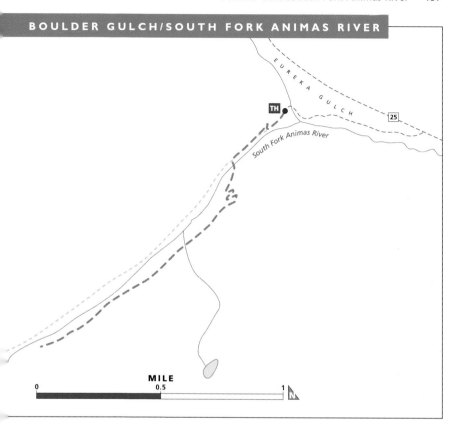

TH

EUREKA GULCH

25

South Fork Animas River

MILE
0   0.5   1

north-facing slope blooms later in the season, with monkshood, triangleleaf
senecio, and lacy-umbelled **cowbane** joined by **brook saxifrage**.

Often hidden in neighboring vegetation, shade-loving **green mitrewort**
requires a hand lens to examine the maroon tracery in its wispy green blossoms.
Grays angelica likes the same environs that support **western red columbine**
early in the season.

At a switchback, look for brook saxifrage and daffodil senecio. Keep
trekking up, coming upon loose rock where **Whipple penstemon** blooms. The
helicopter seedheads of **sweet cicely** like the shelter of spruces, and as the route
eases, conifer shade opens to accommodate undistinguished **alpine hawkweed**.

Wide sky overlooks **American bistort** and subalpine daisy. A little seasonal
waterway causes the route to dip, passing the tri-toothed leaf ends of **sibbaldia**,
a rose family member, along with larkspur, tall scarlet paintbrush, Porters lovage,
white geranium, and triangleleaf senecio. **Mountain death camas** has greenish-
tinged white stars on a straight stalk that curves like a shepherd's crook when
in bud. Orange sneezeweed's lax rays lead to a thick colony of poisonous **false
hellebore**, interspersed with small but cheerful **golden draba** and pale lavender

delicate Jacob's ladder. Minute **rock primrose** thrives in stonier places where the competition is less

Alpine avens and beauty cinquefoil appear where the trail grows fainter. Retain the same southwesterly direction to arrive at Coulter daisy, yarrow, geranium, and cow parsnip. Vegetation-stripping avalanches clear paths for wildflowers, including two that produce only disk flowers: hairy **Parry** or **rayless arnica** and smooth **rayless senecio.** Aspen sunflower grows near both subalpine and **edible valerian.** **Ritter** or **yellow kittentails,** an endemic, quickly matures its barely yellow tubular flowers into plump green seedpods.

Blues soon dominate in the form of **Colorado blue columbine,** larkspur, and tall chimingbells as you dip into a ravine, led by purple fringe on the left. Upslope, an interesting iron-stained geologic formation catches the eye.

The next meadow passes tall scarlet paintbrush along with other flowers previously encountered. Head into spruce forest sheltering daffodil senecio and broadleaf arnica. Pocket meadows in the conifer wood harbor snowy **bittercress** and cowbane.

Leave the shade on a gently ascending trail that passes lots of creamy **bracted lousewort** and subalpine daisy. Lining a waterway are flowers already seen, with the addition of late blooming **sawtooth senecio.** After you cross, look for yellow monkeyflower, willowherb, and pale blue **American speedwell.**

Erosion wears at the ravines to the north. Harebell rules on this side as you look upstream into the colorful gash the stream has carved. A grassy sector supports fireweed, **orange agoseris,** and pale green-yellow **alumroot.**

Many-rayed goldenrod signals a rocky tread underfoot. Look here for **blueleaf cinquefoil, Rocky Mountain gentian,** and in a slightly boggy swale, **little pink elephants, marsh marigold, queen's crown,** monkshood, and **star gentian** later in the summer. Little rose gentian, with its fringed throat, likes the environs as well.

The drier far side resumes the stony tread. More defined, the path winds through spruces to approach a flower-studded patch of false hellebore. A vast meadow soon stretches before you. Make your way through the well-watered stretch, keeping to clumps of vegetation.

Negotiating this boggy area rewards you with a rocky trickle lined with queen's crown, little pink elephants, and **green bog orchid.** A rushing Animas tributary offers even more flowers. The sound of the river rises as **meadowrue** accompanies an easygoing push over a dry hillock, offering a view the river.

The brook on the left, engulfed in pretty wildflowers, ushers in a patch of white **cottonsedge,** or **bogwool,** looking like a spill of windblown cottonballs. Coursing noisily on the right, the South Fork plunges in a brief falls. Find yourself a nice flat boulder and enjoy the solitude at this turnaround point, in the shadows of 13,552-foot Tower Mountain and 13,325-foot Storm Peak.

Highland Mary Lakes Trail

*Wildflower
Hike 25*

*Pristine Highland Mary Lakes are a
just reward for an aerobic hike.*

moderate to somewhat difficult	*Trail Rating*
6 miles out and back	*Trail Length*
San Juan National Forest/Weminuche Wilderness, east of Silverton	*Location*
10,800 to 12,000 feet	*Elevation*
July to August	*Bloom Season*
late July to mid-August	*Peak Bloom*

Directions

From Silverton, drive east on CO 110 approximately 4 miles to
Howardsville and turn right (south) at the second bridge onto
FR 589/CR 4. At mile 1.7 from the turnoff, bear right where a sign
indicates a dead end. At mile 4.5, just before the trailhead, the
road dips down to a four-wheel-drive creek crossing. The other
side has an abrupt climb, and if your vehicle isn't equipped for
this kind of crossing, park to the left before the creek. You'll be
able to see the crossing descent and the trailhead area beyond.

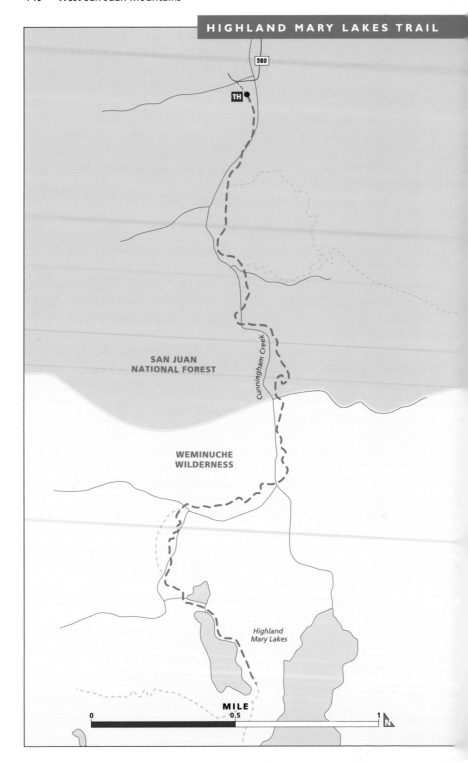

300

TH

SAN JUAN
NATIONAL FOREST

Cunningham Creek

WEMINUCHE
WILDERNESS

Highland
Mary Lakes

MILE

0   0.5   1   N

The 3 miles up to the charming first Highland Mary Lake are challenging but well worth the effort. Gaining 1,200 vertical feet, the trail follows Cunningham Creek to an alpine lake anchored by a picturesque island, with a larger Highland Mary Lake shimmering just yards away. This remarkable hike is also a who's who of subalpine flora, giving you lots to look for along the way.

Parking is open at the actual trailhead, but a creek crossing just 0.2 mile short of it can be a challenge, with an abrupt farside bank. You would be best crossing with a high-clearance, four-wheel-drive vehicle. Probably the easiest place to park prior to the creek is on the level tailings pile just beyond the left turn descending to the creek, assuming you've tackled the last rough mile of access road. Parking prior to that mile is available.

False hellebore carpets the valley floor near the sign-in register box and signboard for the Weminuche Wilderness. After filling out information, begin hiking up, noting the diverse reds of **king's crown** and **tall scarlet paintbrush** under a willow on the left. Underneath spruce, look for **delicate Jacob's ladder**. On the right are **fireweed**, **orange sneezeweed**, **beauty cinquefoil**, **edible valerian**, and the red-bracted, paired black fruits of **twinberry honeysuckle** bushes.

Two fleabanes occur as you rise, fine-rayed white **Coulter daisy** and wider-rayed, lavender-pink **subalpine daisy**. At a sign prohibiting motor vehicles, look for **tall chimingbells**, **triangleleaf senecio**, and a **leafy Jacob's ladder**, a tall and purple polemonium.

Small bloomers such as **pussytoes** and **alpine bistort** make way for more prominent flowers, such as **yarrow** and, on the left cutbank, late-blooming **Parry goldenweed**. Check right for ferny-leaved **Porters lovage**, once sought by resourceful American Indians for its many medicinal properties.

Across the creek are **green gentian** and **Colorado blue columbine**, while on the near side are native **tall burnt orange false dandelion**, **rayless senecio**, **Whipple** or **dusky pentstemon**, and **thickbract senecio**.

A slope leads down to the rugged gorge narrowly bordering the creek, and the ascent becomes steeper and rockier. Nearby, a glade features **shrubby cinquefoil**, **pink-headed daisy**, Porters lovage, **bittercress**, Colorado blue columbine, and tall chimingbells. The track levels through a willow carr, coming across avalanche debris featuring tall scarlet paintbrush's vivid bracts and **mountain parsley**'s snowflakelike umbels. Avalanche-path flowers such as pink **wild onion** and diminutive **rock primrose** thrive here.

Ascending, the route passes **golden aster**, and later orange sneezeweed, paintbrush, and Porters lovage. As you rise toward the top of the waterfall, look for **subalpine larkspur**'s dolphin-shaped buds. **Wild geranium** and **rosy paintbrush** appear among the vegetation. A rocky and more serious climb introduces **nodding** or **daffodil senecio**'s yellow and somewhat disorganized rays. Spruce shade suits **heartleaf arnica** and the white curls of **parrot's beak lousewort**, sometimes called **rams-horn** for obvious reasons.

Topping out by a rock sporting brick red king's crown, hike up to a level area where golden triangleleaf or **arrowleaf senecio** and beauty cinquefoil complement powder blue tall chimingbells.

At a sign that divides the paths of horses and hikers, go right to overlook a pretty waterway lined with common fireweed's cousin, **riverbeauty**, or **alpine fireweed**. Its compact nature, blue-green leaves, and love of moisture make it a lush species. Colorado blue columbine thrives in the vicinity, as do larkspur, arrowleaf senecio, and rosy paintbrush. Look around the small glen for **slender-tipped clover**'s rosy heads, pink-headed daisy's refined pale rays, and delicate **brook saxifrage**, its starlike blooms suspended on wiry stems. **Cowbane**'s lacy umbels add to the airy effect.

Cross the stream on stones for another closer look at riverbeauty. The trail narrows to find spires of common fireweed near equally tall **aspen sunflower**, finally leveling in a flowery meadow populated by thickbract senecio and **alpine milkvetch**. Up next are a pair of valerians, dainty-headed, blushed **subalpine valerian** and lackluster edible valerian.

To the left, a sheer wall overlooks orange sneezeweed and tall chimingbells as you prepare to step up, via roots and rocks, passing occasional daffodil senecio. A steep climb reveals more Colorado blue columbine and both rosy and tall scarlet paintbrush.

Wildflowers abound on the trail to Highland Mary Lakes.

To mount the cliff, prepare for some high steps. **Blueleaf cinquefoil,** **queen's crown,** and **mouse-ears** accompany your progress. Rocky tread takes hikers up to a warm palette of king's crown, paintbrush, pink-headed daisy, and **many-rayed goldenrod,** while a pretty cascade pitches off to the right.

The route eases, cooled by shade before entering another sunny opening yielding bottlebrush heads of **American bistort** and Colorado blue columbine. Damp soil on the left supports **Parry clover,** cowbane, **little pink elephants,** and earlier-blooming **Parry primrose.** Look among willows for late-blooming **star gentian**'s dusky purple silken petals.

Bedrock lifts you to discover classic white flowers of **fringed parnassia** and more star gentian on the left. On the right, a moss-lined seep hosts little pink elephants, **green bog orchid,** queen's crown, and more prim parnassia, each pearly blossom aloft on its own stem. The whites of bittercress, cowbane, and brook saxifrage dominate among the willows.

After negotiating a bit of mud, note **bracted lousewort,** its creamy helmeted beaks whorled on a sturdy stalk. Mud and rock send hikers up to the gorge rim for a fine waterfall profile. The route then wends through conifer woods to encounter **twistedstalk** and more brook saxifrage.

Tightly hemmed by willows but leveling, the trail heads for a pocket meadow where **alpine avens'** brassy five petals sit over leatherfern-like leaves. The stream nearly touches the trail, highlighting lacy cowbane, **yellow monkeyflower,** and rich pink Parry primrose.

Turn a corner to see another cascade, as well as **Fendler sandwort.** Looking like an unambitious clover, trailside patches of teal **sibbaldia** promise to turn salmon with the cool days of autumn. Keen-eyed observers may spot a foot-high specimen of **alpine campion,** its dusky rose petals barely showing beyond its striped, inflated calyx.

Back in spruce shade, look for familiar flowers, as well as **northern paintbrush,** delicate Jacob's ladder. king's crown, daffodil senecio, and the tiny, dark blue flowers of **alpine veronica.**

ALPINE FIREWEED
Chamerion subdentatum

This vivid purple-pink member of the evening primrose family favors upper subalpine streamsides, hence the more poetic name, riverbeauty. The broad, blue-green leaves framing the bright petals and sepals are numerous, giving this less common fireweed an understated bushy appearance, unlike its tall, spired cousin, common fireweed.

At a creek crossing, watch for subalpine arnica and Parry clover. Just after this is the main Highland Mary Lakes stream, demanding a careful crossing, too. From here, a serious ascent begins: Use small steps to even out your breathing.

Views of the tiered mountain to the left open up as the willows fall back momentarily, revealing many-rayed goldenrod. A bedrock sector features gray mats of pussytoes, blueleaf cinquefoil, and some king's crown. A dip puts the trail back on broken rocks as it aims for a level stretch of good tread, allowing hikers to glimpse deep purple **monkshood.**

A lithic knob signals another water crossing, where queen's crown, subalpine daisy, arnica, little pink elephants, and paintbrush abound. After traversing a muddy stretch, the trail rises once more, showcasing hot pink Parry primrose. A winding ascent takes you up to meet **black-headed daisy, moss campion,** slender-tipped clover, and subtle purple **pinnate-leaf daisy.**

Along this rocky pitch grows **Parry lousewort,** each creamy beak supported by a striped calyx. Search for a spur to the left, which immediately sends hikers across a jumble of angled rock, where you may catch sight of marmots or pikas. This route might be hard to see, but if you continue up on the obvious trail, you will eventually face an arduous crossing of the rock jumble at least two to three times the distance of the closer crossing; both require cautious foot placement.

Once across, stay on the near side of the outlet creek, making your way up to a logical place to cross the watercourse and noting a narrow but worn trail on the far side. Follow the entrenched trail to find lovely examples of moss campion as you make your way to a rust-colored bit of rockfall. Traveling the regained trail, pass a creek lushly lined with Parry primrose, brook saxifrage, queen's crown, **marsh marigold,** Parry clover, and bittercress on the right. A low slope on the left displays copious riverbeauty.

Finally, the trail levels and you are rewarded with the first Highland Mary Lake, shimmering around a krummholz-covered islet. Beautifully pigmented tall scarlet paintbrush spatters the nearside lakeshore. The far shore seems to drop off a lip, making this Highland Mary Lake a hanging lake. A couple of strides crosses the outlet creek of the first Highland Mary. Twist up to overlook two little tarns on the right.

Here, look for **draba, alpine blue violet,** Colorado blue columbine, king's crown, paintbrush, and, in protected places, the whites of marsh marigold, **snowball saxifrage,** and **mountain candytuft.**

Giant carved steps take you up the outcrop, highlighting tundra plants such as alpine avens, black-headed daisy, blueleaf cinquefoil, daffodil senecio, and **western paintbrush.** When the outcrop peters out, step up to pleasant walking and a view of the second, larger Highland Mary Lake. This scenic point makes a ideal turnaround point if you are inclined.

Bullion King Lake

A serene alpine lake, complete with waterfall, makes for a grand conclusion to this hike.

easy to moderate	**Trail Rating**
4.25 miles out and back	**Trail Length**
San Juan National Forest, west of Ouray and Silverton	**Location**
11,550 to 12,600 feet	**Elevation**
July to late August	**Bloom Season**
July to early August	**Peak Bloom**
From Ouray, travel south on US 550 approximately 14 miles to Red Mountain Pass. Just over 0.5 mile after the pass, turn right (west) on FR 822. If you do not feel confident tackling a rough, rocky road, park at mile 0.75 in a tall spruce grove and begin walking up. For others with high-clearance vehicles, continue to mile 1.5, parking by the stand of small spruces just before a road to the right joins at an acute angle and FR 822 steepens.	**Directions**

The name Bullion King Lake testifies to this area's mining heritage, which began in 1878 when the first wagonloads of gold ore went over 11,018-foot Red Mountain Pass. To the wildflower lover, this route offers its own riches, including an abundance of flowers, beautiful views, and a good chance of solitude, especially on weekdays. Folks with four-wheel-drive can go farther on FR 822, but they will miss out on a lot of wildflower pleasure.

Drive partway up the rough, narrow access road to wherever you are comfortable taking your vehicle—obviously, the less you drive, the longer your hike. At about 0.75 mile, there is a grove of tall spruces on the left, with a well-trammeled floor and a meadow filled with little pink elephants behind it. Drivers may park here or go on up via a couple of switchbacks to mile 1.5, parking near a patch of short spruces.

The hike itself begins at the juncture of two roads and travels up FR 822 as it climbs a flower-lined route, parts of which narrow considerably between a cliff and a drop-off. The ascent is fairly steady until it flattens upon approach to the mine tailings. It then curls up gently, though sometimes rockily, to even out at lake level.

Except at the lowest spruce-shaded spot, parking is a bit of a challenge no matter where you begin your trek. Be sure to watch for storms as you hike.

This description begins where two roads meet at an acute angle. The first flower you notice is golden **subalpine arnica** fanning down open slopes, while to the northeast, Red Mountain commands the horizon. Where the acutely angled road aims right, continue straight ahead, bearing left as the road ascends. **Orange sneezeweed** rises over the masses of arnica.

A small slide of iron-stained rock on the right features **king's crown**, both **blueleaf** and **beauty cinquefoil**, **white geranium**, **Parry goldenweed**, mounded **rock senecio**, little **pink willowherb**, and **subalpine larkspur**. Krummholz spruces cling to cracked rock where **purple fringe**, **wild onion**, and charming **yellow monkeyflower** bloom, joined by little, dark blue **alpine veronica** and more narrow-flowered pink willowherb.

Dark red king's crown, with its succulent leaves, and native **Coulter daisy** thrive. On the right, the rock face ends, making way for a pretty meadow of subalpine arnica, cinquefoil, and orange sneezeweed, accented by cool **subalpine daisy**, a fleabane. Showy swabs of **rosy paintbrush** perk up the color scheme.

Under a hoary spruce, look for **cowbane** and **triangleleaf senecio**. The road inclines steadily, passing **sibbaldia**, with its tri-toothed, blue-green leaves, on the right cutbank. The last stand of small spruces finds **pussytoes**, lush subalpine larkspur, and **Colorado blue columbine**.

A steeper grade pulls the route uphill, passing wine-colored tubes of **dusky penstemon** and, by the spruces, **delicate Jacob's ladder**. Having turned a hairpin curve, look for **Ritter** or **yellow kittentails** to the right. Lots of **pink-headed daisy**, with its angora-like buds, joins Coulter daisy, its yellow eye surrounded

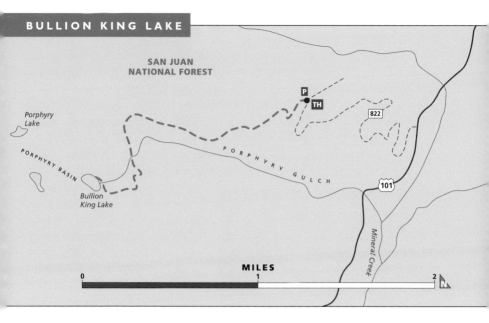

by long white lashes. **Alpine avens**' blossoms look a lot like those of cinquefoil, but with leaves resembling leathery fern fronds.

At the next turn, as you rise on gray rock, be sure to take in the view of the mountains. Then look for both pink **wild geranium** and white geranium, and on the left, **golden aster**. **Black-tipped senecio** and purple fringe both favor the lithic soil. Trek up to a pewter-colored outcrop where clumps of lavender **pinnate-leaf daisy** complement mounds of golden aster, while **slender-tipped clover** tucks its roots into nooks and crannies. **Alpine sorrel** offers its vitamin C–charged, ultrasour leaves.

The roadway narrows considerably and ascends as it traverses a steep slope along a lengthy cliff with a drop-off opposite into Porphyry Gulch. Downslope, sinuous white water courses through the gulch, which features rosy paintbrush. Your uphill trek is rewarded by a level sector featuring a sweep of crenellated ridges and rounded rock. The next outcrop features **alumroot**, **edible valerian**, and dusky penstemon. Rose family cousins alpine avens and beauty cinquefoil boast similar blooms. Yellows continue with another rose clan relation, **shrubby cinquefoil**, accompanied by **western paintbrush**. **Many-rayed goldenrod** and Parry goldenweed are here as well.

Rugged volcanic rocks serve as backdrop for larkspur, arnica, and **Porters lovage**. Meadows feature brick red king's crown, swabs of rosy paintbrush, and magenta **fireweed**. An eye-popping pink and yellow sweep on the left combines arnica and more rosy paintbrush.

A rivulet running through rocks on the right supports **Parry primrose**'s yellow-eyed, pink blossoms, with **brook saxifrage** and **bittercress** as foils. At a creek crossing, cowbane offers a lacy counterpoint to showy Parry primrose and paintbrush.

An amazing mountain view and waterfall is fronted by orange sneezeweed, Coulter daisy, and **yarrow**. Back on the right bank, moisture encourages **little pink elephants** and purple fringe. **Yellow stonecrop** displays succulent leaves.

Where the route flattens, note the sizable clumps of alpine avens; its ladderlike leaves will turn wine red in autumn. When you reach a rocky knob on the left, pause to overlook a ragged little gorge. Pinnate-leaf daisy, slender-tipped clover, wild onion, and **alpine sandwort** dot the knoll. **Old man of the mountains'** huge heads greet early-season visitors.

ALPINE LOUSEWORT
Pedicularis scopulorum

Related to little pink elephants, alpine lousewort in quantity is a find. The soft, rose-pink, hooded flowers are called galeas. Each canine-toothed blossom sits in glistening wool on a short spike 4 to 6 inches high. The leaves are deeply pinnate and fernlike. This less common member of the snapdragon or figwort family prefers wet places in subalpine and alpine ecozones. The specific name, *scopulorum,* means "of the Rockies."

The road takes you down to the water, where a collapsed old mining structure languishes. On the right, threaded by a trickle, little pink elephants surrounds **marsh marigold** and **queen's crown**. In the thick grasses of the swale, look for the fragrant, rosy heads of **Parry clover**.

Cross a shallow waterway and curve up to meet perfumed early bloomer **alpine phlox**, its cushions tucked in the layered rock on the right. Blueleaf cinquefoil, sibbaldia, and alpine sandwort grow here as well, joined by a bit of pink **moss campion**.

Arrive at the white tailings, which, if moist, feel as slippery as clay. A flat segment takes hikers to a rivulet lined with Parry primrose and marsh marigold, whose each white tepal—so called because the petals and sepals cannot be differentiated—has a steel blue reverse.

Stony underfoot, the road takes you closer to cliffs where old man of the mountains grows amongst **black-headed daisy** and amethyst **alpine violet**. Bedrock leads to a trail at a 45-degree tangent that will cross a creek.

Subalpine daisy and **bistort** lead the way, passing **different-leaved senecio**, a high-elevation species.

The creek's banks feature the pink and white of primrose and bittercress. A little falls spilling down from its Bullion King Lake source tells you the hike is nearing its goal. Rise to rejoin the road by an iron pipe, where snowbanks often linger. The four-wheel-drive road ends here. Make your way to the left through huge rocks to find the trail. An upcoming overhanging bank not only presents showy moss campion, but, for the sharp-eyed, tiny lavender-blue **moss gentian**, also called **compass gentian** because it resembles the mariner's compass rose found on antique maps.

Execute a hairpin curve, heading for a ragged ridge to find

Alpine flora at Bullion King Lake

rock senecio. Tundra lies before you, populated with black-headed daisy, Parry clover, and needly-leaved **San Juan alpine draba**. Continue over golden granite to meet **McCauleys buttercup**, its lacquer yellow petals hiding youthful sepals covered with black hairs. Note also the rosy pink whorls of **alpine lousewort**, a less common cousin of little pink elephants.

Late-season snowbanks sometimes exhibit red algae. Looking up at a hanging meadow, note the lovely display of alpine lousewort and waxen western paintbrush, a pleasing duet.

Broad and quiet here, Bullion King Lake's outlet creek travels through tundra interspersed with bare patches, where you might find **dwarf clover**, its florets blooming singly instead of in the head typical of most clovers. Lilac **single-headed daisy** pops up sporadically. Look in the alpine vegetation for the lollipop heads of **snowball saxifrage** and pink or white **pygmy bitterroot**, which opens translucent blossoms in a cradle of succulent linear leaves.

Follow the trail directly to the bedrock shores of Bullion King Lake, accompanied by pert black-headed daisy. Beautifully set in eroded dove gray and rust rock, the lake's clear waters reflect the sky. Walking to the right reveals a waterfall on the far side, shooting down a ragged, volcanic rock cleft. On the near shore, the outlet creek carves itself an escape from the rough rock. Enjoy this gorgeous spot for as long as you like before turning around.

Wildflower Hike 27 # Clear Lake

The route to ruggedly set Clear Lake is lined with wildflowers.

Trail Rating	easy to moderate
Trail Length	3 miles out and back
Location	San Juan National Forest, west of Silverton
Elevation	11,600 to 12,000 feet
Bloom Season	July to late August
Peak Bloom	late July to mid-August
Directions	From the Silverton junction on US 550, go north 1.7 miles to FR 585 and turn left (west). Follow FR 585 approximately 4 miles, angling right (north) onto Clear Lake Rd./FR 815. The Clear Lake Rd. sign recommends four-wheel-drive vehicles only, but high clearance and caution may be adequate. Continue 2.8 miles and park by the switchback.

This trail offers an easy and scenic way to access a high-mountain lake gem cradled in a theatrical setting. Though it is possible to drive to Clear Lake, the best wildflower viewing is had on your own feet. The Clear Lake access road switchbacks often. On a switchback that heads left at mile 2.8, park and start your journey on an easygoing grade. The route flattens near the top, then mounts a knoll to view the lake.

Wildflowers accompany the 1.5 miles to Clear Lake from beginning to end. Parking is limited to a couple of vehicle spaces at a switchback point, but most folks in four-wheel-drive vehicles take the rough road to the lake. Drive as far as you are comfortable, then park at will. The hike is above treeline so keep an eye on the weather, especially in the afternoons.

Begin at the switchback where you leave your vehicle parked and start your ascent. Roadside, look for **fireweed**, white-headed **yarrow**, and **tall scarlet paintbrush**. **Orange sneezeweed** and **white geranium** grow here as well.

Looking upslope, note **aspen sunflower** among fireweed spires. Closer to the road is late bloomer **Parry goldenweed** and its golden flowers, while on the left, **tall chimingbells** rises over dark-stemmed **western golden ragwort**. Where **elderberries** are forming, look for lavender-rayed **showy** or **aspen daisy**. Ubiquitous **beauty cinquefoil** grows alongside **silverleaf scorpionweed**, with its coiled inflorescences.

Neck-craning is needed to spot **green gentian** spikes shooting up among aspen sunflower and spruce trees. Closer at hand, **king's crown** displays its dark red heads. True to its name, **black-tipped senecio**'s phyllaries are, indeed, edged with black. At a rusted gatepost, a small rockfall is studded with **wild blue flax**, **pearly everlasting**, and aspen daisy. On the slopes, **Colorado blue columbine** thrives, and **wallflower** puts in an appearance as well.

The volcanic San Juans are sometimes marked by sandstone

HAYDENS PAINTBRUSH
Castilleja haydenii

A San Juan Mountains tundra endemic, softly luminous Haydens paintbrush has linear-lobed bracts. The actual toothpicklike flowers sport minute lips and four stamens. This high-elevation paintbrush is named for Ferdinand Vandiveer Hayden, who led the U.S. Geological Survey in the Rocky Mountains in the early 1870s. The Latin genus name commemorates Domingo Castillejo, an 18th-century Spanish botanist.

formations such as the Cutler Formation, which bands the South Mineral Creek drainage below. As you travel up the roadway, thirteener peaks such as Vermilion and the Golden Horn dominate the western skyline.

Guarding a rocky-soiled cutbank, tall **Indian warriors** lifts red-streaked helmets above ferny foliage. Black-tipped senecio favors well-drained earth, as does **Whipple** or **dusky penstemon**, with its wine-colored tubes. Rusty fallen rock tells of enough moisture to support **cow parsnip** and **sandwort**'s little, white, starlike blooms.

A showy embankment offers **rock senecio**'s golden daisies, as well as the bright yellows of western golden ragwort and black-tipped senecio blooming in a mass of fireweed. To the left you see richly pigmented, purple-blue **subalpine larkspur** and, at your feet, the fine white rays of **Coulter daisy**.

Spruce shade announces **rayless** or **Bigelow senecio**'s smooth, tuck-and-roll heads. Bare until its terminal flowers cluster, yellowish-green **alumroot** is pale in comparison to wildfire swabs of tall scarlet paintbrush decorating the slope on the right. To the left is Lower Ice Lake Basin, its rock formations ornamented by waterfalls.

On the right are sunny **arnica**, plain **edible valerian**, and lavender **delicate Jacob's ladder**. Damper soil is indicated by tall chimingbells, while in the sloped vicinity, king's crown, sassy **purple fringe**, quiet wallflower, rock senecio, and clumps of Colorado blue columbine threaten to outshine green flowered **Grays angelica**.

Along an inside curve, look for native **tall pale agoseris**, also known as **tall pale false dandelion**, sharing space with nonnative common **dandelion**. Orange sneezeweed and soft-haired **subalpine arnica** punctuate **pussytoes** mats knitting the cutbank's loose soil. Cow parsnip dominates the foreground, while the marvelous peaks to the west rise in the background.

Passing **thickbract senecio**, you arrive at a few spruces almost at treeline, with a waterfall visible in the background. Nature uses her considerable talent wisely, clothing a slanted meadow with the gold, blue, and white of senecio, arnica, orange sneezeweed, aspen sunflower, **alpine avens**, tall chimingbells, larkspur, Colorado blue columbine, and **Porters lovage**, accompanied by rubbery-looking spikes of green gentian.

As the spruces fall behind you, look for white **Canada violet**, as well as pink **wild onion**, with dainty and pink-headed **subalpine valerian** above it. **Mountain death camas**' off-white stars share ground with patches of succulent-leaved king's crown. Alongside the road, an outlet stream emanating directly from a mine points up to the rosy, rounded heads of **slender-tipped clover**.

At a patch of purple fringe, look upstream to find **yellow monkeyflower**. Two wildflower-filled ravines feature Colorado blue columbine, slender-tipped clover, larkspur, and subalpine valerian.

Hiking on a road means the grade is usually not overtaxing. You soon approach a series of switchbacks and the promise of a pleasant incline for the

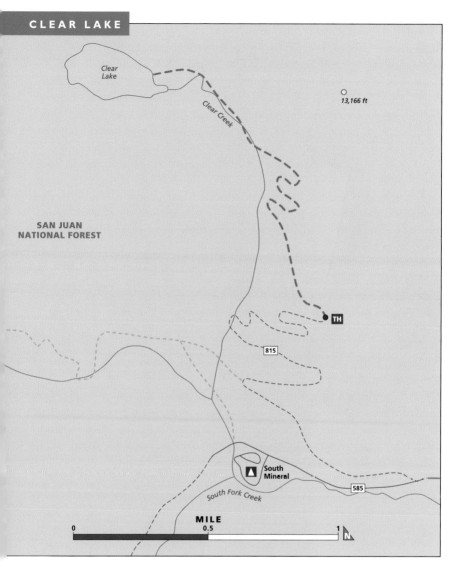

remainder of the hike. One of these switchbacks presents lush king's crown along a cutbank and, where moisture permeates the bank, look for a bit of white **fringed parnassia**, its bare stems rising over glossy basal leaves. Plush tall chimingbells and larkspur lead to a flat segment featuring mining remains. At this point, the road becomes rougher.

An outcrop around the next curve contains a seep where snowy **bittercress** and airy **brook saxifrage** accompany yellow monkeyflower. Continue to rise to yet another switchback, enjoying the view of the Golden Horn.

With the ledge of the Cutler Formation across the way, a stone-paved hillside features lime green mounds of rock senecio. **Western paintbrush** dabs an uphill slope with color. The next corner's outcrop is populated with sand-wort, light purple **pinnate-leaf daisy**, starry **yellow stonecrop**, and the broad blooms of **old man of the mountains**, or **alpine sunflower**.

A gorgeous cascade flows down from the rugged bowl that holds Clear Lake. Soon, the roadway dips toward the fast-dropping outlet creek. On the right, keep an eye out for **Haydens paintbrush** along a fractured, head-high rockface. With narrow, dark leaves and lined, luminous pink bracts, Haydens paintbrush is particular about where it grows and is partial to high ridges.

As the elevation approaches 12,000 feet, the heart rate increases as does the stoniness of the tread. On a level segment, look left for **alpine mouse-ears** and lushly leaved and bracted **rosy paintbrush**. Turn a corner to find **little pink elephants**, each head mimicking perfectly its namesake. Light-hearted brook saxifrage grows next to staid bittercress, a watercress cousin, and shocking pink **Parry primrose**.

Back on the left, a wet area features **marsh marigold**, **queen's crown**, **bistort**, orange sneezeweed, tall chimingbells, Parry primrose, and king's crown. Pass a short spur road on the left that crosses the creek to a meadow; the boggy area beyond holds white **cottonsedge**, or **bogwool**, a late-summer bloomer. Level walking makes it easy to spot a colonizing species of yellow monkeyflower and, across the way, a fresh flood of **subalpine daisy**. A waterway emerges from under a rock pile, while on the left, the little outlet from a sublake is lined with the pink and white of Parry primrose and marsh marigold.

A rock ledge frames vivid pink cushions of **moss campion** and white **black-headed daisy**; to understand the common name, peer under the rays for the ruff of purplish-black hairs. On the left, the ledge presents **McCauleys buttercup** at its base. From above, this buttercup's petals are the typical lacquered yellow; the sepals underneath are covered with coarse, blackish hairs.

On the other side, the moss campion finds companionship in alpine avens, **alpine sandwort**, **sibbaldia**, and more black-headed daisy. **Snowball saxifrage**, an early bloomer, lifts its crowded lollipop heads above a rosette of leathery leaves. Lavender **single-headed daisy** appears as well.

Follow the lake's shore to admire lush rosy paintbrush and **Parry clover**'s rosy heads. The rocky bank opposite presents **sky pilot**, an early blooming cousin of Jacob's ladder with equally skunky foliage offset by sweet-scented, bluish-purple flowers bursting with neon stamens. A pink and gold flat on the right is crammed with rosy paintbrush and senecio; on the left side are pink paintbrush, Parry clover, and little pink elephants. White bistort makes its stand. The last turn up toward the knoll overlooking Clear Lake features tall chimingbells and more bistort.

Continue up the knoll, where Haydens paintbrush finds a happy roothold overlooking uniquely set Clear Lake. Serene in its ragged bowl, this alpine lake calls for a moment of rest and relaxation before retracing your steps.

Ice Lake Basin

*Breathtaking scenery accompanies
you to rugged Ice Lake Basin.*

moderate to difficult	***Trail Rating***
6 miles out and back to Lower Ice Lake Basin; 7 miles round-trip to upper basin	***Trail Length***
San Juan National Forest, northwest of Silverton	***Location***
9,850 to 12,257 feet	***Elevation***
early July to August	***Bloom Season***
late July to early August	***Peak Bloom***
From the Silverton junction on US 550, travel north 1.7 miles to FR 585. Turn left and continue 4.5 miles to the South Mineral Campground. Park in the adjacent lot on the right for the trailhead.	***Directions***

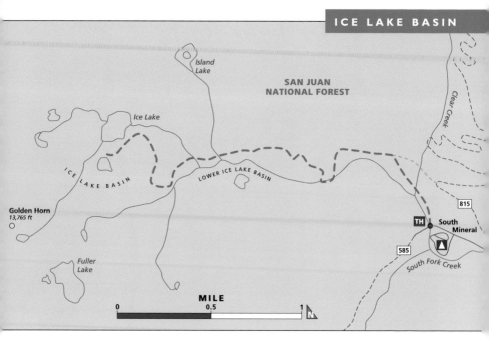

ICE LAKE BASIN

Island Lake

SAN JUAN NATIONAL FOREST

Clear Creek

Ice Lake

ICE LAKE BASIN

LOWER ICE LAKE BASIN

Golden Horn
13,765 ft

815

TH   South Mineral

585

South Fork Creek

Fuller Lake

MILE
0   0.5   1

N

The scenic, uphill climb to Ice Lake Basin in one of the outstanding wild-flower hikes in the San Juan Mountains. Flowers are abundant and views are breathtaking, though this is not a hike for the faint of heart: Be prepared for 3 or more miles of fairly difficult hiking with a 2,400-foot elevation gain. Several stream crossings add to the challenge.

The trail begins gently, heading up through forest by switchbacks, then gets serious in its ascent until it reaches flower-filled Lower Ice Lake Basin. Reaching the upper Ice Lake Basin requires a strenuous additional climb but is well worth the effort.

Trailhead parking is generous for early arrivals, but fills as morning wears on. As always, be attentive to building thunderstorms, best avoided by getting an early start.

The trail to Ice Lake initially splits a meadow of lavender **fleabane daisy, many-rayed goldenrod, wild geranium,** and **leafy Jacob's ladder. Orange sneezeweed**'s lazy rays grow near prolific **yarrow**'s tidy white heads and **silver-leaf scorpionweed**'s coiled inflorescences. **Meadowrue,** or **false columbine,** makes a green foil for many-rayed goldenrod's myriad stars.

Under aspen shade, look for shy **purple** or **water avens** in the vicinity of a small stream. Keeping this less common avens company are **cowbane, tall chimingbells, monkshood, triangleleaf senecio,** and some **bittercress. Aspen daisy, cow parsnip, yellow monkeyflower,** and **brook saxifrage** are also denizens of the damp habitat.

Flanking the route are tall **Indian warriors**, while late in the season, **Parry goldenweed** sends up green leaves with unorganized bursts of gold, daisy-type flowers. Rocks and spruce roots form the path where pale lilac **delicate Jacob's ladder** produces sweet flowers and the skunky foliage characteristic of polemoniums.

Passing **pink willowherb** along a level segment, the trail arrives at another seep, where yellow monkeyflower, **white geranium**, and **yellow avens** flourish. As it curves away, the route approaches 8-foot-tall monkshood, **twinberry honeysuckle**, and scouts of **tall scarlet paintbrush**. An S-curve takes the trail by the creek, to arrive at a damp spot supporting cowbane and more purple avens, also known as **chocolateflower**.

Switchbacks continue the ascent. Leaving the creek, note sunny **heartleaf arnica**, tall **aspen sunflower**, and **wild strawberry**. An uprooted tree shelters **green bog orchid**, while nearby on the left, **least wintergreen**'s pale, greenish bells hang from a straight stalk.

At a creek crossing, look for more monkshood, triangleleaf senecio, cowbane, cow parsnip, and bittercress. White **Canada violet** flowers demurely as you look downhill in the forest shade, which supports yet another wintergreen, **pink pyrola**, also called **bog wintergreen**.

Meander up a hillside meadow of wild geranium, **rayless senecio**, orange sneezeweed, **Coulter daisy**, leafy Jacob's ladder, and **cinquefoil**. **Mountain parsley**'s long stems lift yellow snowflake umbels alongside **fireweed**'s magenta spires. Crawling among red strawberry runners is purplish **alpine milkvetch**.

Root-covered and rocky, the route parallels the creek as it flows around flowered, midstream islands. Trailside grow **elderberry**, twinberry honeysuckle, and **currant** shrubs. Cross the stream via a handy log or beam, noting substantial cow parsnip and dainty-flowered tall chimingbells. A verdant meadow area is full of familiar wildflowers in purple, white, and gold.

Willows shelter cousins yellow avens and purple avens; the former's petals are overt on upright heads, the latter's, covert on nodding flowers. A curve in the route brings another switchback. Early-season hikers enjoy **western red columbine** along the way. **One-sided wintergreen** appreciates the mossy shelter of a gnarly old root on the left.

Returning to open skies reveals aspen sunflower, soon complemented by purple-blue **subalpine larkspur**. Recrossing the brook means another colorful array of subalpine life zone flora, including green bog orchid guarded by poisonous monkshood. The route inclines more seriously, offering waterfall views before turning away. Greet another flowery meadow featuring **pink-headed daisy**, Indian warriors, and toxic **false hellebore**.

After rising on a steep slope and a switchback, conifer woods offer shade and views of a snow-filled cirque gracing a mountain nearly 14,000 feet high. Continue up until you reach a brief spur on the right, spattered with **golden aster** and leading to a plunge of white water and a derelict bridge.

Back on the main trail, check out **sweetvetch**, or **chainpod**, for pretty pink racemes of pea-type flowers or its connected, flattened pods. Yellow mountain parsley and tall scarlet paintbrush brighten the way, as does aspen daisy and many-rayed goldenrod.

Spectacular views accompany the climb up to the 1-mile mark. The trail continues to ascend, passing a collapsing mining structure decorated by tall scarlet paintbrush. **Wolf currant** shrubs precede a stiff pitch as water courses down narrow rock ledges. An avalanche path devoid of trees provides a clean slate for flowers such as **western golden ragwort**, many-rayed goldenrod, and rayless senecio. Complementing the golds is azure **wild blue flax**. On hot days, the fragile petals drop by afternoon.

Ahead is a series of switchbacks that rise through a rugged volcanic landscape. As you climb along the rocky trail, watch for palmate-leaved **beauty cinquefoil**, which shares billing with **silvery cinquefoil**. The trail continues up, switching back in short increments and passing meadowrue, sweetvetch, and fireweed, and the occasional specimen of **purple fringe** and sprawling **sandwort**. Entering a dry streambed, the route eases.

Soon, you are greeted with a profusion of flowers, including paintbrush, cow parsnip, **Porters lovage**, tall chimingbells, and larkspur. Pink-headed daisy leads the route up onto forest duff, passing Canada violet and pale yellow **bracted lousewort**.

As the trail enters forest shade, it steepens quite sharply. Surprisingly well vegetated, the spruce-dominated forest shows

PURPLE AVENS
Geum rivale

An unlikely looking member of the rose family, purple avens is a tall plant with three to seven hanging, purplish-bronze flowers that resemble Asian temple bells. Each is made of sepals and bracts hiding violet-tinted, clawed petals. The leaves consist of five to nine leaflets. Fond of wet, subalpine places, purple avens is also called water avens and chocolateflower, referring to a chocolate-like beverage American Indians derived from the roots. Purple avens roots were also made into an eyewash treatment. The species name, *rivale*, means "of brooksides."

off pink-headed daisy and aspen sunflower. Stony tread returns the trail to a whole slope of white, gold, blue, and red, featuring many now-familiar flowers as well as **king's crown**, blooming in deep red.

Whipple penstemon's dusky purple tubes lead to yet another well-watered segment with paintbrush, leafy Jacob's ladder, golden aster, and late bloomer **sawtooth** or **sawleaf senecio**.

Cliffs overlooking a creek signal a breather as you level to pass another flowery stretch where, in late summer, royal blue chalices of **Rocky Mountain gentian** thrive. **Ritter kittentails**, an early bloomer in palest yellow, now sports lumpy, plump, green stalks. Nearby are generous clumps of **slender-tipped clover**, sending up round, rosy heads from blue-green, three-part, tapered leaves.

Flanked by more slender-tipped clover, the trail showcases grand views of crenellated peaks. At this point, you have hiked an elevation gain of about 1,400 feet. Stony tread leads through shoulder-high wildflowers colorful enough to suit a Gauguin painting. Porters lovage, which was once valued for its pharmaceutical use, dominates here, along with larkspur, paintbrush, fireweed, and tall chimingbells.

Wildflowers are everywhere here at mile 2, where open skies nurture a lovely little meadow anchored by king's crown. Shady woods signal a steeper ascent, bordered by the creamy white petals of **fringed parnassia**, dusky purple **star gentian**, and a few green bog orchids. Damp underfoot, the trail comes to a small stream populated by yellow monkeyflower, more fringed parnassia, pink willowherb, and brook saxifrage. Early-season hikers find **Parry primrose** blooming here. You have arrived at Lower Ice Lake Basin, a goal in itself as far as wildflowers go. But press on; the best is yet to come.

In the distance, Vermilion Peak and Golden Horn each push 14,000 feet, and soon, a rockfall supports a startling array of flowers. Twinberry honeysuckle grows near a rock ringed by **Colorado blue columbine**, **alpine sorrel**, and purple fringe. Somewhat barren soil supports **pussytoes** mats and many-rayed goldenrod as you round the foot of the rockfall, heading toward level track and the rich, deep red, flat heads of king's crown.

Off to the left is a view of pristine Lower Ice Lake Basin. Waterfalls cascade from several levels, including a crudely carved cleft to the right; even farther right, another falls passes mining tailings where people once sought to wrest valuable minerals from the earth.

Cross a brook, being sure to glance left and downstream to catch **river-beauty**, better known as **broadleaf** or **alpine fireweed**. A cousin of common fireweed, it is compact and brilliantly pink and sports blue-green leaves. Soon a wider, livelier creek requires you cross on stones, possibly using a grassy island supporting both king's and **queen's crown**. A seep presents pink **wild onion** and willowherb. Look to your left to spot an unusually angled waterfall.

Ascending again, the track heads for a sheer cliff, its base lush with masses of neon yellow arnica, complemented by purples of larkspur and monkshood.

A fallen chunk of the cliff announces beautiful Parry primrose, right at your fingertips. Marsh marigold, brook saxifrage, and bittercress grow here as well.

Above treeline now, the route steepens before easing, passing subalpine daisy and more Colorado blue columbine. Begin to note the ragged peaks that will be your backdrop at Ice Lake Basin, still a fair ascent ahead. Tundra plants thrive, including tightly mounded alpine sandwort, sky pilot, and aspen sunflower. Black-headed daisy's white head hides a fuzzy collection of almost black hairs. Hugging the tundra earth, alpine parsley keeps its tight yellow umbels low in the harsh alpine environment, while soft pink starbursts of pygmy bitterroot, sometimes called least lewisia, emerge from succulent, linear-leaf nests.

The last segment of the trail levels as it threads past luminous paintbrush, including high-altitude western paintbrush. You have arrived, earning your reward of lovely Ice Lake cradled at 12,257 feet by a rugged basin. Above you, from left to right, are 13,761-foot Fuller Peak, 13,894-foot Vermilion Peak, 13,769-foot Golden Horn, 13,738-foot Pilot Knob, and 13,767-foot Ulysses S. Grant Peak.

After checking the skyline for building thunderheads, meander another hundred yards or so to a picturesque second lake, where you can enjoy a snack or simply solitude before returning the way you came.

Ice Lake is surrounded by a plethora of paintbrush.

Rico-Silverton Trail

Wildflower Hike 29

Blanketed in vivid wildflowers, South Park is a place of high-country beauty.

easy to moderate	**Trail Rating**
4.5 miles out and back	**Trail Length**
San Juan National Forest, west of Silverton	**Location**
10,650 to 11,600 feet	**Elevation**
July to September	**Bloom Season**
late July to mid-August	**Peak Bloom**
From the Silverton junction on US 550, travel north 1.7 miles to FR 585. Go 7.8 miles to the road's end. The last 2.8 miles to the trailhead are rough and rocky and include multiple creek crossings; a high-clearance vehicle is recommended.	**Directions**

Every hike in the San Juan Mountains presents a unique personality, especially when it comes to wildflowers, and Rico-Silverton Trail No. 507 has wildflower personality to spare. Broad South Park meadow, with its vivid, expansive displays of intense rosy paintbrush and bright gold blooms, makes for some of the best wildflower viewing in the region. In fact, every foot of trail on this hike is accompanied by lovely blossoms. Even the last 2 miles of the access road offer great viewing in late July and early August.

The trail begins at the South Fork of Mineral Creek, then gently ascends into level South Park. The route continues up and ends, for this description, at just over 2 miles, culminating in a cascading waterfall. The entire trail is 25 miles, and for those who wish to hike beyond the narrative, it climbs to intersect the Colorado Trail, and later ascends again to a pass at over 12,000 feet.

Parking at the road's end is available almost anywhere in a flat meadow, but is best in worn areas close to the trailhead.

Cross the South Fork of Mineral Creek on the available log to the trailhead sign. Beattie Peak soars behind you at 13,342 feet. Wildflowers start at the signpost with lush **Colorado blue columbine, subalpine arnica, orange agoseris, edible valerian, tall chimingbells, rosy paintbrush, monkshood, subalpine larkspur,** and **Whipple penstemon.**

Rocky and rising, the trail passes **beauty cinquefoil, Coulter daisy, rayless senecio,** and **orange sneezeweed,** all contributing their colors to the dominating purple-blue of subalpine larkspur. An avalanche-stripped slope opens the mountainside to flower-nurturing sun. Dull gold **rayless arnica** and lavender-pink **subalpine daisy** thrive.

Ahead, the parade of colors continues. Snowflakes of yellow **mountain parsley** join the whites of finely rayed Coulter daisy and the bottlebrush-shaped heads of **American bistort.** Not so colorful is **Grays angelica,** looking like a drab green visitor from an alien planet's flora. Lacy **cowbane** and **red onion** frame a view of the Bandora Mine behind you.

Rosy paintbrush draws attention, but look also for smaller flowers, such as **homely buttercup** and mustard family member **golden draba.** Glance left for a particularly lavish display of color, which includes more rosy paintbrush. The bracts and modified leaves give the plant its color; the actual flowers look like green toothpicks. Plump green spikes of odd-looking **Ritter** or **yellow kittentails** make an interesting sighting.

While avalanche paths open space for flowers, they devastate the forest, as evidenced by a tangle of fallen conifers, easily negotiated thanks to Forest Service personnel. Look in this area for **heartleaf arnica, false hellebore,** and tri-toothed **sibbaldia.** Populating the avalanche path on the left are plenty of rayless arnica's nodding heads.

Off to the west, views are spectacular. The trail, once a two-track road, features **marsh marigold** right down the center. Bistort and **triangleleaf senecio** send hikers into spruce forest where tall chimingbells abound in pink buds and blue bells. The shade also supports white **parrot's beak lousewort**, its cousin **bracted lousewort**, and subalpine daisy.

A sign tacked to a tree tells you to go left. On the right, both **pink** and **white willowherb** beg to be noticed, along with **daffodil senecio**. The ascent resumes with an arrangement of **brook saxifrage** and cowbane joined by tall chimingbells interspersed with snowy **bittercress**.

The left side of the trail passes a low mossy bank yielding **green mitrewort**, or **bishop's cap**, a saxifrage family member. You need a magnifying glass to appreciate the maroon tracery woven into its frangible green snowflakes. Soon the trail rises rapidly and rockily. Look left to find **globeflower** still in bloom. **Twistedstalk**'s reflexed hanging bells will mature into red-orange berries. Farther up, brook saxifrage lightens a boldly hued garden. An open area where the trail eases features **Porters lovage**, red onion, and brassy **alpine avens**.

A slide of angular rock tapers off to present lush columbine clumps, while willows shelter monkshood and bistort. A small stream supports bright pink **Parry primrose**. The trail trail climbs, eventually coming to a sign that points the route right. The single track, lined with soft duff, drifts slightly down to find **lesser wintergreen** thriving in old-growth shade.

When the trail intersects rushing South Fork Mineral Creek, watch for patches of globeflower as well as uncommon white **northern true saxifrage**, with tiny, ivy-shaped leaves. The best way to cross the considerable volume is a series of worn boulders that form an informal dam just upstream. Hikers can, using caution, step from stone to stone to reach the far side. Other crossing options are possible as well.

SHY WOOD NYMPH
Moneses uniflora

A dweller in deep forest shade and particularly at home in mossy environs, shy wood nymph is a wonderfully fragrant flower. Like a wavy-edged star, the five-lobed flower bows to the earth, hence the appropriate common name of this wintergreen family member. Other names include star pyrola and single delight, the translation of its Latin scientific name. The genus portion is derived from the Greek *monos*, meaning "one," and *hesis*, meaning "delight." The Latin species name, *uniflora*, is self-explanatory: one-flowered.

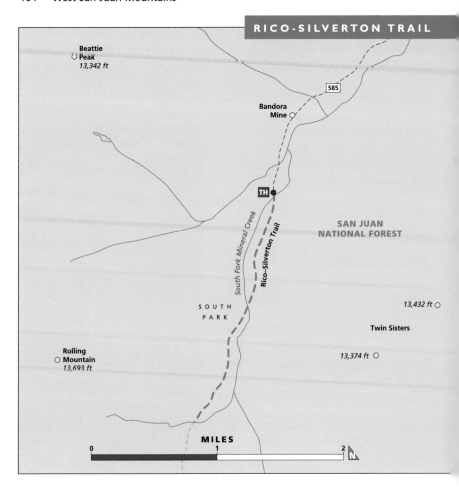

Greeting you on the far side are large heads of **Parry clover**, round, rosy, and fragrant. Shortly up the trail, on the inside of a curve, look near an old, rotting stump for the ivory, ruffle-edged stars of **shy wood nymph**, bowing a wonderfully perfumed head. Hiding here under leafy neighbors are over three dozen nymphs.

As you hike, look left for twistedstalk, its crooked stems hiding reflexed, splayed bells hanging from a right-angled pedicel under the leaves. Patches of arnica, orange sneezeweed, and rosy paintbrush hint at the glorious views ahead. On the way, a specialty clover of the San Juans, **slender-tipped clover**, displays tapered blue-green leaves and rosy heads topping long stems.

The level trail leads through the edge of the spruces to a willow-encircled pond. **Twinberry honeysuckle** marks your entry into a breathtaking expanse of wildflowers. Parry clover, under ideal conditions, produces heads the size of

Ping-Pong balls. Lots of pink-lavender subalpine daisy spreads wide rays alongside willow-sheltered monkshood. Subalpine arnica, orange sneezeweed, and beauty cinquefoil bathe the meadow with golds, accented by rosy paintbrush. Acting as subtle foils are **white geranium** and Coulter daisy.

The trail is not strenuous, but don't be tempted to rush: Stroll instead, absorbing the magnificent variety of colors. Hikers soon reach a meandering creek, best crossed at a narrow spot amongst willows. Beyond, stretching into the distance, is gorgeous South Park, a paradise of wildflowers with radiant rosy paintbrush among golden arnicas and senecios. The Twin Sisters are to the left (east) and part of Rolling Mountain is to the right (west).

Granitic boulders stud the meadow, sheltering low-growing white **alpine rock primrose** and **mountain candytuft**, the latter featuring four petals in a cross shape. Pale lilac **delicate Jacob's ladder,** palest yellow Ritter kittentails, and shorter tall chimingbells quiet the color scheme. Whitish, burgundy-based paintbrush hybrids grow near rayless senecio and marsh marigold.

The trail heads gently up to a round-ledged outcrop, led by **queen's crown** and cowbane. The granitic outcrop also supports **mountain death camas'** greenish-white stars.

Make your way up the wet trail through willows to a place of sedges and rushes, where queen's crown appreciates the extra moisture, as does delicate, wide-eyed **American speedwell**, or **brooklime**, blooming in the palest of blues. Off to the southwest, a keyhole cleft on Rolling Mountain deserves a glance.

Pushing through the last willows prior to crossing a rockslide, note Whipple penstemon's wine-colored tubes and little **black-headed daisy**. Make your way across the granite pile, passing a large slab encrusted with lichen; a crevice on the far side harbors a single cushion of brilliant pink **moss campion**, a relative of carnations.

On the far side of the slab, little purple **alpine violet** clusters in tundra-type vegetation, as do **fringed parnassia** and ground-hugging **alpine parsley**. **Yellow monkeyflower** thrives near a mossy trickle. Rising, the track meets plenty of **wild onion**, sporting soft pink, pointy tepals. Mountain candytuft's cross-shaped flowers are scented, as is the case for most members of the mustard clan. Buttercup take you to a bright meadow full of wildflowers now familiar.

Steepening considerably over loose rock, the route passes straight-stemmed **aspen sunflower** and a slanted meadow of mountain death camas. Hybridization of pale yellow **northern paintbrush** and rosy paintbrush results in an unlimited pink palette.

A distinctive, almost pink-colored waterfall marks the turnaround point of this hike. For hearty hikers, the trail rises to meet the Colorado Trail near a 12,580-foot pass, promising grand views.

Wildflower Hike 30

Molas Pass East/ Colorado Trail

Broad wildflower meadows fan out from the Colorado Trail on this beautiful hike.

Trail Rating	moderate to difficult
Trail Length	4 miles out and back
Location	San Juan National Forest, north of Durango
Elevation	10,600 to 10,200 feet
Bloom Season	late June to August
Peak Bloom	early July
Directions	From Durango, take US 550 north approximately 44 miles and turn right (east) into a large parking area following milepost 65. From Silverton, head south on US 550 about 6 miles, turning left (east) into the parking lot.

Wild blue flax, echoing the color of the sky, complements the gorgeous mountain vistas on this section of the Colorado Trail (CT). A long view of the Durango & Silverton Narrow Gauge Railroad lends this hike a certain romance, but be prepared as well from some challenging brief climbs. For the seasoned hiker, the elevation gain and loss hardly registers; the casual day-hiker may find the short descents and ascents somewhat arduous. But tackling them promises gorgeous flowers and a potential glimpse into Colorado's railroading history. To get oriented to the mountains that soar above this trail, make a point of stopping at the Molas Pass Overlook adjacent to US 550 and locating the peaks on the interpretive signage.

Beginning gently, Molas Pass East/Colorado Trail weaves through rolling terrain until an outcrop drops you sharply onto loose tread, further descending through aspens. The route then levels for a long way through a sloping meadow, followed by a nontaxing descent to an outcrop overlook, where, three times each summer morning, the Durango & Silverton Narrow Gauge locomotive puffs alongside the Animas River; the last northbound morning train passes far below at just about noon.

Parking is generous at the area adjacent to US 550.

The parking area and access road already offer a variety of wildflowers, including **shrubby cinquefoil**, lavender **fleabane daisy**, and **alpine milkvetch**. **Yarrow** unfolds its white heads as **mountain parsley** mimics golden snowflakes.

Looking into nearby willows turns up **tall chimingbells**, **aspen sunflower**, **orange sneezeweed**, and **northern paintbrush** in cool yellow. Further investigation adds snowy **bittercress**, cowled **monkshood**, and a touch of red **king's crown**.

Locate the Colorado Trail sign and pause a moment to take in the grand panorama around you. Look ahead for the thirteeeners of the Grenadier Range, in addition to Electric Peak and Snowdon Peak. Then turn to catch Grand Turk and Sultan Mountain. Northwest is the rolling, tiered terrain of the Molas Highlands.

As you proceed, compare valerians—the dainty-headed **subalpine valerian** in powder pink and its less attractive cousin, **edible valerian**, nearby. A field of yellow reflects the sunshine. Saucy as it is delicately flowered, subalpine valerian goes by a couple of other names, including **hemispheric** and **hairy-fruit valerian**. Still clinging to its springtime bloom is **marsh marigold**, a member in the hellebore family. A seasonal streambed, confined by a culvert running under the trail, supports flowers such as freckled **yellow monkeyflower**, lacy **cowbane**, and **yellow avens**.

A stand of stately spruces is home to tall chimingbells, white-topped **Porters lovage**, lavender **delicate** or **subalpine Jacob's ladder**, a member of the phlox family, and **rock primrose**, its miniscule blossoms suspended on wiry stems. A trail kiosk for the Weminuche Wilderness anchors the spruce grove.

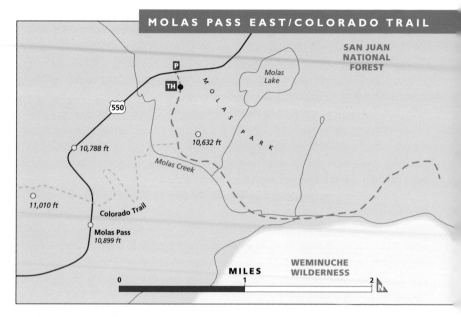

The magnificent mountain backdrop welcomes you to an open area where the trail descends a bit, passing the lovely spurs of **Colorado blue columbine**. This regal, honeysuckle-scented flower won the contest for Colorado state flower in 1899. Molas Lake, owned by the city of Silverton, gleams off to the left as the route drifts down.

A logo sign points the CT two ways; this description heads south, where little mats of **alpine sandwort** hug the lithic soil. **Rosy pussytoes**, soft as kittens' paws when they first appear, grows near **wild blue flax**. Heading over waterbars, the CT encounters **alumroot**, once prized in England as a source of secret ink that could be read only under running water.

Dipping into a swale presents a plethora of **pink plumes**, a coy member of the rose clan whose heads come in threes, each displaying pointy, dusty rose sepals. Other labels are **prairie smoke** and **old man's beard**, referring to the dusty pink, wildly coifed seedheads.

Opposite a red sandstone bank, clumps of **Fendler sandwort** present delicate stars over thin, grasslike leaves. Here, another CT sign helps keep you on track. Drift down to pass **mountain death camas** rising among grasses, as mountain parsley contributes a flurry of yellow snowflakes. Tightly foliaged alpine sandwort appears near purplish alpine milkvetch. Ubiquitous **wild strawberry**'s red runners find new territory in which to root.

You are soon rewarded with more wild blue flax, its silken petals so fragile that they fall as the day heats up. However, the stems are tough as nylon line and provided innovative early peoples with fibers for cordage, snares, and nets. The gold blossoms of shrubby cinquefoil offer complementary yellow. Fine-rayed, white **Coulter daisy** is a native neighbor.

A few small aspens provide dappled shade for pale yellow northern paintbrush. Listen for the sound of running water as you near a small cliff dropping into a drainage to the right. Check for **New Mexico senecio** as the trail makes a switchback down. In the rock, **wallflower** offers its scented, soft yellow, cross-shaped flowers, and **cliff** or **red globe anemone** offers cerise tepals, a term used when petals and sepals cannot be differentiated.

The sound of falling water might induce you to go right on a spur, passing bright pink, pea-type flowers of bushy **sweetvetch**. Enjoy overlooking a small cascade before heading back to the main trail, which steepens considerably. Make your way down past crumbling rock ledges where greenish-yellow alumroot, light lavender **showy** or **aspen daisy**, and buttery wallflower line the trail.

The trail threads through a copse of quaking aspens where perfumed **wild rose** waits. Petite **spreading fleabane** and **aspen daisy** grow near **snowberry** shrubs dangling blushed tubes.

The trail continues to descend sharply, reaching social trails where this route heads left, drawn toward slopes covered with wild blue flax. Scatters of rosy pussytoes mark the way down to another aspen copse, this one featuring **many-rayed goldenrod**. Straitlaced aspen sunflower's typically east-facing heads take the trail out of the aspens.

At last the trail flattens out, the dominant wild blue flax accented by white yarrow, orange sneezeweed, pink plumes, gentle wallflower, and shrubby cinquefoil. Arrive at a Colorado Trail signpost and continue on. Early-season hikers enjoy the quiet purple grace of **wild iris**. Damp soil nourishes monkshood's purple-cowled sepals, as well as cowbane's delicate heads and tall chimingbells' dangling corollas.

SAFFRON SENECIO
Packera crocata

At home in moist subalpine meadows, saffron senecio has toothed basal leaves and distinctive, striped red and gold button buds. This notable senecio, with its red-orange heads, makes a choice find. Borrowing its common name from the stigma color of the saffron crocus, a valuable culinary spice, this groundsel or senecio is far less common than its many cousins. John Packer, a Canadian botanist, is honored by the genus name.

Ladylike subalpine valerian leads to a seasonal waterway where smaller flowers, such as **pink** and **white willowherb**, share space with bright yellow monkeyflower. Look up the drainage for pink plumes and the maroon, barrel-like heads of **rayless** or **Bigelow senecio**.

The trail rises gently before entering a conifer stand. On the way, search the bunchgrass for the red and gold buds of **saffron senecio**, which resemble small buttons. As you locate the first saffron senecio among the prolific grasses, more will catch your eye.

Spruce shade suits **meadowrue** and early-blooming **few-flowered false Solomon's seal** with its tiny, starlike blossoms, explaining another common name, **star Solomon's seal**. Nearby, rock primrose keeps a low profile.

The trail eases over a small rise before topping out in the company of sandwort. Roots and rocks assist the trail's incline, as **heartleaf arnica** presents leafy colonies supporting a few brassy suns. In sunny openings, red globe anemone displays cerise cups in the company of pale northern paintbrush and pink **wild geranium**. Shade enhances the lanternlike heads of **western red columbine**.

Subalpine arnica, with its softly haired leaves, accompanies the trail around a curve to a post with the CT logo. Look for **tall scarlet paintbrush**, more western red columbine, **twinberry honeysuckle**, and **green gentian**. **White geranium** shows well in shade. Here and there, you might spot mountain death camas in its curved bud stage. The flowerstalk will straighten as it gathers strength to bloom.

Where some scraggly aspens struggle in an opening, a strong social spur aims right, up a rocky knoll. This is the overlook that reveals the Animas River flowing below, cutting the deepest gorge in the San Juans. Across to the southeast, peaks rise from the base of the canyon to heights exceeding 14,000 feet. At the right time, you might see the Durango & Silverton Narrow Gauge train chugging its way up to let backpackers off at the Needleton stop.

Regain the main trail to head for some stately, white-trunked aspens which shelter tall scarlet paintbrush. Just a little farther is a moss- and lichen-covered outcrop draped with needly mats of **dotted saxifrage**.

From here, the trail drops clear down to the Animas River—a goal for backpackers perhaps, but for wildflower hikers, this is a good turnaround point.

West Lime Creek Trail

West Lime Creek Trail is a pleasant jaunt beside a lively stream.

easy to moderate	***Trail Rating***
6 miles out and back	***Trail Length***
San Juan National Forest, north of Durango	***Location***
10,000 to 10,400 feet	***Elevation***
late June to September	***Bloom Season***
mid-July	***Peak Bloom***
From Durango, go north on US 550 about 38.5 miles. The trailhead is located 0.4 mile beyond milepost 60, halfway between Coal Bank and Molas Passes. From Silverton, head south on US 550 just over 11 miles. Park roadside on the far outside of the curve.	***Directions***

West Lime Creek Trail No. 679 offers a little bit of everything: A lively crystalline creek, hopscotching forest and meadow, and a wide variety of wildflowers. The first hundred yards of the trail are the only challenge to a route that pleasantly meanders above West Lime Creek, rising gently as it goes. About 3 miles in, the trail is challenged by a bog. From here, you can opt to trail-find to a horsetail waterfall with an approximately 25-foot drop. The Forest Service tries to keep the trail clear of fallen trees after winter. A colorful selection of wildflowers abounds, giving you lots to look for and identify.

Parking is extremely limited on the side of busy US 550, making a weekday the best time to hike West Lime Creek.

Park carefully near a sign indicating 10,000 feet elevation. The trailhead is marked by signage. Rough and loose, the path descends briefly at the beginning on volcanic ash compressed into rock. Here, **black-tipped senecio** thrives in its favorite rocky ground. **Wild raspberry** takes you to a fork where West Lime Creek Trail bears left downhill to parallel the stream; the uphill fork heads into private property.

Twinberry honeysuckle, also known as **black twinberry**, grows trailside in the company of whitish **yarrow** and yellow **beauty cinquefoil**. **Wild strawberry** spreads via red runners and competes with gray-green mats of **pussytoes** and starry white **spergulastrum**, a sandwort. Add to that mixture **wild geranium** in pink and coil-headed **scorpionweed**. Directly below runs clear West Lime Creek.

Let your eyes travel upslope to find exquisite **Colorado blue columbine**. A rockfall is home to **false columbine**, or **meadowrue**. **Cliff** or **red globe anemone** shows cerise tepals while the stream heads for a cavern exit under the highway.

Lemony **wallflower**, each flower configured as a cross, grows alongside more bright cinquefoil, **American vetch**, **mountain parsley**, and **golden aster**, which is an aster in name only. Pinks are represented by blushing and delicate-headed **subalpine valerian** and the assertive pink of bushy **sweetvetch**. Purple comes in the form of winsome **blue violet**.

In the shade of a willow glade, look for Colorado blue columbine, sweetvetch, **edible valerian**, **tall chimingbells**, **cowbane**, and simmering flames of **tall scarlet paintbrush**. Complementing the blue columbine are colonies of **heartleaf arnica**.

Stony tread enters a spruce stand and changes to soft duff as you pass lilac **delicate Jacob's ladder**. Smaller, earlier-blooming **western red columbine** glows like embers. As the trail enters a dry watercourse, look for head-high **green gentian**, or **monument plant**, **white geranium**, **many-rayed goldenrod**, and **fireweed**. The lower slope is composed of Colorado blue columbine, barely pink subalpine valerian, and bright paintbrush.

Lifting above the creek, the trail highlights royal blue **Rocky Mountain gentian** in late summer, along with **mountain death camas** and cliff anemone, which matures into cottony seedheads. West Lime Creek supports damp-loving

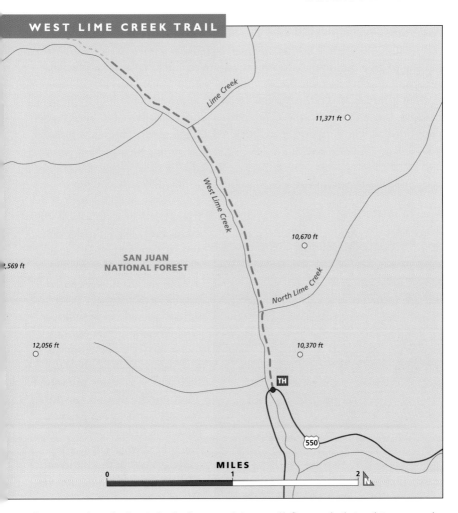

flowers such as **little pink elephants**, plain, small-flowered **alpine bistort**, and classically simple **fringed parnassia**. A mossy seep nurtures **green bog orchid**. Look for western red columbine under conifer shade.

A flat segment takes you past a hillside of **rayless senecio**'s smooth barrel heads and mountain parsley's filigreed snowflakes. Scattered around are **orange agoseris** and **orange sneezeweed**, both composites but nothing alike. Spruce shade introduces distinctive and endemic **Ritter** or **yellow kittentails**. A little uptick sees the creek cascading into a pool where columbine decorates the sheer walls. At this point, the trail crosses just above the creek, signaled by a red arrow painted on a creekside rock. Stepping-stones cross the waterway and send you up a stony pitch to a drier aspect, where mountain parsley and **alumroot** claim rootholds under a cap of volcanic rock.

Orange sneezeweed and orange agoseris, with blooms similar to burnished copper, lead into a small stand of spruce trees, while **elderberry** and twinberry honeysuckle lead out. Wallflower, a scented early bloomer, and beauty cinque-foil are found trailside. The trail prepares to go down to meet West Lime Creek, passing **prickly mountain currant**, its salmon-colored, salverform blossoms maturing into bristly red fruit.

A giant block of rockfall debris creates an intimate little fall of white water. Stacked, broken ledges to the right support white **Canada violet, bittercress,** paintbrush, columbine, and some brick red **king's crown**. This is the place to give endemic Ritter kittentails a close inspection, noting its large basal leaves and small clasping leaves along the straight stalk. Its pale yellow tubes stand perpendicular to the stem.

RITTER KITTENTAILS
Besseya ritteriana

Endemic to the San Juan Mountains, Ritter kittentails sends up a packed spike of small, pale yellow, minutely-lipped flowers. A denizen of rocky meadows near timberline, this member of the snapdragon or figwort family has spinachlike, toothed basal leaves, and much-reduced leaves lining the stalk, which may grow up to a foot high. Dr. Charles E. Bessey, teacher to fellow botanist Per Axel Rydberg, is honored by the genus name; the species name commemorates B.W. Ritter of Durango, Colorado.

Moisture lovers such as **triangleleaf senecio**, purple **monkshood**, tall chimingbells, and lacy cowbane thrive in a shady spot where the trail draws close to the creek. Willows bend over **rosy paintbrush**, snowy bittercress, and **brook saxifrage**.

Way up to the right, a mossy seep drips off a ledge of rock; watch creekside here for brilliantly pink **Parry primrose**. Then prepare to meet **tasselrue** trailside, with its big palmate leaves and little buds that look like folded ivory cups. The fringed effect on this buttercup relation is produced by ribbony bits of stamen parts.

The trail ascends briefly by a small falls, which is followed soon by a bigger falls as West Lime Creek squeezes between ledges to take a 12-foot drop. Damp trail takes you by two species of green bog orchid and tidy clumps of fringed parnassia, each round bud lifted singly on a bare stem. A trickle pours down through thick emerald moss, providing a home to little pink elephants and more orchid varieties.

A grassy slope hosts fireweed, while white tones are represented by parsley family members **Porters lovage** and **cow parsnip**. A rounded mountain and neighboring peak, still showing snow, make for stunning views. In a steep, grassy meadow, look for the yellows of **aspen sunflower**, orange sneezeweed, beauty cinquefoil, and wallflower. The trail continues to rise flanked by rayless senecio and **alpine milkvetch**. Cruising back into conifer shade brings white Canada violet and cowbane, as well as **false columbine**, soon yielding to the real thing, western red columbine. Leveling in the open, the view widens to include a third crest.

Paralleling West Lime Creek, the trail's pleasant character gives you time to consider the San Juan Mountains' volcanic origins, said to be some 70 million years ago. Note outcrops of compressed ash layers and distinct crossbedding. Before a stony track lifts you into shade, observe the dusky, wine-colored tubes of **Whipple penstemon**.

Moist soil supports **tall western larkspur**, Porters lovage, and cow parsnip, accented by triangleleaf senecio and monkshood. Forest duff softens footfalls along a level section that soon enters West Lime Creek's narrowing valley. Before crossing a tributary, note the round, rosy heads of **Parry clover** on the right.

The route crosses Lime Creek on stones and chunky logs, then enters a meadow where the path is sometimes obscure. Warm hues of aspen sunflower, orange sneezeweed, cinquefoil, and mountain parsley highlight the 13,000-foot-plus summits of the Twin Sisters. The meadow is home to little blue melissas, which flit about looking for a place to "puddle," their method of gathering moisture and minerals from the soil. Ascending gradually, you pass many-rayed goldenrod and **New Mexico senecio**, along with **wild onion** and subalpine valerian, both in pink.

A spruce wood shelters **parrot's beak lousewort**, while a wide, open slope showcases rushing West Lime Creek. A downslope outcrop supports king's crown and valerian. Lined by cinquefoil and diminutive alpine milkvetch, the route takes you to another bit of falling water.

The creek continues minus the added volume of the tributaries you have passed, making it quieter as it introduces tiny, bright **golden draba**, each cross-shaped flower giving away its mustard lineage.

A rocky rise brings on more golden draba before the trail eases to expose starry **sandwort**. Follow a glaciated ridge to find the purplish little pea-type flowers of alpine milkvetch.

Rosy paintbrush lines the route as it vanishes into a bog. This is a natural turnaround point, but for those wishing to go on to the 25-foot horsetail falls, the bog can be circumvented by climbing to the right and making your own way up for another 0.3 mile or so. For others, locate a big, meadow-anchoring rock just back down the trail and perch on its flat top for a snack and relaxation.

Wildflower Hike 32

Pass Trail to Engineer Mountain

Wildflowers foreground cloud-cloaked Engineer Mountain on the Pass Trail.

Trail Rating	easy to moderate
Trail Length	5.4 miles out and back
Location	San Juan National Forest, north of Durango
Elevation	10,680 to 11,750 feet
Bloom Season	July to August
Peak Bloom	late July to mid-August
Directions	From Durango, head north on US 550 31 miles to Coal Bank Pass. Take a left (west) on the first dirt spur after the pass for trailhead parking. From the Silverton junction of US 550, go south approximately 15 miles to the spur road, turning right (west) for the parking area and trailhead.

Located between Durango and Silverton at the summit of Coal Bank Pass, Pass Trail to Engineer Mountain is a great way to explore scenic, wildflower-filled expanses in just over 5 miles round-trip. The trailhead access—right off US 550 where the Coal Bank Pass restrooms appear—is almost opposite the trailhead spur road.

Well-defined Pass Trail starts with an easygoing ascent and maintains it fairly steadily, with only a few steeper climbs to its junction with Engineer Mountain Trail at mile 2.5. Hikers can turn around here or tackle a bit more strenuous incline, heading to a great slab of red sandstone on 12,968-foot Engineer Mountain's flank, the turnaround point for this description.

Bright flowers are literally everywhere, whether filling a subalpine slope, decorating a pocket meadow, or lining a waterway. Parking is usually adequate in the graveled area just west of US 550, especially on weekdays.

Popular Pass Trail begins in a magnificent natural garden. Even the parking area is surrounded with huge heads of **cow parsnip** in close formation, interspersed with **subalpine larkspur**, **triangleleaf senecio**, **tall chimingbells**, and **wild geranium**, all thriving in moist soil. As you begin along the trail, note **orange agoseris** and yellow **beauty cinquefoil**. Odd **Ritter** or **yellow kitten-tails**, with large, shallowly scalloped basal leaves and stalk-climbing smaller leaves, is almost hidden in the colorful crowd.

Peering over head-high bloomers, towering spikes of **green gentian** are scattered amidst more subalpine larkspur, **aspen sunflower**, **Porters lovage**, **orange sneezeweed**, and robust cow parsnip. This parsley or carrot clan member is less commonly called **bear cabbage** due to its popularity with bears. The delicate white rays of **Coulter daisy** are practically overwhelmed by **false hellebore**.

Purple, blue, and white dominate at eye level, while trailside color includes **Whipple** or **dusky penstemon**. Almost colorless in comparison is **waterleaf**. Where the vegetation thins a bit, glance uphill for a display of red, white, blue, and gold dominated by **tall scarlet paintbrush**. **Pink-headed daisy** is recognizable by its angora-like ruff. If the opportunity arises to examine green gentian, take at look at its fascinating four-merous flowers, the same rubbery pale green as the rest of the spike.

Among the abundant wildflower varieties, be sure to look for maroon-headed **rayless senecio** and bright aspen sunflower, its stems straight as sticks. A drainage dip showcases the vivid red bracts and modified leaves of tall scarlet paintbrush, while a bit farther up, a ravine introduces you to clumps of **sweet-vetch**, **wild onion**, and late-blooming **goldeneye**.

Ascending gently, the trail passes **golden aster**, orange agoseris, **yarrow**, and yellow **mountain parsley**. Weathered spruces lead to a smattering of **monkshood** sheltered under willows. A seasonal waterway studded with boulders presents lacy **cowbane**, a dainty cousin of cow parsnip and lovage. Orange sneezeweed foregrounds Potato Hill to the south—which, at 11,871 feet, is hardly a "hill."

A small trickle supports graceful **Colorado blue columbine**, while an uptick into spruce shade offers wild onion and the purple thimbles of **harebell**. Lots of ladder-leaved sweetvetch, also known as **chainpod**, begs inspection of its distinctive seedpods. **Edible valerian** is not showy, but it appears frequently along the trail.

The gradient increases, passing softly haired **subalpine arnica**. Cousin **heartleaf arnica** colonizes under nearby spruces. **Mountain death camas** grows alongside **parrot's beak lousewort**, its coiled white blossoms lending it another moniker, **rams-horn**. The route evens to expose a view of the Hermosa Cliffs off to the south.

Curve up to find **wild rose** and a hillside of sweetvetch, with some late-blooming **Parry goldenweed** also putting in an appearance. **Rayless** or **Parry arnica** makes up in numbers what it lacks in show. Straight-stalked, ferny-leaved **bracted lousewort** shares a neighborhood with cousin parrot's beak lousewort.

SWEETVETCH
Hedysarum occidentale

A showy, potent pink pea family member, bushy sweetvetch plants can grow up to 3 feet tall. Also known as chainpod, its seedpods are joined like links in a chain, looking rather like sequins hooked together. In southwestern Colorado, it is found up into the subalpine zone. Sweetvetch roots are favored by bears and were also a food source for American Indian tribes.

Denser understory arrives on approach to a couple of rock steps, represented by Porters lovage, tall chimingbells, and white-starred mountain death camas. Switching back and forth, the trail greets coolly pink **subalpine daisy** and the yellows of mountain parsley and aspen sunflower, sometimes called **five-nerved**, due to the vein pattern in the leaves. Arnicas, including heartleaf, subalpine, and rayless, are abundant.

Little clusters of sunny heads top **thickbract senecio** as it accents a red, white, and blue garden of Porters lovage, cowbane, mountain death camas, tall chimingbells, larkspur, monkshood, and, upslope, tall scarlet paintbrush. Putting in two showy appearances are **king's crown** and **rosy paintbrush**. Along this pleasant section of trail, **daffodil senecio** dots the understory, along with **delicate Jacob's ladder** and **many-rayed goldenrod**. Be sure to note a

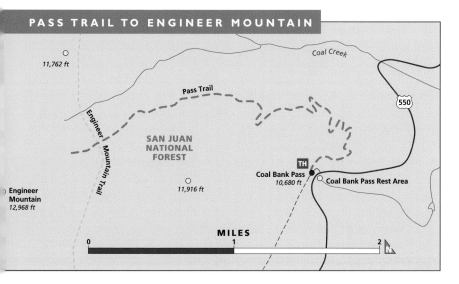

patch on the left of **pearly everlasting**, with its straw-textured bracts. On the right, a seasonal watercourse nurtures **pink willowherb** and cowbane. Next up, close enough to compare, are both smooth rayless senecio and hairy rayless arnica.

Pass Trail steepens as it passes **twistedstalk**'s zigzag stems, kinked pedicels, and dangling bells on the way to a mossy stretch. On the upper side, **subalpine buttercup** highlights tiny, snowflake blossoms of **green mitrewort**, a saxifrage family member. The other side shows subalpine larkspur, Porters lovage, triangle-leaf senecio, and some daintily inflorescenced, blushing pink **subalpine valerian** with stamens standing out like minuscule pins in a cushion.

A few rocky paces take hikers by bracted lousewort, mountain death camas, and white **Canada violet**. On the right, sweeps of tall chimingbells lend a blue cast to the forest, soon to be supplanted by brick red king's crown.

Back on the opposite bank, subalpine valerian comes on strongly, interspersed with subalpine daisy's lavender-pink rays. The keen eye might discern **western red columbine** on the right bank, blooming later than is typical. A few paces more turns up Colorado blue columbine.

On the upside of the rising trail is paper white **bitttercress**; on the downside, king's crown. The ambling trail switchbacks, coming across **northern true saxifrage**, with tiny white flowers and equally tiny ivy-shaped leaves. This find is tucked into the rocky bank on the right, for the dedicated to spot.

Flattening out along a damp area, the trail displays several familiar flowers along with **yellow monkeyflower** and pea-soup green **Grays angelica**. Surrounded by a grassy meadow, a small pond invites hikers to examine thick-bract senecio, **alpine veronica**, **little pink elephants**, and the pink-floreted, round heads of **queen's crown**. In the shallows, the aquatic wildflower **marsh trefoil**, or **buckbean**, forms a green raft, its fringy white flowers blooming early.

Venerable spruces lead to a bright sidehill meadow presided over by aspen sunflower and orange sneezeweed. An open spot offers a chance to pause and admire the mountains.

Turning a corner brings you to tiny-flowered **golden draba**, a mustard family member displaying the typical cruciform flowers, in the brassy company of **alpine avens**, of the rose clan. Traverse the meadow, noting thickbract senecio's golden heads.

As it gains elevation, Pass Trail showcases **different-leaved senecio** and false hellebore, along with rosy paintbrush, **marsh marigold**, **Parry clover**, and little pink elephants. Logs take you over a section of muddy bog as the trail continues to be damp in places. Wet weather makes much of the Pass Trail a slippery affair.

American bistort waves its bottlebrush heads on the way to a seasonal waterway where pink **Parry primrose** lines the drainage. Cloaking a hillside ahead, buttercup and marsh marigold reveal an upcoming seep. It emerges directly from under a hill to nourish yellow monkeyflower tucked around angular rocks.

Coming from forest into scattered spruce parkland, the wildflower displays keep getting better, tending to a gold-accented, mostly pastel theme. Rising ahead is the impressive bulk of Engineer Mountain, with its bands of maroon Cutler Formation sandstone, and above that, gray palisades. Up to the left, a rocky waterway supports delicate Colorado blue columbine.

The route divides into two tracks under the triangular subpeaks of Engineer Mountain, its grand profile commanding the rose and gold landscape. Brilliant wildflower combinations keep hikers enthralled as the track curves up, headed left around a willow carr to arrive at a junction. At this intersection, you may choose to turn around, or hike a steep additional 0.25 mile toward Engineer Mountain to a big slab of red sandstone, which is ideal for a snack and contemplation.

Potato Lake via Spud Lake Trail

Wildflower Hike 33

For easygoing entry into a magnificent mountain setting, try Spud Lake Trail to Potato Lake.

easy	**Trail Rating**
2.5 miles out and back, including lake loop	**Trail Length**
San Juan National Forest, north of Durango	**Location**
9,360 to 9,800 feet	**Elevation**
mid-June to August	**Bloom Season**
late June to early July	**Peak Bloom**
From Durango, take US 550 north approximately 28 miles to FR 591, also called Old Lime Creek Rd., located 0.4 mile past milepost 51. Turn right (east) and continue 2.9 miles to the unsigned trailhead on the left. Park just past Scout Lake.	**Directions**

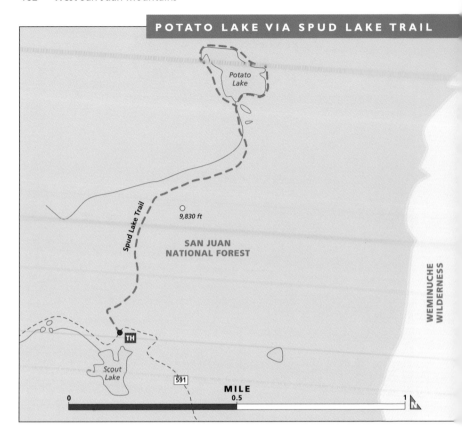

POTATO LAKE VIA SPUD LAKE TRAIL

Potato Lake

9,830 ft

Spud Lake Trail

SAN JUAN NATIONAL FOREST

WEMINUCHE WILDERNESS

TH

Scout Lake

591

MILE
0.5

0   1

Scenic, floristic, and easygoing, Spud Lake Trail No. 661 leads to prosaically named Potato Lake, where the majestic Twilight Peaks serve as backdrop. This gentle ascent to the lake is as undemanding as, say, a potato, but offers the wildflower lover an exciting array of species. Additionally, kids will enjoy passing many beaver ponds, some anchored by old lodges.

The trailhead, unsigned but marked by a pair of log posts, is just around the corner from Scout Lake, often covered in pond lilies. Spud Lake Trail begins on a slight incline and ends at the lake, gaining an easy 440 feet over 1.2 miles. Wildflower highlights include a fringed flower called buckbean, which, like the lake, is much prettier than its name.

Parking for a few cars is available at the trailhead and supplemented by informal parking across from Scout Lake.

Since scenic Scout Lake is right around the corner from the Spud Lake Trailhead, this description starts at Scout, which offers a surface covered with **yellow pond lily**. In the interstices, **water smartweed** floats, preparing for a mid-July bloom of hot pink spikes. If Scout's waters are still, you might see 12,504-foot Grayrock Peak reflected on its surface.

Pale pink heads of **Geyer onion** are sprinkled lakeside, as are both **beauty cinquefoil** and **silvery cinquefoil**, the latter with grayish, pinnate leaves. **Wild iris** grows nearby. Small flowers such as **rock primrose** and blue **alpine veronica** are both found on a granitic thumb poking into Scout Lake.

Taking leave of the lake, cross the road, angling northeast, and note violet-tinged **Rocky Mountain penstemon** decorating an outcrop. Head between the two log posts that indicate entry to Spud Lake Trail. Behind the posts, the trail begins on its rockiest segment. Brilliantly pink **wild rose** and muted pink **snowberry** bushes join the light pink umbels of Geyer onion. Not to be outdone, **tall scarlet paintbrush** offers its red bracts and modified leaves. **American vetch** presents its few magenta, pea-type flowers.

Within a few yards, the trail tread smoothes out as it passes pleated **false hellebore**, moisture-loving **white geranium** and **tall chimingbells**, and yellow **mountain parsley** and **heartleaf arnica**.

Turning up a bit, the route passes the white, frothy clusters of **northern bedstraw** on the left, while on the right, the tendrils of American vetch overtake neighboring vegetation. Forming blueberry-like fruits, **serviceberry** provided food for early peoples, as did **creeping grapeholly**, with its tart, bluish-black fruits. Beauty cinquefoil adds a touch of gold.

Dappled aspen shade shelters **snowberry**, while wild rose presents five pink petals. Look left for the refined white rays of native **Coulter daisy** and tall **aspen sunflower**. **Fireweed** spires will bloom with four magenta-pink petals and four darker sepals in between.

The western skyline is dominated by Grayrock Peak, while trailside, **Porters lovage** presents its ferny leaves and white, umbellate inflorescence characteristic of the carrot or parsley clan. Willows shelter **blue violet** as the trail turns.

A slight dip reveals a brief social spur that offers a look at Grayrock. Joining Grayrock is pyramidal Engineer Mountain, just 32 feet shy of being a thirteener, and Potato Hill at almost 12,000 feet high. Return to the trail to note **pussytoes** lifting papery, rosy bracts over silver-felted leaf mats and **hawksbeard**, with its thin, hairy, straight stems rising above a rosette of equally hairy leaves. The narrow heads produce short, dull gold rays.

Before the trail steps up a bit, examine the base of a chunk of granite for soft pink Geyer onion. The gently rising, somewhat stony path brings limber pines with their resinous, rounded-scale cones and **many-rayed goldenrod** blooming to the left. Rocks stud the way. A small beaver pond is surrounded by aspen stumps chiseled by the animal's big incisors. Stroll a little higher to find several more dams, some with old lodges.

At a large pond anchored by a derelict beaver lodge, look right under a spruce for the emberlike blooms of **western red columbine**. Past the last dam and some willows, another spruce boasts a specimen of green **woods orchid**, its interesting flowers as green as its broad, alternate leaves.

Opposite some willows, false hellebore unfolds, accented by pale pink subalpine valerian, Out of the damp earth, blue violet pokes up its edible heads. A few casual logs span a bog as the trail comes to **twinberry honeysuckle**, dangling paired, dull gold tubes cupped in reddish bracts, as well as white **Canada violet**. Head-high young aspens shelter **subalpine arnica** with its softly haired opposite leaves.

A lichen-covered boulder shelters more western red columbine and the tiny stars of rock primrose. Look in spruce shade for **Colorado blue columbine** and **false Solomon's seal**, with a zigzag stem of lustrous leaves terminating in a creamy white terminal raceme of thin-petaled stars.

Off Potato Hill's left shoulder, Engineer Mountain appears in a gap where you can compare cousins, subalpine and heartleaf arnica. The former blooms later, with several heads rising from the leaf axils, while the latter is typically single-headed. On a rocky tread, the trail highlights **sandwort** and a bank on the right shows hanging gold tubes of **many-flowered puccoon** as well as clumps of short lavender **fleabane daisy** as well.

The trail passes above another beaver dam, this one constructed in more a grassy meadow than a pond, and the view west catches the ski runs of Durango Mountain Resort. On the right, in the shade of Douglas firs, false Solomon's seal thrives. Close by grows **few-flowered false Solomon's seal**, with sparse, thready blooms. These cousins grow close enough for comparison.

Hikers are in for a treat—jewel-like Potato Lake. The loop around it is best done clockwise. Begin curving west, on the fishermen's trail, to catch **golden aster**, **meadowrue**, blue, tiny-flowered alpine veronica, and **twistedstalk**, with its suspended, split-lobed bells. Continue on to find soft-leaved subalpine arnica on the way to a seep area featuring **green bog orchid**. In

BUCKBEAN
Menyanthes trifoliata

More descriptively called marsh trefoil, this species—the only of its genus in this region—populates ponds as far south in Colorado as the Gunnison Basin. Its succulent rootstock sinks roots in pond mud, sending up three-parted leaves and small, intriguing flowers, the five whitish petals fringed with angled hairs. With its delicate flower, buckbean looks like a Venus flytrap. This interesting plant's cousins are tropical.

drier zones, look for scree-loving sandwort, with five pointed petals dipping into green centers.

Then look to the lake for a yard-wide islet, almost afloat. This is the first encounter with **buckbean**, or **marsh trefoil**, which sports five extremely fringed petals. Among the ivory petals are black anthers that look like bits of cracked pepper. Leathery, oval, three-part leaves clasp a thick stem. There will be a number of places, some more accessible, to see this interesting wildflower as you continue circling the lake.

On the dry side of the narrow path, the off-white beaks of **rams-horn**, or **parrot's beak lousewort**, uncurl. More finely fringed buckbean populates a soggy islet near a defunct beaver lodge.

Here and there, yellow pond lily lifts thick stems to open its golden globes above the surface. **Goldenrod** leans a budded stalk, ready to open pert yellow flowers, while a quartz-studded granite outcrop is anchored by **currant**, serviceberry, and both herbaceous beauty cinquefoil and woody **shrubby cinquefoil**.

Redtwig dogwood shelters under spruce, while trailside, late-summer hikers can expect **Rocky Mountain gentian**. Travel on to a spot where emerald moss nurtures a brigade of green bog orchid. A trickle flowing from underneath red alders is the place to see cowbane and more green bog orchid.

As you travel east, fleabane daisy competes with a wonderful view of the Twilights rising 13,000 feet into the sky. Almost as successful and equally alien as the ubiquitous **dandelion**, **oxeye daisy** populates the next trail sector, along with **pearly everlasting**.

A damp area presents a stubby member of the mint family, **self-heal**, or **prunella**. Nestling in reddish bracts, its tiny, two-lipped flowers are tinted darker purple on the top lip, lavender on the bottom lip. A scree area is home to many-flowered puccoon and more beautiful Colorado blue columbine.

Continuing on takes you to another ramshackle beaver lodge completely surrounded by pieces of grass bog, where more buckbean flourishes. Tall chimingbells' pink buds and blue corollas share a rocky embankment with Canada violet and **twinberry honeysuckle**. This is an easy spot to compare Colorado blue columbine with meadowrue. Coming up is a hybrid pink columbine, nearby its blue cousin. Red paintbrush in the vicinity also may be the result of crossbreeding.

When you've finished enjoying the loop, retrace your steps to your vehicle.

Wildflower
Hike 34 # Purgatory Trail

The Durango & Silverton Narrow Gauge Railroad
puffs across the Animas River.

Trail Rating	moderate to somewhat difficult
Trail Length	8 miles out and back
Location	San Juan National Forest, north of Durango
Elevation	8,700 to 7,700 feet
Bloom Season	June to September
Peak Bloom	late June to early July
Directions	From Durango, go north on US 550 approximately 26 miles to milepost 49. Turn right (east) into a small, dirt parking area directly across the highway from the Durango Mountain Resort entrance. The sign here is marked for Trail No. 593.

Conveniently located adjacent to US 550 about midway between Durango and Silverton, Purgatory Trail No. 593/511 is used mainly by backpackers headed for overloved Chicago Basin. But this trail holds many pleasures for day-hikers as well. By dropping over 1,000 vertical feet, anyone may get an up-close view of the historic Durango & Silverton Narrow Gauge Railroad running deep in the Animas River Canyon in late mornings and late afternoons. It is quite an experience to watch the black locomotive powering up the grade, pulling cars full of thrilled passengers much as it did over a century ago.

This trail, then, is as much about trains as wildflowers—maybe more, if your goal is to watch the authentic coal black engines pass you, either from a trackside curve or from the Cascade/Animas footbridge where, midspan, you can see the train pass over a girder bridge upstream.

Starting out gently, Purgatory Trail's initial descent sector is relatively tough, more from loose rock underfoot—this is a pack trail—than the incline. Next comes the pleasant crossing of well-named Purgatory Flats. From here, the trail descends through a canyon carved by Cascade Creek. The final switchbacks drop hikers onto the level floodplain of the Animas River.

Wildflower species are typical of upper montane and are nicely displayed on the Purgatory Flats stretch. On the footbridge's far side, scarlet bugler penstemon adds an unexpected touch.

Parking is quite limited, as some vehicles are there over several nights, so arrive early to secure a spot.

Wildflowers begin with the cheerful, but alien, **oxeye daisy**, which has marched into the mountain West like an invading army. **Shrubby cinquefoil** and **mountain parsley** complement the dark blue tubes of **Rocky Mountain penstemon**, all natives.

Left of the green metal gate, a worn path through white-barked quaking aspens starts hikers out on the Purgatory Trail. Flowering whites are represented by **yarrow**, **white geranium**, **fleabane daisy**, and **mouse-ears**, its clever cleft petals forming dainty ears.

Water slowly weaves through alders and willows to the left. **Aspen sunflower** abounds along the even trail until **wild rose** and **wild strawberry** send the route on a downward drift. More aspen sunflower highlights **tall scarlet paintbrush**, both preparing the way for the elegant **Colorado blue columbine**, with its delicate honeysuckle scent.

Coming into forest, you can expect **heartleaf arnica**, along with red paintbrush, Colorado blue columbine, and white-umbelled **Porters lovage** for an informal red, white, and blue theme. A sign for Purgatory Trail affirms you are on the right route.

Mountain ashes shelter paintbrush by a Weminuche Wilderness signboard. **Alpine milkvetch**'s small, purple-tinged flowers grow near cousin **American** vetch's larger magenta blossoms. A turn heads the trail down, passing **Canada violet** in the company of **western red columbine** and heartleaf arnica.

The substantial leaves of **false Solomon's seal** are the texture of polished leather and march up slightly zigzagged stems that terminate in creamy racemes of minuscule stars. Search conifer shade for the occasional **spotted coralroot orchid**. **Tall chimingbells** and **meadowrue**, or **false columbine**, like the north-facing aspect as well. The route treads comfortably alongside **thimbleberry**, generous with its maplelike leaves but frugal with its white blossoms.

Declining more steeply, the trail passes **Indian warriors**, its red-streaked helmets, called galeas, perched above fernlike foliage. The route curves in the direction of running water to a switchback where **twinberry honeysuckle** grows, its red-bracted pairs of dull gold tubes maturing into inedible black berries. Loose pebbles underfoot complete for attention with glowing tall scarlet paintbrush.

Bordering the small creek are **snowberry** shrubs. **Tall coneflower** and **cow parsnip** appear trailside as the route parallels the creek. Lush **false hellebore** shares riparian habitat with tall **western larkspur**, **baneberry**, and **redtwig dogwood**. Continue on the north bank to meet **orange sneezeweed** and complementary lavender **aspen daisy** under a stand of its namesake trees.

Heading down over loose rock asks for careful foot placement—take this descent slowly. Pass a seep to find tall coneflower, lacy **cowbane**, **Coulter daisy**, and a bit of **prunella**, or **self-heal**, a two-lipped, two-tone member of the mint family. The waterway drops over stones to present **many-rayed goldenrod** and **pearly everlasting**. Electric blue damselflies float by **serviceberry** as the trail continues to descend rockily. Aspen sunflower leads hikers from dappled aspen shade into the open to encounter **common evening primrose** and, near slabs of granitic rock, droopy-leaved **spreading dogbane** dangling dainty, blushed bells. A bit of pink **hyssop** can be spotted in the vicinity, as can **buckthorn**, with creamy, minute flower clusters.

Tropical-looking **green gentian** leads to a conifer-shaded turn, and an outcrop with views of the Twilights, the West Needle Mountains, and Potato Hill. Tidy **golden aster** signals a very rocky decline. When the trail eases, look by a ravine for the sky blue petals of **wild blue flax**. As you face a gorge to the south, watch for more spreading dogbane, an oleander relation with softly perfumed bells. A few ponderosa pines turn the rockbound trail northerly to a lush glen of redtwig dogwood and wild rose. Underneath struggling aspens, **chokecherry** forms racemes of tart fruits.

Purgatory Trail briefly levels, then resumes its stony descent to arrive at richly pigmented Rocky Mountain penstemon. A final descending pitch earns hikers the long, even, southerly cruise of Purgatory Flats. Birdsong and grasses accompany you to a little creek where serviceberry and wild rose thrive.

As you traverse Purgatory Flats, enjoy the dynamic combo of blue Rocky Mountain penstemon and red **scarlet gilia**. A social trail heads left to a derelict log structure, while the main trail goes right. **Silvery cinquefoil** joins forces with dots of fleabane daisy, while aspens shelter white **northern bedstraw**. After crossing Purgatory Flats' drier stretches, the trail enters a riparian area dominated by narrow-leaved cottonwoods. Overhung by willows are **edible valerian**, shrubby cinquefoil, twinberry honeysuckle, **senecio**, and **yellow avens**. Like soldiers from a strange green army, stalks of green gentian stand sentinel here. These plants spend years gathering energy to send up a robust flowerstalk, only to die afterward.

On a west heading, pass **beauty cinquefoil** and cross a boggy spot where tall chimingbells and cow parsnip share space with **yellow wintercress**, its tiny petals forming a cross shape as mustards tend to do. Narrow-leaved cottonwoods shade the trail as it crosses a creek on old logs. Push through the trees to the main trail as you navigate a muddy segment, a good place to detect elk prints.

A small rockfall offers a home to **rayless senecio** and spires of **white checkermallow**, a hollyhock and okra relation. In the vicinity of rock walls hung with mats of **dotted saxifrage**, look out for **king's crown** and hyssop, a square-stemmed mint. **Alumroot**'s long, bare stems and small, green-yellow flowers stand above neat basal leaves. Nearby, **Rocky Mountain gentian** blooms in royal blue.

Arriving at river level under open skies brings thimbleberry, redtwig dogwood, **elderberry**, and Rocky Mountain maple trees trailside. Riparian influence shows in moisture-lovers such as tall chimingbells, cow parsnip, and tall coneflower. Baneberry's glassy orbs shine as you come upon a jumble of fallen rock.

An incline above the narrowing creek is accompanied by occasional tall scarlet paintbrush and wild rose. Soon **harebell** will dangle its purple thimbles. On the uphill bank, western red columbine precedes a solid lithic wall fronted by thimbleberry and meadowrue.

High above the creek, the trail comes to ledges producing

WHITE CHECKERMALLOW
Sidalcea candida

Related to hollyhocks, cotton, and okra, white checkermallow is found in wet places in the montane and lower subalpine zones. Its Latin species name means "white," in reference to the racemes of delicate flowers. Tall and unbranched, with big, coarsely palmate leaves, this member of the mallow family exhibits the typical fused pillar of stamens with myriad colored anthers.

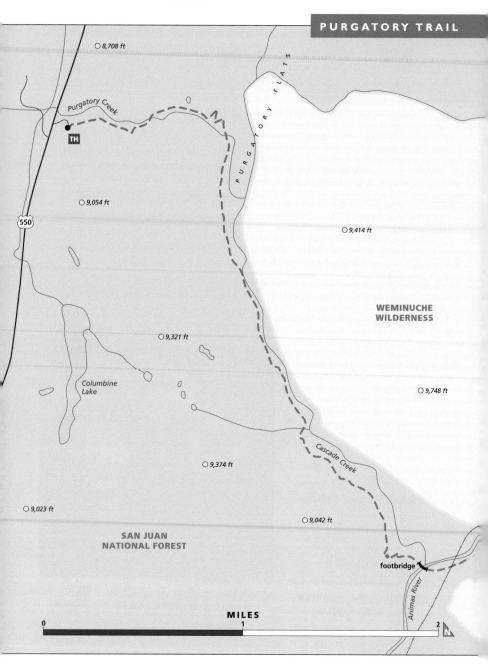

king's crown. A brief flattening of the route is followed by an ascent, passing the lax, golden tubes of **many-flowered puccoon**. Alternating shade and sun take Purgatory Trail higher, as Cascade Creek carves a path to join the Animas River below. Outcrops shaded by ponderosa pines serve as bases for **creeping**

grapeholly, whose neon yellow flower clusters bloom early and mature into sour, blue-black berries.

Stony tread curves gently down by **narrowleaf paintbrush** and aspens. It is at about this point in the descent that hikers may start to see **scarlet bugler penstemon**'s long, slender tubes. Fond of rocky soil, this tall, slim-foliaged member of the snapdragon family displays a reflexed lower lip.

The tread, shaded by Douglas firs and pines, softens underfoot as it passes bright pink **sticky geranium**. Begin switchbacking down the remaining elevation loss, coming to a welcome floodplain where **buckthorn** and scarlet bugler penstemon dot the floor. A rock cairn sends trekkers right, toward the Animas River footbridge.

The footbridge, guyed by hefty cables, is a handsome span with the pellucid green Animas rushing underneath. At this point, you can look upriver to a dark girder bridge that, at the right times, frames the black locomotive of the nostalgic Durango & Silverton Narrow Gauge Railroad. Typically, about three trains run per day in summer, with 11 a.m. often a good time to catch the train from the bridge. The West Needle Mountains rise in the background.

On the far side of the Animas footbridge are the Cascade Wayside Shelter tracks, accompanied by a series of interpretive signs and scattered scarlet bugler penstemon. A series of riverside picnic tables invite you to enjoy a snack in the roaring company of the beautiful Animas before tackling the ascent back to your vehicle.

Purgatory Flats offers a welcome respite in the descent to the Animas River and the Durango & Silverton Narrow Gauge Railroad tracks.

Wildflower
Hike 35 *Lake Hope Trail*

Dramatic peaks and glorious wildflowers
are yours along the Lake Hope Trail.

Trail Rating	moderate
Trail Length	6 miles out and back
Location	San Juan National Forest, south of Telluride
Elevation	10,800 to 11,880 feet
Bloom Season	late June to September
Peak Bloom	July (late July if snowpack is heavy)
Directions	From Telluride, take CO 145 south approximately 10 miles, turning left (east) 0.6 mile past milepost 61 onto FR 626 at Trout Lake. Continue 1.7 miles, bearing left onto FR 627 and following the rough road 2.5 miles to the trailhead. Parking is limited. High clearance is helpful.

Set in a talus and scree cradle at nearly 12,000 feet, Lake Hope may have floating ice on its surface as late as July. This popular hike offers a bit of everything, from stunning views to gorgeous wildflowers. The 2.5 miles of access road are rough and sometimes rocky, but taken slowly by a competent driver it's passable for most vehicles. High clearance is helpful, though.

The hike begins in forest, soon crosses a creek, then gradually wanders through conifer shade and sun. A serious ascent via a multitude of switchbacks, mostly shaded, takes you above treeline, rewarding you with a pristine high-alpine lake.

Parking is available if you're here early, but later arrivals can park roadside.

Heading east through thick forest, Lake Hope Trail begins uneventfully, offering the occasional **heartleaf arnica** in a sparse understory. Increasing sun brings **parrot's beak lousewort**, or **rams-horn**, each coiled blossom swirling above fine-toothed, uncut leaves. **Porters lovage**, with deeply cut, fernlike leaves, attracts multitudes of pollinating flies to its fine-flowered umbels. Adding color are **tall scarlet paintbrush**, **rayless senecio**, and hairy **rayless arnica**, the last two eschewing showy ray flowers. Watch here, too, for **Whipple** or **dusky penstemon**, said to exude a carrion odor to attract flies.

Warm hues are represented by **orange sneezeweed** and the dandelion-like heads of **orange agoseris**, as well as pink **wild geranium**, daintily inflorescenced **subalpine valerian**, and **pink-headed daisy**.

Soon you approach the first creek crossing, helped by stones. Paintbrush, **tall chimingbells**, and **subalpine larkspur** welcome you to Poverty Gulch, where a crenellated background ridge has the romantic name of Golden Horn. The water's edge presents **yellow monkeyflower**, some snowy **bittercress**, and brick red **king's crown**. In the vicinity, look for petite **golden draba** and brassy **subalpine arnica**, with its softly haired leaves. Tall **triangleleaf senecio** produces sparse gold flowers. Turning west, the trail meets golden **mountain parsley** and creamy **bracted lousewort**.

Forest shade filters enough sun to support the pink heads of **subalpine daisy**, looking more like an aster than a fleabane, while spruce shade suits lilac **delicate Jacob's ladder**. A rockfall is the place to find mats of **dotted saxifrage** showing miniscule blooms suspended on wiry stems. Soil pockets formed from tumbled stone support **Colorado blue columbine** as you encounter **elderberry**'s frothy heads. Crossing lichen-encrusted angular rock you'll see rockbrake fern. Here, too, the sour, kidney-shaped leaves of **alpine sorrel** send up red-bracted heads. Big-headed **old man of the mountains**, or **alpine sunflower**, also thrives among the rocks.

The next drainage requires a descending zigzag, passing white **Canada violet** growing in deep, rich soil. **Cow parsnip**, triangleleaf senecio, and wild geranium clothe another moist spot, accompanied by **wolf currant**. Look up-slope for the blues and whites of tall chimingbells, subalpine larkspur, Porters lovage, and **cowbane**. Delicate **brook saxifrage** requires an observant eye to spot its tiny blossoms.

Rocky and rising, the trail showcases the magnificent peaks before you. On a level sector, pause to enjoy the view. Across the glacier-carved, U-shaped valley to the northwest is distinctive Lizard Head, rising to over 13,000 feet high. Continue up the rocky tread to spruce krummholz—a word meaning "crooked wood" in German—sheltering lots of dotted saxifrage. A trio of cascading, segmented falls makes a gorgeous vista.

Moisture supports tall chimingbells, with bracted lousewort, subalpine larkspur, wild geranium, and **wild strawberry** nearby. **One-sided wintergreen** sees the forest taper off as you approach another rockfall, where you encounter **wild raspberry** and butter yellow **wallflower**.

PARROT'S BEAK LOUSEWORT

Pedicularis racemosa ssp. *alba*

Parrot's beak lousewort can be found in the cool shade of dry, coniferous forests in montane and subalpine life zones. Its curled white flowers are the reason for its other common name, rams-horn. Unlike other louseworts, rams-horn has entire leaves, finely and evenly toothed. The unbranched clumps sport dark, sometimes red-tinged foliage. Another common name for this plant is sickletop lousewort.

The trail soon crosses a rivulet—not difficult for booted feet—with a lovely waterfall competing for attention. Watch for **stinging nettles** if your legs are bare.

Rockslide soil pockets cultivate king's crown, which, in turn, leads to **slender-tipped clover**. Where the tread becomes easier, look for **western red columbine** still in bloom. Prior to crossing another tributary, gaze uphill for a patch of red paintbrush. The creek served as a chute for an avalanche that once cleared great swaths of the forest. The waterway's banks display **false hellebore**, creamy **globeflower**, and king's crown.

On the far side of the creek, take a moment to look across to the San Miguel Mountains, where Lizard Head stands in the company of Sunshine Mountain. A flat trail has a blue, gold, and white combination of tall chimingbells, orange sneezeweed, Porters lovage, larkspur, senecio, and fuzzy-leaved subalpine arnica. Anchoring the left side are the whites of brook saxifrage and cowbane. The right side features vivid pink, early-blooming **Parry primrose**, **pink willow-herb**, and some yellow monkeyflower.

Yet another trickle from the east supports paintbrush and **twistedstalk**, with its reflexed split bells dangling from kinked

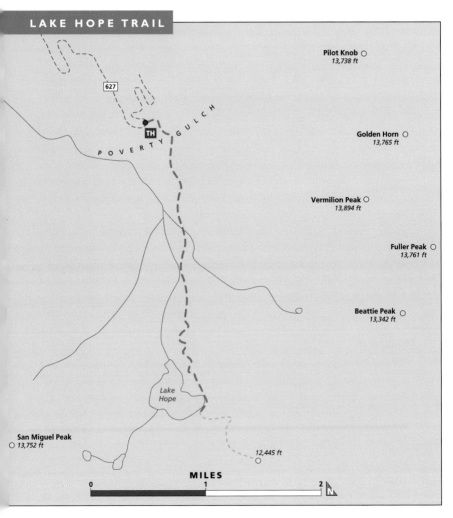

pedicels. Near rotting logs, look for **green mitrewort**, or **bishop's cap**. A less common cousin, **sleighbells**, or **one-sided white mitrewort**, grows here as well.

Forest shade brings about an even-tempered trail that crosses over a noisy creek by a plank bridge. Trail and rivulet share a bed, and, though shallow, the running waters make sturdy boots necessary. Delicate pink heads of subalpine valerian precede a pair of cascades where intensely pink Parry primrose grows.

The trail bends left to expose green mitrewort before ascending over roots and rocks. Parallel the closer cascade through forest until the route crosses the rushing water by rocks or a log upstream. Pushing close to a small gorge, hikers find **delicate** or **subalpine Jacob's ladder**, as well as bittercress, tall chimingbells, and twistedstalk.

A series of switchbacks assists you as the Lake Hope Trail rapidly gains elevation. Watch in a sheltered turn for the pearl buds and smooth, emerald basal leaves of **fringed parnassia**. As you cross a rockfall, keep an eye out for the delicate, nearly translucent **alplily**, as well as **alpine avens**. The north-facing bank retains snow long enough to keep **marsh marigold** and globeflower dormant longer. Jade green Trout Lake shimmers far below, while nearby both **subalpine** and **caltha-leaved buttercup** shine. Switchbacks take you between rockfalls, highlighting hot pink Parry primrose. Not showy at all, but a member of the rose family nonetheless, **sibbaldia** has minutely petaled, chartreuse flowers and tri-toothed leaves; its most colorful time arrives in fall, when the cloverlike leaves turn salmon colored.

Early bloomer **wild candytuft**, with its white, sweet-scented, cruciform flowers, decorates the rocky track. At a mossy corner, look for **Canada violet**, lilac delicate Jacob's ladder, and **white geranium**.

Even if the switchbacks seem endless, avoid the temptation to cut across them. Unsightly shortcuts leave the area vulnerable to erosion. Momentarily leveling, the route encounters **snowball saxifrage**'s lollipop-like white heads and, around the corner, sibbaldia, king's crown, and **alpine** or **Baker's parsley**.

A heavy snowpack may leave lingering snowbanks on this north-facing slope, making hikers glad of sturdy footgear. An open spot brings a view of a waterfall, as well as vibrant Parry primrose, white marsh marigold, and creamy globeflower.

Where the track nearly touches Lake Fork, Lake Hope's outlet creek, the richly saturated petals of Parry primrose command attention. Still ascending, the trail passes through areas of recent snowmelt, entering acres of marsh marigold, buttercup, and alpine avens. An easier grade allows you the opportunity to examine high-country flora such as alpine parsley. Its glistening green leaves look like those of a miniature holly.

Views expand upon approaching treeline. Alpine parsley's small umbels are ringed by flimsy green bracts, while bright **rosy paintbrush** displays softly haired, broad bracts of outrageous hues. Up on the ridges, patches of spruce krummholz, flattened by prevailing winds, survive in their innovative fashion.

The trail levels and a patch of trailside **little pink elephants** signals Lake Hope just ahead. Winter resists summer here, and the green, almost teal, waters of the lake might still show some late-melting ice. Little pink elephants and orange sneezeweed take the trail northeast above the lake to meet **wild onion**, tall chimingbells, king's crown, subalpine daisy, and golden arnica.

Upslope is a perfect outcrop from which to enjoy Lake Hope and the silver stream falling into it. In the rock crevices, look for vivid pink **moss campion**, both **blueleaf** and **snow cinquefoil**, **alpine sandwort**, **bistort**, and minuscule **yellow draba**. When you're ready, retrace your steps to the trailhead.

Lizard Head/ Wilson Meadows Trail

*Wildflower
Hike 36*

*The towering crest
of Lizard Head
from the Wilson
Meadows Trail*

Resembling the spiny head of an ancient reptile, Lizard Head is one of Colorado's most distinctive peaks. But though drivers can spot its profile from CO 145 heading south from Telluride, it is best appreciated on foot. The Lizard Head Trail promises wonderful views of the mountain, as it begins in stands of aspens with a rich understory, then rises via a series of switchbacks to a saddle. A right-bearing path takes you toward Wilson Meadows where, just before the trail drops somewhat precipitously over bare ridges, you are rewarded with a stunning view of the Lizard across the valley. Wildflowers are many and varied from start to finish, and parking is generous at the trailhead.

moderate	*Trail Rating*
5 miles out and back	*Trail Length*
Uncompahgre National Forest/Lizard Head Wilderness, south of Telluride	*Location*
10,280 to 11,000 feet	*Elevation*
late June to August	*Bloom Season*
late June to July	*Peak Bloom*
From Telluride, head south on CO 145 approximately 12 miles to Lizard Head Pass, turning right (west) on the Lizard Head Trailhead spur to the parking lot.	*Directions*

Dramatic summits dominate the view from the trailhead, but be sure to notice **false hellebore**, bright **beauty cinquefoil**, and graceful **Colorado blue columbine** in the vicinity. **Leafy Jacob's ladder**, with its namesake foliage structure, presents winsome, purple, flared, funnelform corollas, each extruding gold stamens. Fat and green by midsummer, **Ritter** or **yellow kittentails** sprouts plump, pale yellow tubes during peak bloom in early summer. Native **Coulter daisy** displays fine white rays, while **orange sneezeweed** offers a rather lax arrangement of rays.

Soon, you encounter a rhubarb relation, **subalpine dock**, with its dark, substantial leaves and showy, reddish-rose panicles of winged achenes, as the individual seeds are called. Also preferring damp ground are trail-flanking **tall chimingbells** and **Porters lovage**, along with marine blue **subalpine larkspur**. **Green gentian** stands tall, pale green in foliage and flower.

Continuing on brings clumps of **wild iris** and **wild blue flax** as well. Down to the right, where willows populate moist soil, more thick subalpine dock and tall chimingbells join the lush subalpine flora. Trying hard not to be noticed is **waterleaf**; trying hard to be noticed is **cow parsnip**; somewhere in between falls **white geranium**. On the hillside, compare the clear yellow-gold of **aspen sunflower** and the warm gold of orange sneezeweed.

Traveling through waist-high wildflowers is a great way to begin Lizard Head Trail. A little trickle sneaks under the route, supporting **yellow monkeyflower**, **pink willowherb**, and **cowbane**. Complementary neighbors **shrubby cinquefoil** and Colorado blue columbine accompany the trail to a corner where the Colorado state flower is abundant, forming a graceful foreground for the peaks to the south. Along the way grows **Indian warriors**, each creamy blossom lined with red. **White peavine** sports reddish-purple nectar guidelines that age to a rusty-tan color.

Glance up to the left, a rocky, verdant area presents pretty, pink, bushlike **sweetvetch**, a pea or legume family member. Nearby, aspen sunflower faces east.

Upon a stony hillside, **cliff** or **red globe anemone** opens cerise tepals and **drop-pod locoweed** offers its purplish, pea-type flowers. Waving grasses line your way across the hillside on a north heading, in the company of **aspen daisy** and **pink-headed daisy**. Endemic Ritter kittentails opens small, waxen yellow tubes in quantity around a plump green stalk lined with small clasping leaves; the lower leaves are spinachlike. **American vetch** spreads its tendrils through the grasses.

At a sign indicating a path to the picnic area, Lizard Head Trail heads straight, lined by Coulter daisy and beauty cinquefoil. On the upside slope, toxic false hellebore is interspersed with ultramarine subalpine larkspur, leafy Jacob's ladder, and wild blue flax. Sparsely flowered **rockcress**, a slim mustard, stands straight near a sign prohibiting bicycles on the Lizard Head Trail.

Hiking into a willow-filled ravine, the trail passes cousins cowbane and Porters lovage. Preparing prodigious buds, **northern bedstraw** clusters will send up frothy, scented inflorescences. Rather rangy **tansy mustard** also pops up occasionally.

Conifers shelter white geranium, pink **wild geranium**, and **golden draba**, a mustard clan member. **Triangleleaf** or **arrowleaf senecio** towers over **homely buttercup**, pink willowherb, and dainty pink **subalpine valerian**. In the vicinity, look for **mountain death camas** and **orange agoseris**' burnt copper dandelion heads.

Mossy stones guide a rivulet lined with snowy **bittercress**. At left is **green bog orchid**, while a drier zone brings the flares of **tall scarlet paintbrush** and **Whipple** or **dusky penstemon**.

Shaded, the trail descends to a little rockfall and its attendant creek. **Wolf currant**, cowbane, and bittercress thrive in the vicinity. The far side presents triangleleaf senecio and tall chimingbells in the shade of large quaking aspens. **Sawtooth** or **sawleaf senecio** accompanies wild geranium along the easygoing route.

LEAFY JACOB'S LADDER
Polemonium foliosissimum

Paired leaflets make up the sticky pinnate leaves of leafy Jacob's ladder, which emit a skunky odor when rubbed or crushed. Pretty, funnelform lavender flowers form a flat inflorescence atop sturdy, hairy-foliaged clumps. Some people have attributed the genus name to the Athenian philosopher Polemon; however, it is also said to come from *polemos*, the Greek word for "war." The Latin species name simply means "leafy." It is found in montane and subalpine meadows and streams.

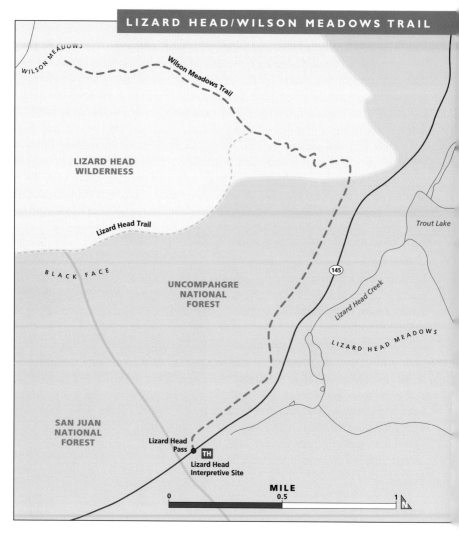

LIZARD HEAD/WILSON MEADOWS TRAIL

WILSON MEADOWS

Wilson Meadows Trail

LIZARD HEAD
WILDERNESS

Lizard Head Trail

Trout Lake

BLACK FACE

UNCOMPAHGRE
NATIONAL
FOREST

145

Lizard Head Creek

LIZARD HEAD MEADOWS

SAN JUAN
NATIONAL
FOREST

Lizard Head
Pass TH

Lizard Head
Interpretive Site

MILE
0   0.5   1

Be on the alert for **rattlesnake plantain orchid** on the left. Each earth-hugging rosette leaf is centered by a whitish midrib; some will send up an erect stalk of miniature, greenish orchid flowers. With a dip, expect **black-tipped senecio**, each clump packed with big, rubbery-looking, mint green leaves. A stony area supports **goldeneye** on the left and **meadowrue** on the right.

The trail ascends again, with forest shade suiting big-headed cow parsnip and Porters lovage, both parsley family members. These two umbelled white flowers are accented by subalpine larkspur's deep purple-blue blossoms and **tall western larkspur**'s stately blue spires.

Where a small stream runs in an avalanche path, look upstream for yellow monkeyflower, with its distinctive, red-spotted lower lip. Also in keeping with the yellow theme are aspen sunflower and orange sneezeweed.

Under conifer shade, triangleleaf senecio and wolf currant line a rockier tread. Open spots allow glimpses of Trout Lake in the distance. Early-season hikers may encounter **spotted coralroot orchid**, its reddish form completely devoid of chlorophyll.

A great jumble of rock flows down the slope where **elderberry** bushes find a roothold. Before a little log-lined seep, **twinberry honeysuckle** shrubs have paired tubes that later become inedible black berries. Whipple penstemon's maroon tubes accent tall chimingbells' cool, icy blue. **Baneberry** displays its red or white glassy orbs, both toxic.

Lavish larkspur is the highlight on the next segment of trail; it is a hellebore, but an especially pretty one. Look also for larkspur's even more poisonous cousin, **monkshood**. While larkspur sepals fuse into a spur, those of monkshood arc into a hood; both keep their scrunched-up petals under purple cover.

An uptick takes hikers to a rockfall where the trail then dips to cross lower down. Negotiate the stony jumble to encounter interesting rockbrake fern. On the far side, more Colorado blue columbine grows near pink **wild rose**.

A sign indicates the Lizard Head Wilderness and Uncompahgre National Forest. Little flowers such as **Canada violet** and golden draba lead up to an avalanche path. Ascending, the route switchbacks over stony tread to find tall scarlet paintbrush.

Trout Lake glistens below as you prepare to mount another switchback, where **fireweed** will later add its vivid spires. At the top of the avalanche chute crossed earlier, aspen daisy prepares for light purple bloom. **Snowberry** bushes lean over **golden aster** as the rocky ascent reaches a small rockfall, where Whipple penstemon extends purple tubes in view of yet more columbine. Forest shelters **heartleaf arnica**, while the grade eases in time to watch for ground-hugging rosettes of rattlesnake plantain orchid. The trail recrosses the avalanche path, offering tremendous views, as well as fireweed, perfumed wild rose, and **scorpionweed**.

Along the steady incline, tall chimingbells accompanies hikers into spruce shade, the favored habitat of **delicate Jacob's ladder**. The next grassy opening sports a bit of early-blooming, scented **wallflower** in yellow, a color shared by golden draba, cinquefoil, **mountain parsley**, and orange sneezeweed. Wands of **alumroot** lift greenish-yellow inflorescences.

The avalanche path seems to own the rising trail as it comes up to **New Mexico senecio**, **sandwort**, black-tipped senecio, and **many-rayed goldenrod**. Fragrant forest gives the trail a rocky character as **prickly mountain currant** protrudes from Rocky Mountain common juniper bushes.

At the top of the chute, false hellebore signals an easier trail grade until, at last, the route levels in a nice gold, red, and white garden. Pink **wild onion** brings you up to a trail division where this narrative heads right, toward Wilson Meadows, in the company of lots of Ritter kittentails, budding mountain death camas, white **mountain candytuft**, and **white peavine**.

On the left, a small murky pond provides damp habitat for **parrot's beak lousewort**, chartreuse **rayless senecio**, and **twistedstalk**. Prepare to cross the neck of a verdant meadow where early-blooming **globeflower** grows near **marsh marigold**. Both **rosy paintbrush** and **Parry primrose** show vibrant pinks. The trail bends down to a log-channeled crossing after meeting **bracted lousewort**'s creamy beaks. Upstream, homely buttercup blooms alongside slim-stemmed **brook saxifrage**.

Check for elk prints in the mud as you watch for **little pink elephants** accompanied by **queen's crown**, green bog orchid, and pearly **fringed parnassia**. Where the forest ends, views of stunning mountain ridges begin. Pause at a sign for Wilson Meadows, a route that heads steeply down before you. For this hike description, the sign is the turnaround point.

And what a point! Lizard Head rises across the way like some antediluvian creature from Jurassic time. Find a spot to gaze upon the giant lizard's lithic head and enjoy its unique formation among other impressive peaks.

Lush meadows and forest understory promise a scenic San Juans hike.

Bilk Creek Upper Falls

Wildflower Hike 37

Solitude, pristine waterfalls, and hillsides of wildflowers grace the Bilk Creek hike.

easy to moderate	**Trail Rating**
7 miles out and back	**Trail Length**
Uncompahgre National Forest/Lizard Head Wilderness, south of Telluride	**Location**
9,800 to 10,900 feet	**Elevation**
June to September	**Bloom Season**
July (later if snowpack is heavy)	**Peak Bloom**
From Telluride, take CO 145 west to milepost 74. Turn left (south) onto Ilium Rd. Go 2.1 miles to the junction with CR 63 and bear right onto Sunshine Mesa Rd./FR 623, following it to its end.	**Directions**

Not far from Telluride, the upper falls of Bilk Creek offer stunning views and an abundance of wildflowers, with oversized columbine lining the way to the best vistas. The first 2 miles are easy, including the hewn log spanning Bilk Creek, though the first mile is rather shy of dramatic blooms. But the next 1.5-mile ascent, much of it via switchbacks, makes up for the initial lack of color with a dazzling array of vivid flowers. Plunging waterfalls are a bonus. Trailhead parking is limited, but weekdays see few hikers.

A Forest Service sign, surrounded by **monkshood, wild geranium**, and **tall chimingbells**, orients you to the hike, stating that Bilk Creek and Lizard Head Trail are 2 miles ahead. Shaded by aspens and conifers, the trail curves by **subalpine larkspur**, cousin to monkshood, and comes out on an old roadbed that travels toward Bilk Creek and the Morningstar Mine.

In the dark forest, white flowers, such as **cow parsnip** and **Coulter daisy**, shine. Golds appear in the form of **heartleaf arnica** and later-blooming, lanky **sawtooth** or **sawleaf senecio**. **Canada violet** likes shade and deep, rich soil; subalpine larkspur enjoys the same, but with added moisture. As the roadway gradually ascends, check out the glassy berries forming on **baneberry**, each becoming either bright red or white as it matures.

A few **Indian warriors** rise in the forest, each sturdy stalk lined with red-streaked, pale beaks. Red arrives in the occasional **paintbrush**. Delicate **northern bedstraw** gathers enough light for a froth of fragrant white flowers.

Wolf currant shrubs overhang the cutbanks, while **Nuttalls buttercup**, diminutive, pale blue **speedwell**, and **twistedstalk** appear at a damp spot. On the drier right, unruly masses of **American vetch** produce prodigious ladder leaves but few magenta flowers.

Thick planks keep your boots dry where **mountain death camas** lifts light green stars in the scant company of snowy **bittercress, cowbane, brook saxifrage**, subalpine larkspur, and **triangleleaf senecio**. The mud here is a fine place to look for elk prints.

A trail junction sends Wilson Mesa Trail right and down, while this hike continues on the roadbed straight ahead toward the Lizard Head Trail. Contouring gently, the route penetrates the forest's sparse understory, where, if you are fortunate, you may hear a bugling elk or witness the graceful speed of a pine marten. Some plants, such as **thimbleberry, one-sided wintergreen**, and aptly named **parrot's beak lousewort**, or **rams-horn**, are at home in forest shade. Early-season hikers should note **western red columbine** in the shade as well.

The sound of rushing water accompanies more sunlight and an embankment of orangy **tall scarlet paintbrush** and magenta **fireweed**. The trail tread becomes rockier as **Whipple** or **dusky penstemon** hangs its wine-colored tubes and **black-tipped senecio** lifts pale, rubbery leaves.

In the distance, you can glimpse a waterfall coursing down from a lofty shoulder of Wilson Peak, a fourteener. Open sky gives way to a brief stint of shade. A steep slope is populated by hefty **green gentian**, flares of tall scarlet paintbrush, **aspen sunflower**, and white-umbelled **Porters lovage**.

The trail narrows, passing an avalanche chute harboring Indian warriors and western red columbine. Broken rock, as thinly layered as a stack of paper and fractured from flaky cliffs above, is home to the beautiful **Colorado blue columbine**. It also sports a specimen or two of **purple fringe**, each stalk solidly filled with purple trumpets extruding bright stamens. Moisture under the rock is sufficient to support bittercress.

As you traverse pale gray and rust stones, note some examples of Colorado blue columbine that are nearly white. Coming into shade brings more larkspur and cow parsnip, lilac **delicate Jacob's ladder**, and western red columbine. Shy in conifer shade and somewhat uncommon is **sleighbells**, or **one-sided white mitrewort**, its minuscule snowflakes lining one side. A glen of tall chimingbells comes next.

Small mats of cliff-hanging **dotted saxifrage** frame a view of lively Bilk Creek. **Orange agoseris**, also called **tall burnt orange false dandelion**, joins **orange sneezeweed**, while gold tones are found in **shrubby cinquefoil** and **goldenrod**. **Wild onion** proffers soft pink.

Before entering willows on a cobbled, watery tread, look in view of a graceful waterfall for **yellow monkeyflower**, which loves wet places. The willows also harbor subalpine larkspur and bittercress, a peppery watercress relation. Rocky underfoot, the route meets a small cascade on the left where yellow monkeyflower, tall chimingbells, and bittercress flourish. Immediately after is a larger falls, whose mossy rocks have dainty-flowered bittercress curving over them.

Another avalanche path clears the way for lavender-pink **subalpine daisy** and diminutive blossoms of **pink willowherb**. Soon, the trail introduces plush swabs of

SELF-HEAL
Prunella vulgaris

Also known as prunella or heal-all, this short, colonizing member of the mint family displays the clan's square stems. Terminal spikes of two-tone, purple, hooded flowers, the lower lip of which is three-lobed and curls in a pout, produce abundant bracts. Self-heal lives up to its medicinal name and is used as a tea for sore throats, mouth sores, fever, and upset stomach. Crushed, the plant served as a wound poultice and antibiotic in the treatment of insect bites. The Latin species name, *vulgaris*, means "common."

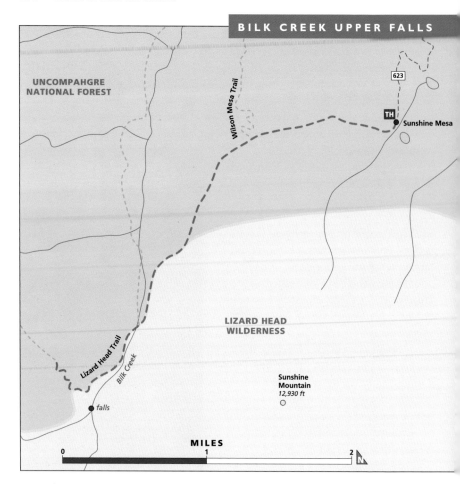

BILK CREEK UPPER FALLS

UNCOMPAHGRE
NATIONAL FOREST

Wilson Mesa Trail

623

TH
Sunshine Mesa

LIZARD HEAD
WILDERNESS

Lizard Head Trail

Bilk Creek

Sunshine
Mountain
12,930 ft

falls

MILES
0   1   2

rosy paintbrush, promiscuous as it is pretty. A late bloomer, **Parry goldenweed** produces small, tidy flowers on clean green foliage, while orange sneezeweed tosses unkempt heads of droopy rays on top of rangy, pale green foliage. Bilk Creek is just below the trail and is crossed in the company of many familiar flowers. Spanned by hewn logs, Bilk Creek signals the junction with Lizard Head Trail on the far side. Nearby stand the remains of Morningstar Mine.

At the Bilk Creek crossing, you have hiked 2 miles. From here, head to a opening in the willows anchored by a sign for Lizard Head Trail No. 505. In the emerald moss, **green bog orchid**, **little pink elephants**, and yellow monkey-flower thrive—as do pesky mosquitos, so don't linger too long.

To continue to Bilk Creek Falls, turn left (south), following the Lizard Head Trail as it passes between an old semi-truck trailer and a dilapidated metal building. The base of the Lizard Head Trail sign sports cheery **subalpine arnica**, while Bilk Creek charges down on your left. Subalpine daisy grows near the Lizard Head Wilderness/Uncompahgre National Forest sign.

A glimpse of water through the spruces tells you Bilk Creek's lower falls is not far.

An avalanche chute narrows and steepens the route considerably as you pass Colorado blue columbine on a sunny south aspect. Rockbrake fern and butter yellow **wallflower** announce a partial view of Bilk Creek's upper falls, as black-tipped senecio, **twinberry honeysuckle**, and **wild raspberry** thrive nearby.

Shrubby cinquefoil flanks the trail, while tiny white stars of **sandwort** keep a low profile. Willows close in, then give way to an outcrop cliff displaying clumps of rose-pink **slender-tipped clover** up on its ledges. Lower on the angular outcrop, tall scarlet paintbrush grows a yard high.

Easier now, the route enjoys the color of Colorado blue columbine, aspen sunflower, shrubby cinquefoil, and the white heads of **American bistort**. Before long, the trail switchbacks higher, making the falls' profile more visible. The wildflowers are almost overwhelming, with the smaller ones such as white **stitchwort** and two-toned purple **self-heal**, or **prunella**, demanding a keen eye.

An old log points the way up to an avalanche of wildflowers, including Colorado blue columbine, aspen sunflower, little pink elephants, **king's crown**, rosy paintbrush, and pearl-budded **fringed parnassia**, a mass of polished, cupped basal leaves lifting bare stems that end in formal white flowers.

Level now, the path approaches a promontory that gives you a look into the whitewater melee of Bilk Creek. You may discover both western red and Colorado blue columbine growing here above the surging water.

Switching back on itself, the trail again briefly overlooks the upper falls, then curves again to offer more lush and abundant flowers. The next part heads through conifer shade, then ascends again, passing now-familiar wildflowers, as well as **edible valerian** and **pearly everlasting**'s white strawflower heads.

Switchbacks assist the ascent, bringing hikers close to rosy paintbrush. Moving between sun and shade, the trail soon brings you near Bilk Creek's upper falls, which plunge as gracefully as a Yosemite waterfall. Near a waterbar, pearly everlasting displays its papery white bracts.

Welcome shade brings not only a gentler grade but soft duff underfoot. However, another uptick lies ahead. The next switchback opens to view a showy flood of blue, white, and gold upslope. Grand vistas of the rugged San Juans accompany each switchback.

A little seep trickles down the trail from finely layered rock and supports a charming small garden featuring a display of fringed parnassia. The next rocky rivulet features brook saxifrage, pink willowherb, yellow monkeyflower, and green bog orchid. Yet another waterway, dominated by white, is accented by tall chimingbells' blue.

This point, just before a sharp incline by a gorge, makes a good place to turn around and retrace your steps. The trail goes on to a slanted bowl, but is less floristic and obstructed by fallen trees. The best of this marvelous wildflower viewing has been yours.

Bear Creek Falls

Cascading gracefully, Bear Creek Falls nurtures Colorado blue columbine.

Trail Rating	easy
Trail Length	4.5 miles out and back
Location	Uncompahgre National Forest, at Telluride
Elevation	8,760 to 9,800 feet
Bloom Season	June to September
Peak Bloom	late June to late July
Directions	In Telluride, walk south on Pine St. and cross the bridge over the San Miguel River to access the trailhead. **Note:** Free parking lots are located at the west end of town, with a courtesy shuttle to the trailhead, or you can use the day-use parking on the east side, not far from the trailhead.

For a hike that literally begins in town, Telluride's Wasatch Trail to Bear Creek Falls boasts a very worthy goal: An impressive waterfall sliding down a tall rockface. The canyon you hike through was once a Ute hunting area, as well as the tribe's chosen place for sacred ceremonies. In the late 19th century, miners made use of the earlier trail to construct a road up the canyon. Today, it is closed to motorized traffic but retains its wide, sociable character.

The 2.2-mile trail ascends at a fairly steady pace, with a few level spots to let you rest. Much of the way is shaded, especially early and late in the day. But the waterfall is out in the open, giving hikers a marvelous frontal view from below, or, with an uphill effort, a cool, close encounter by the pool at the base. While montane wildflower species accompany the entirety of the walk, the last segment of trail is most floristic.

Parking in Telluride can be a bit challenging on weekends, especially during events: See the note in the directions above.

Wasatch Trail begins where Pine Street ends, marked by a handsome carved wood sign about the origins of the Bear Creek Preserve. Immediately behind a gate, the wide roadway starts up, shaded by aspens, alders, and narrowleaf cottonwoods. Here, **Indian warriors** rises in the understory, its helmeted blossoms faintly streaked with red. Also common are the strapping basal leaves and sturdy bloomstalk of tropical-looking **green gentian**, or **monument plant**, a favorite of elk. **Redtwig dogwood** forms its sparse fruits, while **twinberry honeysuckle** displays paired black fruits shown off by a parasol of red bracts.

A trickle runs over the roadway, supporting white, wide-headed **cow parsnip** downhill. Bears love

PINK-HEADED DAISY
Erigeron elatior

Also known by the common name beautiful daisy, pink-headed daisy displays angora-soft hairs that envelope the nodding buds. Though the phyllary hairs appear pink, the hue is in fact due to red crosswalls. A summer bloomer, this tall fleabane likes aspen and spruce-fir forest but at high elevations may be found in the open. Some Native American tribes powdered fleabanes to dust on wounds. The species name, *elatior*, means "tall."

its salty stalks, inspiring a lesser known common name, **bear cabbage**. Slender monkshood rises tall to present its royal purple, cowled flowers. And **white geranium**, which will faithfully follow most of the trail, opens five pale petals lined in deep red.

As the route continues on a gradual incline, **baneberry** is visible, its frothy whitish inflorescences morphing into shiny green berries that will eventually ripen into red or white. Yellow umbels of **mountain parsley** brighten the scene, as does **tall scarlet paintbrush**.

Headed east before it turns south, the route comes across magenta spires of **fireweed**, coloring a whole slope leading down to a pond on the left, next to the San Miguel River. The airy heads of snowy **northern bedstraw**, sweet scented and reluctant to mat, made it useful for filling pioneer mattresses.

Overhead, **mountain ash** readies its berry clusters for an orange-red finish, as fragrant **wild rose** basks nearby. **Elderberry** provides food for birds, while **serviceberry** fruit, bluish-black when ripe, is edible but best left for wildlife. Slightly rougher, the wide track passes **cinquefoil**, tall scarlet paintbrush, and pink **wild geranium**, needing less moisture than its white cousin. **Wolf currant**'s matte leaves, similar to grape leaves, line the way.

Medicinal **yarrow** grows alongside **false Solomon's seal**, the latter's slightly zigzagged stems lined with substantial, shining leaves. Clambering over its neighbors via tendrils is **American vetch**, which opens only a few purple, pea-type flowers. Equally miserly with flowers is **western golden ragwort**.

Ascending easily, the trail finds Rocky Mountain maple hanging over more baneberry and **meadowrue**. Early-season hikers should look for the bright lanterns of **western red columbine** along the shaded north bank.

A trickle on the right near a glass sign case harbors monkshood, attractive but totally toxic, as are most members of the hellebore family. **Cowbane** and tall **triangleleaf senecio** like damp environs as well. Though the way is wide, **stinging nettles** grow here and are prolific on the last segment before the falls.

The route turns south and Bear Creek tumbles down a small gorge of its own making. Another rivulet from the right, diverted through a culvert, announces upcoming **sawtooth** or **sawleaf senecio**, blooming a bit later than most of its brethren. Under aspen and alder shade, **yellow avens**' brassy petals soon give way to softly burred seedheads.

Leveling, the trail approaches leafy colonies of **heartleaf arnica** on a slope providing glimpses of Bear Creek as well as pink wild rose. Downslope among aspens, check out **Coulter daisy** and **orange sneezeweed**.

The tread increases in rockiness as well as incline. An angular tabletop rock on the right supports a bit of **one-sided wintergreen** on its mossy right flank. Paintbrush flares vie with soft buds of **pink-headed daisy**. Toward the creek, look at conifer bases for **twinflower**, its tiny, paired, blushed bells dangling on a wiry stem over a mat of small, shining, round leaves. Green, strappy leaves clothe **Parry goldenweed**, a late bloomer.

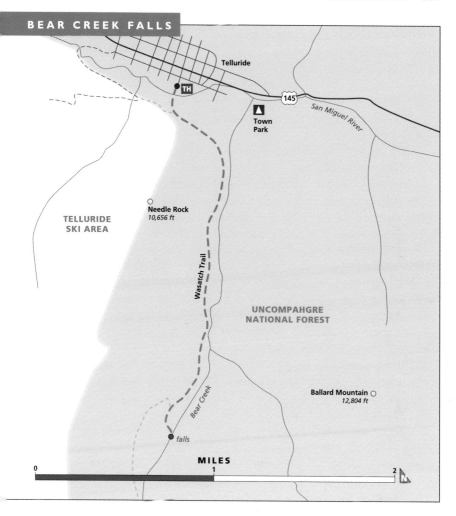

Under aspens, light purple **harebell** blooms, and will do so until frost. **Wild raspberry** prepares you for a rocky and rising track as you travel in the company of **aspen sunflower**. Spruce shade on the left produces twinberry honeysuckle and more wild rose. Then the route eases briefly, and Coulter daisy appears, as white as the bark of the aspens it blooms under. White geranium flanks the roadway near **Whipple penstemon**'s purple tubes.

A marvelous view of spiky peaks straight ahead brings on **rayless arnica** on the right. Easing, the trail opens to sunny skies, nurturing more aspen sunflower, each facing east due to a chemical in their stems that constricts the heads to greet the rising sun. At this point, **snowberry** bushes still present narrow pink tubes.

A plethora of cowbane and other damp lovers, including **brook saxifrage** and **yellow monkeyflower**, inhabit a road-crossing trickle. Under willows on the right, look carefully for upright stalks dangling rosy parasols above round-leaved rosettes; you have found **pink pyrola**, sometimes called **swamp wintergreen** for its predilection for boggy places.

Red dirt underfoot brings hikers in the vicinity of an explosion of green gentian, which spends years gathering energy to send up the impressive flower-stalk, its first and only. Sawtooth senecio, a tall late bloomer, signals the next rise. Woolly and ferny, the gray-green foliage of yarrow keeps company with Whipple penstemon.

Ascending again, Wasatch Trail passes mountain parsley and furry pink-headed daisy. When the route flattens some, look for sparsely foliaged western golden ragwort and, to the east, a waterfall cascading in the distance. A grassy meadow features lots of light purple **leafy Jacob's ladder** flanking a social spur, which then leads to a formation of reddish rock edging crystalline Bear Creek. Whipple penstemon and **beauty cinquefoil** like the environs as well. Resume the ascending main trail, which sports yellow avens, cowbane, and, under a tangled willow clump, western red columbine. A nearby trickle on the right has **green bog orchid**, tiny **pink willowherb**, and a few yellow monkeyflowers.

Leveling once again, the trail comes to lichen-encrusted rocks bordered by **orange agoseris** and **tasselflower**. You might notice a deceptive spur on the left. Instead, bear right and up. Bear Creek Falls is just ahead. Bear Creek's sheer-walled canyon is open to the sky, meaning flowers increase.

A sign points the Wasatch Trail up to the right as the roadway for this hike continues straight ahead, encountering the cute but invasive import **butter and eggs**. Native **scorpionweed** takes its descriptive name from the coiled inflorescences.

Bear Creek Falls is soon before you, plunging some 50 feet over a ledge of dark rock. This may be far enough for some hikers; those who wish to get closer may continue right up to the base. At this point, the roadway narrows to a trail headed right to reach the base of Bear Creek Falls.

Climbing up to a dry watercourse highlights many now-familiar flowers, including western golden ragwort, yellow monkeyflower, and **milky willowherb**. This last bit of trail is tight and adventurous for those who venture to the rock-strewn bottom of Bear Creek Falls. The full impact of the plunging water is appreciated here. Across the churning creek is a mass of **tall chimingbells** mixed with **Colorado blue columbine** and, in the background, evidence of man's efforts to wrest valuable minerals from the earth.

On the falls' dripping ledges, **fringed parnassia** grows on the right, with its pearl buds and fringed white flowers. Up on the right, on Cutler Formation rock, rich pink **broadleaf** or **alpine fireweed** flourishes. This low, almost bushy cousin of common fireweed is partial to wet places, earning it its other name, **riverbeauty**.

Spend a moment and appreciate the beauty of Bear Creek Falls before returning the way you came.

Lower Blue Lake

*Wildflower
Hike 39*

*A turquoise lake and a rainbow of wildflower
color make lower Blue Lake a remarkable hike.*

moderate to difficult	*Trail Rating*
6.6 miles out and back	*Trail Length*
Uncompahgre National Forest/Mount Sneffels Wilderness, north of Telluride	*Location*
9,400 to 11,000 feet	*Elevation*
late June to August	*Bloom Season*
late July	*Peak Bloom*
From Ridgway, head 4.8 miles west on CO 62 and turn left (south) on Dallas Creek Rd., also signed as CR 7. At 2.1 miles, bear right on FR 851, continuing to the end of the road, for a total of 9.1 miles from highway to trailhead.	*Directions*

The San Juan Mountains are chock-full of gorgeous wildflower hikes, but perhaps none are so popular and, at peak bloom, so lovely as lower Blue Lake. In a good snow year, the peak is likely to occur in the last half of July, with the third week of the month being prime. A rugged surround of mountains shelters the aquamarine lake, which serves as a just reward for the hike's first half, an uphill forest climb. Throughout the second, easier half, wildflowers reign, culminating in gorgeous lower Blue Lake itself.

Arrive at Blue Lakes Trailhead early for a decent parking spot.

Begin your hike behind a yellow metal gate with a sign announcing the trailhead. In the distance are the scenic peaks of the Mount Sneffels Wilderness, which form the backdrop of this 6.6-mile round-trip excursion.

A trickle flowing from the right helps support white **cow parsnip**, golden **triangleleaf senecio**, **yellow avens**, **cowbane**, and, against the moist bank, **yellow monkeyflower**. **American vetch**'s magenta-pink, pea-type flowers grow near **white checkermallow**, a relation to hollyhock and cotton. Small, white-flowered plants include scented **northern bedstraw** and ferny **yarrow**.

A wilderness information sign sends the Blue Lakes Trail right and the Blaine Basin Trail left. Bear right and enjoy the fantastic view of 14,150-foot Mount Sneffels. Traveling parallel to the East Fork of Dallas Creek, the trail passes more white checkermallow. **Aspen daisy** highlights a single track leading to a small falls sounding off to the left.

On an upward trend, the route passes pink **wild geranium**, **tall scarlet paintbrush**, and stately **larkspur**. **Sawtooth** or **sawleaf senecio** starts the trail off on an undulating course.

A trickle on the right presents cowbane, **twisted-stalk**, and **brook saxifrage**. A few yellow monkeyflowers point out nodding **pink willowherb**. **Parry goldenweed** helps finish off the yellow season, and **arnica**

RATTLESNAKE PLANTAIN ORCHID
Goodyera oblongifolia

When this deep-shade forest orchid blooms, it does so in a loose spiral of hairy, greenish-white flowers. The erect stalk rises over a rosette of mottled leaves with white midribs in a pattern thought to resemble a snake's rattles. This North American native may colonize via rhizomes. Its evergreen leaves once served as poultices for cuts and sores. John Goodyer, a 17th-century British botanist, is honored by the genus name.

and **fireweed** share trailside billing. Early-season hikers encounter **western red columbine** here.

Nothing like a little moisture to encourage **green bog orchid** and **fringed parnassia**, sometimes mistaken for a white buttercup. Keep an eye out along a dry watercourse for satiny **little rose gentian**, a later-summer bloomer.

The upside slope suits **silverleaf scorpionweed** just fine, as it does white, fine-rayed **Coulter daisy**. Pass over a couple of culverted rivulets where **tall chimingbells** dangles pink buds that morph into blue bells.

Aiming away from Dallas Creek, the trail ascends stonily, passing **rayless arnica** to curve around to a small purple, white, and gold garden of tall and spare **monkshood, cow parsnip,** Coulter daisy, yellow avens, and senecio, with a touch of blue tall chimingbells and brook saxifrage. On the mossy left bank, **one-sided wintergreen** bends a short stem of greenish bells, while **green mitrewort**, or **bishop's cap**, sends up an erect stalk of olive-colored blooms.

As you climb, look for **heartleaf arnica**, which brightens the forest shade. Deepening shadows along the next rising sector suit **rattlesnake plantain orchid**. Each rosette leaf is divided by a white midrib that fades outward in the pattern of snake rattles.

The ascending route eases somewhat where lilac **delicate Jacob's ladder** accompanies towering, midnight blue larkspur. Aspen trees and conifers form a mixed wood where **white peavine** and **meadowrue** line a comfortable stint leading to a flat.

Soon an uptick carries the trail along a grassy slope marked by **elderberry** bushes and **orange agoseris**. Level cruising follows a quartet of whites in Coulter daisy, northern bedstraw, white geranium, and yarrow.

This is a good spot to check out the smoothly fluted drum heads of **rayless senecio** in both maroon and chartreuse, both varieties eventually exposing gold disk flowers. Then get ready for a challenging forest ascent. For the next few paces, rattlesnake plantain orchid lays its leaf rosettes singly on the barren floor on both sides of the trail. The erect stalks show pale green buds in various stages of development, with the lower ones unfurling the small orchid blooms. Magnification assists appreciation.

Switchbacks help Blue Lakes Trail attain its 1,600-foot vertical elevation gain. Level at last, the trail passes vest pocket gardens along the way to a slope of rich blue larkspur, tall chimingbells, cow parsnip, and the ever-present wild geranium.

Encouraged on by tall scarlet paintbrush on a well-drained tread, hikers reach the Mount Sneffels Wilderness sign. As the route continues up, look for **parrot's beak lousewort** and ivory-headed **shy wood nymph**. The sound of running water signals the cheerful yellows of **orange sneezeweed** and **mountain parsley**. Moisture nurtures more tall chimingbells and larkspur trailside. Shy wood nymph's cousin one-sided wintergreen guards a tree emblazoned with the hiking sole-and-heel icon. Forest duff sends up early-blooming **spotted**

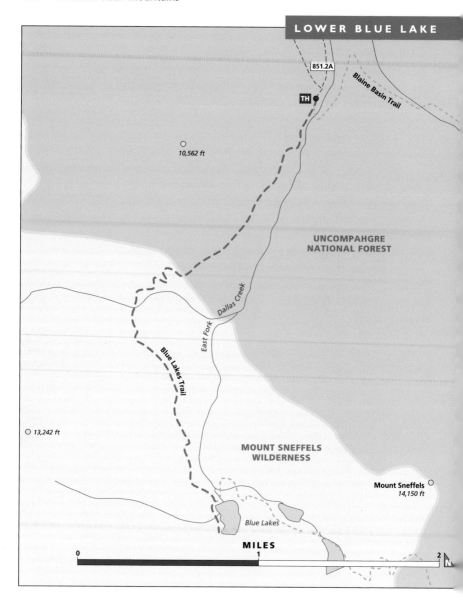

851.2A

Blaine Basin Trail

TH

10,562 ft

UNCOMPAHGRE
NATIONAL FOREST

East Fork

Dallas Creek

Blue Lakes Trail

13,242 ft

MOUNT SNEFFELS
WILDERNESS

Mount Sneffels
14,150 ft

Blue Lakes

MILES

0   1   2

N

coralroot orchid, its reddish stalk incapable of making chlorophyll. **Mountain candytuft** and **rockcress** represent the mustard clan.

Delicate Jacob's ladder accompanies you on a lift in the route before a drop takes you down to the creek and another shot at one-sided wintergreen. Stronger ambient light allows wildflowers to line the stream, including **aspen sunflower**, yarrow, **Porters lovage**, **harebell**, larkspur, and tall chimingbells. Orange agoseris adds a coppery note. **Bittercress** and cowbane thrive in a seep on the right, and dangling harebell tints a slope purple.

At a creek crossing, look right for western red columbine. Spires of blue **lupine** on the bank await your successful crossing, as does triangleleaf senecio and cowbane. Softening the floral scene, **Canada violet** precedes a colony of **false hellebore**. Adding bright accents are golds of orange sneezeweed, rayless arnica, American vetch, and wild geranium.

At the meadow's end, the trail resumes its rocky, ascending character. **Subalpine daisy** adds a warm lavender hue to the dominant lupine blue. Stars of **mountain death camas** share space with swabs of **rosy paintbrush**.

Begin a set of forested switchbacks adjacent to an avalanche path, where wildflowers enjoy the open sky, including Grays angelica, the native oddity of the carrot family. Through a gateway of spruces, check down to the right for another little grouping of shy wood nymph, sometimes called **single delight**; cousin one-sided wintergreen is here as well.

Prepare to reenter forest as the route passes **nodding** or **daffodil senecio**. A weathered rock claims a mat or two of **dotted saxifrage**; it is again found by a knotted old root in the company of **pussytoes**.

Under expansive skies, the trail passes **goldenrod**, aspen sunflower, and Porters lovage. **Green gentian** spires punctuate an upslope display of red, white,

Spectacular hues encourage high-country hikers on their way to lower Blue Lake.

and blue. A little falls area finds familiar flowers such as **pink-headed daisy** and **Whipple penstemon**. Standing above the creek, you are treated to dazzling color, whether upslope or down. Tall scarlet paintbrush competes with rosy paintbrush as the trail heads into forest once more. Look for **bracted louse-wort** in the shade.

Spruce shade and late-melting snow support a plethora of creamy **globe-flowers**. **Homely buttercup** and **marsh marigold** lead to a small footbridge. Nearby, a white water cascade squeezed between two rocks shows off a fine grouping of **Colorado blue columbine**. **Bistort**'s waving white wands conduct you through more delightful gardens as a wildflower-lined ascent introduces **purple fringe**, its funnels showing bright gold stamens.

Mounds of succulent-leaved **rock senecio** herald an honest-to-goodness waterfall with a palette of red, blue, and gold in the foreground. Offsetting the bright pigments are pastel Colorado blue columbine and pink-headed daisy.

Waist-high wildflowers line curves that present both orange and **tall pale agoseris** growing next to one another. These natives are known as **tall pale false dandelions**. With coarse volcanic cliffs above, a ravine showcases lupine, tall chimingbells, **subalpine arnica**, and bistort.

Downslope, be alert for scented **Parry clover**'s round, rose heads. Also sweet are the tiny white flowers of mountain candytuft. Pocked with angular boulders, an upcoming avalanche chute showcases **alpine avens**, **golden draba**, and delicate Jacob's ladder.

A showing of rosy paintbrush brightens a rock-studded meadow where snow lingers late. The most common fleabane of high elevations, **black-headed daisy** has white rays subtended by blackish hairs. Strolling an even section takes you to a sign indicating lower Blue Lake is straight ahead.

When you reach the lake, proceed counterclockwise around the shore. Aim right, skirting the marshy lakeshore, to find **little pink elephants** and monkshood. The outlet waters may attract the slate gray American dipper, or water ouzel, as it bobs for insect larvae harvested underwater. A flat rock with an outstanding view of peaks, lake, and flowers makes a good place for a snack before the lakeshore grand finale.

Just beyond the snack rock, a social path leads directly to lower Blue Lake through myriad wildflowers. Start at your feet, with small pink willowherb and **alpine veronica**. Easier to spot are the hot pink hues of rosy paintbrush and **Parry primrose**. Larkspur leads to the aquamarine lake's edge.

Continue to a shallow but lively inlet creek, then retrace your steps to enjoy this blossom-filled hike in the other direction.

Wetterhorn Basin Trail from the West Fork Cimarron River

Wildflower Hike 40

Stunning views along the Wetterhorn Basin Trail

moderate to difficult	*Trail Rating*
6.2 miles out and back	*Trail Length*
Uncompahgre National Forest/ Uncompahgre Wilderness, southeast of Ridgway	*Location*
10,500 feet to 12,600 feet	*Elevation*
July to August	*Bloom Season*
late July to early August	*Peak Bloom*
From Ridgway, head north on US 550 1.7 miles to Owl Creek Pass Rd. and then turn right (east). After approximately 13.5 miles, turn right (south) on West Fork Cimarron Rd./FR 860. Parking is available where the four-wheel-drive road begins. Passenger cars should stop here, or you may continue on the rugged road to mile 2.4 right before a creek crossing. High-clearance vehicles should be able to go the additional 1.2 miles to the trailhead, where parking is also available.	*Directions*

West Fork Cimarron Road is lined with subalpine wildflowers, making the drive to the trailhead a beautiful preview of the hike to come. The length of the route depends on where you park: You may start walking where the well-maintained road ends, or start just before the West Fork Cimarron creek crossing. With a high-clearance vehicle and a competent driver, you could also continue across the creek and up another 1.2 rough, rocky miles to the equally rough parking at the trailhead. From this point on, however, it's flowers, flowers, and more flowers, until the grand finale at West Fork Cimarron's cascade-fed basin.

The trail, signed as Wetterhorn Trail No. 226, gradually ascends to a meadow, then meanders south through forest and washes before climbing to the basin's head. From here, the route to the 12,600-foot pass heads moderately uphill until a final section sends hikers steeply toward the saddle; this section is not long, but it earns a strenuous rating.

Parking is crudely accommodated on a rocky area if you choose to drive to the trailhead.

An alluvial rock fan where the parking is located starts the hike off with views northwest of 12,152-foot Courthouse Mountain and, behind it, aptly named Chimney Rock. West Fork Cimarron basin showcases a crescent of interestingly shaped peaks, beginning on the left with 13,144-foot Precipice Peak, then Redcliff at 13,642 feet and Coxcomb Peak at 13,656 feet.

The rock outflow is sporadically studded with **black-tipped senecio, Whipple penstemon,** and **orange sneezeweed.** On the periphery, **thickbract senecio** gets a roothold, as do **larkspur** and **silvery lupine.** Joining the colorful array are **tall chimingbells,** pink **wild geranium,** and less showy **false hellebore, rayless senecio,** and **Colorado thistle.**

At the base of the sign-in register for Wetterhorn Basin Trail are the pretty purples of larkspur and silvery lupine. Though not much in the way of color, **edible valerian**'s loose clusters of flowers relax high above strappy basal leaf clumps.

A small rockpile, decorated with **king's crown,** lupine, and tall chimingbells, perches left of the single-track trail. At your feet, yellow snowflake umbels of **mountain parsley** float over no-nonsense **yarrow,** a plant that can acting as an insect repellent, blood coagulator, and antiseptic.

Easygoing, the path passes both rayless senecio's smooth foliage and **rayless arnica**'s hairy foliage. Off to the right flows West Fork Cimarron River. Trailside, both **orange agoseris** and **tall pale agoseris,** also known as **tall burnt orange false dandelion** and **tall pale false dandelion** respectively, display warmly rayed heads. A damp area supports the blues of tall chimingbells and larkspur, complements to golden **triangleleaf senecio.**

A rivulet presents Whipple penstemon and wild geranium near a whole bank of silvery lupine. This palmate-leaved member of the pea family is seldom out of sight throughout the hike. **Wild onion, rosy paintbrush**, straight and sturdy **bracted lousewort**, and both colors of rayless senecio add to the variety. **Pink-headed daisy** and dots of **spreading fleabane** lead to a trough waterway where tiny-flowered blue **alpine veronica** meets **little pink elephants** and **green bog orchid** among scattered willows on the right. As the trail gets a little rocky underfoot, note the similarity between the tri-toothed leaves of **sibbaldia** and **wild strawberry**. The latter sends out red runners to find new territory.

The trail through the West Fork basin travels under open skies, passing brick red king's crown, brassy **cinquefoil**, and swab-headed **American bistort**. Flanked by little seeps decorated with **yellow monkeyflower**, the trail crosses high ground and leads toward forest. More little pink elephants grows near alpine veronica's diminutive flowers and pink wild onion. Patches of **alpine avens**' coinlike heads add a spot of sunshine.

Heralding a good-sized tributary, carpets of round-headed rosy **Parry clover** thrive near **heartleaf arnica**. The stony waterway is home to **pink willow-herb** and more yellow monkeyflower, sporting minute spots on each lower lip. Parry clover accompanies you up the far side, as does delicate white **starwort**.

Curving along the forest perimeter on a stony uplift, the route passes **snowball saxifrage** and lavender-blue **delicate Jacob's ladder** under spruce shade. Where **blueleaf cinquefoil** blooms in gold, check behind you for a fine view of Courthouse Mountain and Chimney Rock.

Daffodil senecio nods its yellow, rather disorganized rays over the tidy red heads of king's crown. Tasked with knitting together loose lithic soil is two-toned **alpine clover**, which tends to form patches of low, gray-green leaves.

Mountain parsley's yellow blooms complement lupine blues as you enter Uncompahgre Wilderness in Uncompahgre National Forest. Nearby, note **Colorado blue columbine**, stately larkspur, and American bistort's large, cotton-swab heads. Black-tipped senecio leads hikers into the forest, where heartleaf arnica and lavender-pink **subalpine daisy** both bloom.

A pocket meadow hosts tall chimingbells, larkspur, rosy

McCAULEYS BUTTERCUP
Ranunculus macauleyi

With succulent, dark, spatulate leaves and fleshy stems, McCauleys buttercup has sepals sporting black hairs. The five shiny yellow petals surround multiple stamens and pistils, each developing an individual seed, or achene. The flower is named for plant collector Lieutenant C. H. McCauley.

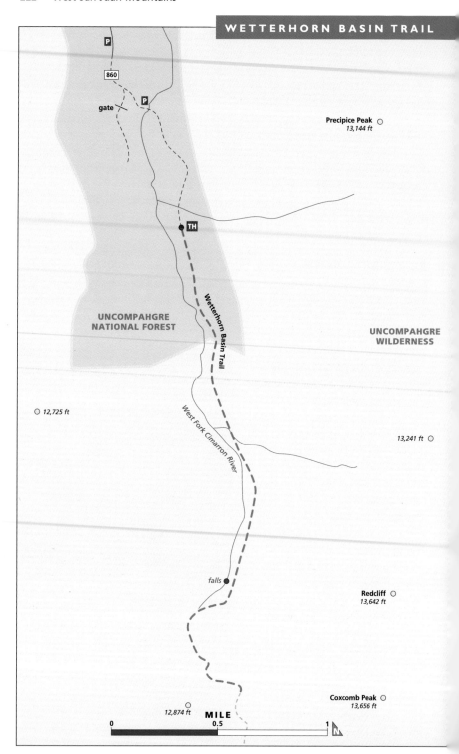

P

860

gate

P

Precipice Peak ○
13,144 ft

TH

Wetterhorn Basin Trail

UNCOMPAHGRE
NATIONAL FOREST

UNCOMPAHGRE
WILDERNESS

○ 12,725 ft

West Fork Cimarron River

13,241 ft ○

falls

Redcliff ○
13,642 ft

Coxcomb Peak ○
13,656 ft

12,874 ft ○   MILE

0   0.5   1   N

paintbrush, and triangleleaf senecio. The blue-green leaves of sibbaldia, a rose family member, support easy-to-miss greenish flowers. Cushioned by forest duff, the trail highlights **green mitrewort**, or **bishop's cap**, each snowflakelike head displaying fine maroon tracery. Dip down where **brook saxifrage** sits high on wiry stems over neatly scalloped basal leaves. Also in the vicinity is **one-sided white mitrewort**, requiring a keen observer to spot.

The sinuous route ascends and flowers appear more regularly, with Colorado blue columbine, subalpine daisy, larkspur, and lupine dominating. **White geranium** and orange agoseris follow. A seasonal waterway nurtures many familiar flowers, as well as both bright rosy and yellow **northern paintbrush**. The West Fork lines its bank with snowy **bittercress**. Elegant Colorado blue columbine nods its honeysuckle-scented heads.

Ascending in the company of **subalpine buttercup**, the route climbs into conifer shade, where **parrot's beak lousewort** thrives. Continue on to find fragrant Parry clover growing near a drainage on the right, with the casual heads of daffodil senecio and winsome delicate Jacob's ladder nearby.

Open skies shine on a spruce-studded hillside where **subalpine arnica** continues the wildflower parade. At the top of the rise, Coxcomb Peak feels much closer, as its boxy profile dominates the skyline. Look for subtle **alpine hawkweed** in the vicinity.

A small creek crossing offers deep pink **Parry primrose**, little pink elephants, and a nice gold and blue garden of senecio, larkspur, and tall chimingbells.

A small waterfall alerts you to upcoming dainties tucked in mossy rocks, such as **white draba** and **northern true saxifrage**. Spruce shade brings alpine clover mats but little else except shade-loving parrot's beak lousewort. The next rocky segment marks a return to open skies.

Familiar wildflowers line the path as spruces thin. Watch for more paintbrush in tones ranging from burgundy to soft rose to outrageous neon pink. A brook offers Parry primrose, Parry clover, and **marsh marigold**. Look for sour-leaved **alpine sorrel**, **rock senecio**, and cool

SAN JUAN ALPINE DRABA
Draba graminea

Brilliant yellow clusters of four-petaled flowers, each configured like a cross, contrast with bright emerald, linear leaves on this member of the mustard family. This particular species is endemic to alpine areas of Colorado's San Juan Mountains, forming fresh-looking mats where snowmelt is delayed. The genus is also known as whitlow-grass. Its Latin species name, *graminea*, means "grasslike."

northern paintbrush. The route parallels the waterway, which supports little pink elephants and subalpine daisy.

Marsh marigold thrives where the route turns rockily up toward West Fork Pass, while Parry primrose signals the arrival of switchbacks. Small flowers in the vicinity include **different-leaved senecio**, a high-elevation denizen, and **black-headed daisy**, whose white rays hide a ruff of purplish-black fuzz.

Willows line the steepening trail, which brings you to some short, matte blue **alpine chimingbells**. Ready for comparison is tall chimingbells, found in sheltered spots. **Alpine parsley** also demonstrates the shorter stature of high-altitude species.

After another creek crossing, look upstream for the blues of chimingbells and columbine, accented by the pinks of paintbrush, clover, willowherb, and primrose, and the golds of avens and senecio.

Comfortable underfoot, the route is flanked by alpine avens, **alpine blue violet**, and copper-rayed orange agoseris. Soon a creek takes over the trail and is crossed by grassy hummocks.

As the trail ascends seriously, listen for the high-pitched voice of the pika, a rabbit relation that makes its home in rock piles. A great chunk of lichen-encrusted fallen rock is surrounded by columbine, making a lovely contrast. Succulent-leaved **McCauleys buttercup** reveals black-haired sepals, especially in its youth.

Switchbacks take you to alpine tundra dotted with black-headed daisy and alpine avens. Rock cairns mark the route under a ragged ridge, where high-elevation **western paintbrush** dominates. Cross a sandy wash and follow the entrenched route as it passes **alpine sandwort** trailside. Chunky boulders hide little vest pocket displays of king's crown and columbine.

Lingering snowbanks may "bloom" with watermelon snow, an algae, as you proceed up to meet **subalpine valerian**, with its daintily blushed inflorescences. Close by, **moss campion** cushions show eye-catching pink, while alpine sorrel likes a rocky roothold.

Where the trail meets a waterway before a cairn on the left, be sure to pause for a view back to Chimney Rock and Courthouse Mountain. **Pygmy bitterroot**, in pink or white, shows charming, translucent starbursts in a nest of succulent linear leaves. **Rockslide daisy** puts in an appearance in its namesake habitat.

Watch your footing as you note a little waterway on the right, a place to examine alpine chimingbells' blue tubes. Mats of **San Juan alpine draba** add vivid patches of yellow in gravelly places where snow lingered. Along a talus slope, look for the lollipop heads of snowball saxifrage.

The route eases before a steep ascent to West Fork Pass. This may be far enough for you; for those who want to top the pass and enjoy its views, press on a few hundred more vertical feet. You may also find fragrant **purple wall-flower** along the way.

Fish Creek Trail

*Wildflower
Hike 41*

*Fish Creek Trail is a good starter hike
for the San Juans' wildflower season.*

easy to moderate	*Trail Rating*
6 miles out and back	*Trail Length*
San Juan National Forest, north of Dolores	*Location*
8,400 to 9,000 feet	*Elevation*
early June to September	*Bloom Season*
late June	*Peak Bloom*
From Dolores, take CO 145 north 12 miles to FR 535, also called W. Dolores Rd. Turn left (north) and go about 12 miles to Fish Creek Ranch Rd./FR 726. Turn left, following this road about 2 miles to the trailhead.	*Directions*

Situated at the end of a road that runs through an idyllic ranching valley, Fish Creek Trail No. 647 is a pleasant hike offering abundant wildflowers. The trail begins in the aspen-covered hillsides of Fish Creek State Wildlife Area, not far from the town of Dolores in the San Juan National Forest. This description travels 3 miles up the well-watered drainage within hearing range, and occasionally sight, of the stream. At about mile 1, you need to cross Little Fish Creek—a bit of a challenge in early summer, but made easier by a skinny log. For some, this creek crossing may be a good turnaround point; others may want to continue another 2 miles to a scenic spot by Fish Creek.

Parking is generous and may be shared by horse trailers.

The delicate petals of **wild blue flax** and golden flares of **mule's ears** start off the wildflower count at the trailhead for Fish Creek, located at the northeast end of the parking area. A background of quaking aspens overlook a stand of **wild iris** as the trail ascends briefly, passing creamy white racemes of **chokecherry**, a member of the rose family. Each pollinated flower in the cluster matures into a tart fruit that is nearly black when it is ripe. The large seeds contain toxins, but the fruit itself is edible and was used by American Indians as an ingredient in the making of pemmican.

As you proceed under ponderosa pines, look for the golden yellow snowflakes of **mountain parsley**, a native that decorates the trailsides faithfully, as does ubiquitous **dandelion**, a non-native. Narrowleaf cottonwoods shelter **white peavine** and lacy-topped **Porters lovage**.

NARROWLEAF PAINTBRUSH
Castilleja linariifolia

The orange-red bracts of narrowleaf paintbrush enliven trails from Montana to New Mexico. The actual flowers are thin, lime green tubes protruding from slender bracts above linear, deeply cut leaves. Reaching heights up to 3 feet tall, this snapdragon family member likes dry meadows and aspen groves. American Indians mixed the roots with minerals to color deerskin black and made a salve for sores from the dried leaves. The genus name commemorates the 18th-century Spanish botanist Domingo Castillejo.

Adding to the display are **tall scarlet paintbrush**, **tall chimingbells**, and **Indian warriors**, or **giant lousewort**, which sports a mass of fernlike leaves and helmeted flowers on tall, sturdy stalks. **Snowberry** bushes dangle small, blushed bells and reddish buds. **American vetch** attracts attention with purple-pink, pea-type flowers and coiling tendrils.

Red dirt underfoot signals more Indian warriors, as well as **salsify**, which seems at home almost anywhere with its light yellow, pointed ray flowers. These finish off as softball-sized, dandelion-like seedheads containing myriad seeds, complete with parachutes ready to sail away.

The trail passes between snowberry and chokecherry, while little white rounds of **whiplash fleabane** face up like expectant children at a party. Towering over **fleabane daisy** is assertively blue **Rocky Mountain penstemon**. Golden tubes of **many-flowered puccoon** nod on foot-high foliage.

At a turn, the trail levels to meet raging red paintbrush and, in a copse of small aspens, lanky **orange sneezeweed**, with its raggedy rays atop pale, milky-green foliage.

Ponderosas and aspens frame a view of emerald Fish Creek valley. This lush locale encourages tall scarlet paintbrush to send its vermilion bracts and modified leaves a yard high. **Serviceberry**, an early-blooming shrub, forms little blueberry-shaped green fruits that will ripen to a deep bluish-purple color.

Tall chimingbells thrive in the moisture often found among aspens. **Meadowrue** and **white peavine** are less picky about conditions. Nearby, **goldeneye** will later present small blooms on a straggly plant.

A large, bearded-looking spruce heralds **aspen daisy**, with its fine-rayed, light purple heads. **Northern bedstraw** shows little blossoms clustered at the ends of the stems like stars in a crowded constellation. The trail opens to the sky, bringing more American vetch and Rocky Mountain penstemon, its tubes showing five stamens—four working, one sterile. **Wild rose** puts forth an intoxicating scent, while another sweet-scented flower also grows trailside: **Red clover**, a nonnative, is often found wherever pack animals pass.

The trail ascends, narrowing as it passes **cinquefoil**. On the left, tucked by a rectangular rock, is **buckthorn**, showing its clusters of fine, whitish flowers. Vegetation hems in the route as more fern-leaved Indian warriors rises, each helmet or galea forming paired teeth at the tip. Common here, chokecherry's drooping racemes precede **tall coneflower**, displaying its conical center of disk florets.

An aspen glen on the left presents an exquisite combination of soft purple wild iris and **Colorado blue columbine**. The latter is in perfect form here in late June. **Sulphurflower**, a buckwheat, opens its tiny round buds into yellow umbels. The trail continues on level terrain, and sunny spots may offer vibrant red, flared trumpets of **scarlet gilia**, a member of the phlox family.

Following a south aspect, this hike flowers fairly early, unlike the north face across the valley, which stays in thick conifer shade. **Subalpine dock** rises

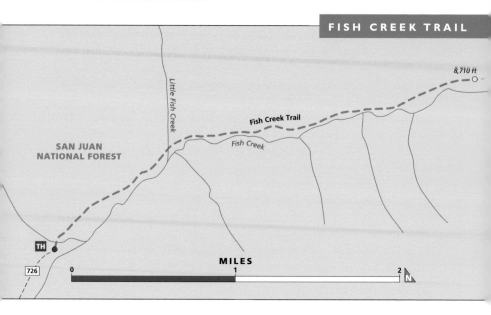

8,710 ft

Little Fish Creek

Fish Creek Trail

Fish Creek

SAN JUAN
NATIONAL FOREST

TH

726

MILES

0   1   2

N

trailside, as does pert **mountain daisy**. Narrowleaf cottonwoods tower over wild
iris on the right, while on the left, **narrowleaf paintbrush** shows its linear bracts
and foliage. Scrub oak shares space with **hawthorn**, whose sweet-smelling,
white blossoms mature into fruits called haws. Almost lost among its bright
neighbors is **bastard toadflax** or **comandra**.

A gate takes you out of Fish Creek State Wildlife Area and into a sloped
ponderosa parkland. Descending slightly, the route enters spruce forest accented
by wild iris and other previously spotted flowers. The trail continues drifting
down to arrive at an open bank where the heart-shaped, white petals of **tufted
evening primrose** spread starkly against red earth. Willows flank a pool of quiet
water on the right, where plate-sized white umbels of **cow parsnip** stand above
huge, coarse leaves. Also look for **tall coneflower**, boasting a disk-flower cone
that elongates with the season.

The trail enters willows via a log-flanked path lined with rushes. Moisture
here nurtures shiny **buttercup**, **twinberry honeysuckle**, and **false Solomon's
seal**. On the right, check for **bittercress**' snowy white, cross-shaped flowers;
the "bitter" tag refers to the peppery bite, more potent after the plant blooms.
An open bench above Fish Creek reveals the cutaway face of a mountain.
Mountain parsley, cinquefoil, and sulphurflower, a valued honey plant, help
to decorate this rock-studded bench.

At a junction with a social trail, bear right. A stony sector lifts the trail to
view the remains of an old log structure to the left. Scarlet gilia's intense red is
met by the deep blue tones of Rocky Mountain penstemon and **early larkspur**.

While Fish Creek flows on the right, Little Fish Creek rushes down from the left, presenting a crossing challenge. If you have had your fill in this first mile, this crossing makes a good place to turn around. Continuing on requires the hiker to ford here or head downstream to find a slender log spanning the creek. A walking stick helps you balance on the log.

Regain the path, crossing over red shale to early larkspur. Mixed conifers offer a shot at viewing false Solomon's seal (the leaf scar is said to resemble the biblical king's seal). Pink **wild geranium** and northern bedstraw draw your attention to **shrubby cinquefoil** bushes down by the creek. Primary colors dominate as you progress.

Meandering, the route passes more sulphurflower, as well as some other now-familiar flowers. **Tiny trumpets'** miniature pink flowers accompany **stitchwort's** cleft white petals. Narrowed by vegetation, the pathway showcases orange sneezeweed, tall chimingbells, wild geranium, and the ever-present mountain parsley.

Following the creek's gentle grade, the trail passes riparian zones where **cowbane** is as delicate as cow parsnip is stout; both are members of the parsley or carrot clan. A red dirt cutbank rises up from Fish Creek, while **leafy Jacob's ladder** grows near abandoned beaver work. Stalks of **aspen sunflower** appear before the trail begins to descend toward a rockslide.

Come up along the left flank of the rock flow and cautiously make your way across the jumble using the roughed-in track and rock cairns. Stony footing leads you to the rockslide's last finger, and a seep nurturing **willowherb** and a bit of **yellow monkeyflower**. Look here, too, for **delicate Jacob's ladder**, with its ladder leaves and pretty flowers.

A slope leading to an abandoned beaver pond and dam is bright with **wintercress**, an early-blooming, bright yellow mustard family member. This is a good place to have a snack and look for wildflowers in the wetland area before turning around.

Hemispheric or **subalpine valerian**, **waterleaf**, **beauty cinquefoil**, orange sneezeweed, **Coulter daisy**, and wintercress accompany the way down to a look at a beaver's past industry. Over by the seep that crossed the trail above, look for white bittercress, yellow monkeyflower, and, perhaps, **green bog orchid**. **Monkshood's** deep purple heads complement **yellow avens'** five-petaled, yellow blooms.

Rest and enjoy the birdsong, wildflowers, and mountain scenery. Then retrace your steps on the Fish Creek Trail.

Wildflower Hike 42

Goble Creek Loop

Showy mule's ears charm the hiker on the Goble Trail.

Trail Rating moderate

Trail Length 3.5-mile balloon loop

Location San Juan National Forest, north of Dolores

Elevation 7,900 to 8,900 feet

Bloom Season May to September

Peak Bloom late June

Directions From Dolores, take CO 145 north approximately 12 miles to W. Dolores Rd./FR 535. Turn left (north) and proceed 9.2 miles to the trailhead and parking area on the left.

While the Goble Creek balloon loop hike does encounter a good number of wildflower species on its climb, it is the sensational mass of golden mule's ears that stuns. The sight, peaking around the third week of June, is well worth the ascent. One caveat: Cattle are grazed in season in these meadows, so don't wait until they arrive on the scene in late June. The 3.5-mile Goble Trail climbs fairly steadily through stands of aspens to reach a rolling landscape dominated by the yellow suns of mule's ears. The ascent and descent comprise about two-thirds of the loop; the remainder rolls across meadowland. Both ascent and descent travel mostly in aspen shade.

Flowers are typical montane-zone species, with wild iris dominating until the multitudes of mule's ears arrive.

A paved pullout beside West Dolores Road/FR 535 is generous enough for horse trailers and hikers' vehicles. You may be sharing Goble Trail with equestrians, so be sure to allow them right-of-way.

Goble Trailhead, found to the west of the parking area and through a gate, is decorated by the cheerful import **oxeye daisy** and its fellow nonnative, **salsify**, both in the sunflower family. On the embankment at the parking area, note dark blue **Rocky Mountain penstemon** and **scarlet gilia**.

Proceed north up a graveled road that parallels Goble Creek. **Wild iris** catches your attention right away, followed by magenta **American vetch**, **snowberry** bushes, and **mountain parsley**, all under narrowleaf cottonwoods. Frothy **northern bedstraw**'s delicate white flower clusters contrast with **golden banner**'s robust, yellow, pea-type blossoms, which hold the keel so tightly that it takes a bumblebee's weight to open them for pollination.

Overhanging the little waterway, **redtwig dogwood** shrubs offer terminal clusters of ivory flowers. Flanking the roadway by a log fence are golden banner, **mule's ears**, and Rocky Mountain penstemon. Look nearby for **wild rose** and medicinal **yarrow**.

A slight incline brings aspens on the right, as well as more wild iris and snowberry bushes, with their pendant blushed bells. Take a moment to sniff fragrant wild rose before the trail takes you past golden **cinquefoil**, **silvery lupine**, and **white geranium**.

The creek runs in an amber-colored bed lined by redtwig dogwood and **cow parsnip**'s broad white heads. The presence of nonnative, sweet-scented **red clover** is a sign that pack animals use Goble Trail. Shooting up a sturdy stalk and dark green, deeply cut leaves, **tall coneflower**, or **goldenglow**, will soon have a cone of disk florets surrounded by droopy ray flowers.

The grade increases where quaking aspens harbor **tall scarlet paintbrush** before it eases to pass **orange sneezeweed**. Riparian influence supports the royal blue of **early larkspur**. Whites are presented by **mouse-ears** and white geranium.

Stony underfoot, the trail looks down on the big, maplelike leaves and snowy blossoms of **thimbleberry**. As the path steepens, watch for **white peavine**

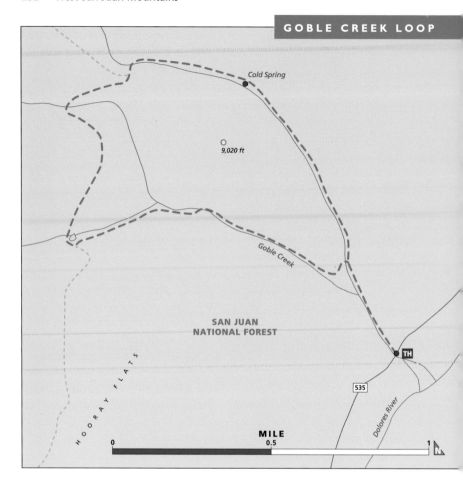

before looking downhill to spires of silvery lupine. This brings hikers to a sign pointing Goble Trail both ways. Having come up the "string," you are now beginning the "balloon" portion of the loop.

Head to the right in sight of golden banner and, beyond it, wild iris and scattered, pale pink **Geyer onion**. Rubbing a leaf tells you it is unmistakably an allium or onion. **Aspen daisy** is budded on its way to blooming. Watch on the right for **self-heal**, or **prunella**, a lavender-pink member of the mint family boasting square stems.

Pass a seasonal streambed hung with **Porters lovage**; it looks similar to deadly poison hemlock. More redtwig dogwood grows here as well.

A magnificent stand of white-barked quaking aspens seems just the right foil for Geyer onion, with its clusters of pointy, tuliplike individual flowers forming a tidy umbel. Upcoming on the right is **leafy Jacob's ladder**, its lilac flowers displaying gold stamens. On the left, cow parsnip's off-white flowers attract flies. Soon to show are **aspen sunflower** and blue **tall western larkspur**.

Under narrowleaf cottonwoods, moist soil supports large **Colorado blue columbine**, its knobbed spurs swept back in a graceful flourish. Aspens tower like the transept of a cathedral, sheltering **Indian warriors**.

The trail rises via S-curves before leveling out in a mixed wood of spruce and aspen trees. More steep climbs are eased by the appearance of lovely **wild blue flax**. Its silken petals may fall by afternoon on a hot day, only to be replaced the next morning by more pointy buds. Early peoples made cordage and snares from the strong stem fibers.

Willows arch over **tall chimingbells** as the trail continues to ascend. Note early larkspur and clumps of aspen daisy, the latter presenting fine light purple rays and golden disks. **Chokecherry** racemes droop as the five-petaled flowers, once fertilized, become nearly black fruit clusters. Tall coneflower's smooth, dark green leaves are abundant.

After crossing a waterway, look for **shrubby cinquefoil**, **willowherb**, and **fireweed**. Cow parsnip, a moisture-loving member of the parsley clan, spreads its broad, whitish umbels. Pale pink **wild geranium** petals, marked with burgundy guidelines, grow in the vicinity, as does tall scarlet paintbrush.

Another uptick in the route sends it winding through white mouse-ears, northern bedstraw, and wild geranium. Snowberry is ever present as the trail heads northwest in company of spruces, making for a mixed woods.

More snowberry lines the way, leading to an opening skirted by aspens, where mouse-ears and its cousin **chickweed** grow. Shrubby cinquefoil and wild iris color this sloped, rock-studded grassy meadow. **Edible valerian** lifts unobtrusive flowers on tall stems, while **orange agoseris**, a native, is shorter and showier. Rich blue early larkspur highlights white geranium and damp-loving **milky willowherb**.

Leaving the sun for shade, the trail presents **buttercup**, more Geyer onion, and **beauty cinquefoil**, with each petal base showing an orange dot. Tall chimingbells grows among snowberry, while **waterleaf** displays black anthers protruding from

SNOWBERRY
Symphoricarpos rotundifolius

A member of the honeysuckle family, snowberry dangles pinkish, paired tubes on a shrub that branches again and again. The paired white berries are attractive to wildlife but considered toxic to humans. Prime habitats include ravines, slopes, aspens, and scrub oak areas from the Canadian Rockies through Colorado. The Greek-derived Latin *symphoricarpos* means "the bearing together of fruit." The species name means "round-leaved."

milky white funnels. Look out for **stinging nettles** as the trail approaches the pole fence protecting Cold Spring. Passing the fence on the left, head north back into even more snowberry.

Climbing again, you pass the occasional **mountain death camas**, its stalk curved like a shepherd's crook while in bud. Also lining the trail are mountain parsley's yellow blooms, white **Canada violet**, and **few-flowered false Solomon's seal**.

As you pass, admire a giant patriarch ponderosa pine scored with bear claw marks on its base. Chokecherry basks in the pine's shelter, as does graceful wild iris. As the trail levels pleasantly, **hawthorn** shrubs arc overhead and flares of paintbrush rise at your feet.

In June, if you are lucky, a cinnamon bull elk may appear through the aspens. White peavine curls its abbreviated tendrils as the trail approaches a rocky little drainage where iris, Porters lovage, golden banner, and Geyer onion hold sway. The now-gentle route finds a gold, blue, and white combination in mountain parsley, early larkspur, mouse-ears, white peavine, and **stitchwort**. Nearby, a crude pole holding pen is brightly decorated with red paintbrush, white mouse-ears, and early larkspur.

You are nearing the high point of this hike. Pass through a wire and pole gate and prepare yourself for the overwhelming sight of countless mule's ears covering the rolling meadows like a universe of miniature suns. Indian warriors leads up to a muddy pool surrounded by pale pink wild onion and wild iris. Look for elk prints near toxic **false hellebore** before treating yourself to a gentle rise that opens to a lovely expanse of rich gold mule's ears and golden banner.

A Forest Service post with a white arrow points straight ahead, through pale pools of **fleabane daisy** and **Fendler sandwort**'s perky white stars. **Silvery cinquefoil** flanks the trail as another brown post aims hikers across a thoroughly gold meadow. Gambel oaks and aspens populate the meadow's borders.

Reddish stems of violet-suffused Rocky Mountain penstemon precede upcoming **yellow paintbrush** which, in turn, precedes a seep, making you glad you wore sturdy boots. Looking downhill, white aspen bark frames tall scarlet paintbrush and early larkspur.

Cross a seasonal waterway and find a sign tacked to a tree for the Goble Trail. Look here for **subalpine valerian**'s dainty-flowered heads before heading to an open, grassy hillside full of larkspur and fleabane daisy. The trail brings another offering of vibrant mule's ears before snowberry and aspens take over, sheltering **sugarbowls**, or **leatherflower**. With finely cut foliage and purple sepals that resemble inverted urns, it also goes by the name **old maid's bonnet**.

Another grand expanse of mule's ears points the way to Nipple Mountain straight ahead. As you begin your descent, summits of snow-creased mountains rise over forested ridges. A sign once again points the way forward on Goble Trail. A steady decline completes the balloon loop, leaving only the "string" upon which you started.

Chicken Creek Trail

*An interesting variety of wildflowers entertain
along the gentle trail to Chicken Creek.*

easy	*Trail Rating*
2.5 miles out and back	*Trail Length*
Mancos State Park, north of Mancos	*Location*
7,900 to 7,600 feet	*Elevation*
May to September	*Bloom Season*
June	*Peak Bloom*
On US 160 heading west from Durango, turn right (north) at Mancos onto CO 184, then, in approximately 0.4 mile, turn right again onto CR 42. Follow it 4 miles to the Mancos State Park Rd. Cross the Jackson Reservoir dam and turn right, back into the park, then left to the trailhead parking. There is a use fee.	*Directions*

Hoping for a short, easy hike in the general vicinity of Mesa Verde National Park? Look no further than Chicken Creek. Starting in Mancos State Park, the colorful descent to meet Chicken Creek is a June winner. This nice section of Chicken Creek Trail No. 615 sees just 300 feet in elevation change, making it an ideal hike for the wildflower enthusiast.

Many wildflower species appear along the way, dominated in June by mule's ears and lupine. Ecozones range from ponderosa parkland to riparian, but mostly stay within the range of scrub oak, juniper, and squaw apple.

Trailhead parking is adequate but requires a fee. A restroom is available near the trailhead.

Chicken Creek Trail begins at a kiosk posted near **wild blue flax**. While perusing the information and getting a trail brochure, check out red-stemmed, yellow-flowered **Schmolls milkvetch**, an endemic. **Fleabane daisy** and **lupine** share space with **snowberry** and upright ivory **Tracys thistle**. Alien **salsify**'s light yellow heads morph into large, softball-sized seed heads. Europeans cultivated the roots, likening their taste to oysters. A patch of **wild iris**, whose roots were used to poison arrow tips, shows how carefully plant parts must be researched.

Spreading **fleabane** adds pale blossoms as the trail rises to ponderosa parkland, where **mountain parsley** and golden **mule's ears** flourish. **Pussytoes** spreads ground-hugging colonies, as does **mat penstemon** with its purple tubes. More wild blue flax complements **many-flowered puccoon**'s little gold trumpets, while **winged buckwheat** leads to scrub oak or Gambel oak on the right. A hillside of mule's ears blooms under the ponderosa pines, its large leaves earning this plant its memorable name. Shiny with resin, they appear varnished. Some Indian tribes used the seeds and fermented roots for food.

PURPLE PEAVINE
Lathyrus eucosmus

Pretty as a garden sweet pea but lacking its fragrance, purple peavine lives in oak woods in the foothills of southwest Colorado. The wide and oval leaflets form a ladderlike configuration, while the upper leaves may have tendrils. The plant was originally thought to be an aphrodisiac, explaining its genus name: Taken from the Greek, *la* means "very" and *thryros*, "passionate." The species name means "attractive."

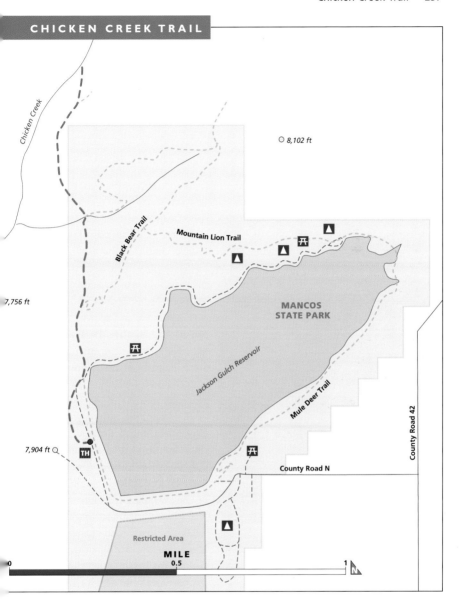

Mancos State Park's Black Bear Trail is designated by a bear paw print on a post. Continue straight ahead for the Chicken Creek Trail, which enters an open meadow filled with lupine's blue-purple spires. **Early larkspur** enjoys the shelter of scrub oak. **Yarrow**, Schmolls milkvetch, and a grand show of lupine persist trailside. Where an old roadway comes up, low mounds of **Easter daisy** blooms for early-season hikers.

Though it resembles garden sweet pea, wild **purple peavine** lacks the fragrance. But it's still pretty in lavender and lilac. Tiny stars of **rock primrose** demand a keen eye. **American vetch** climbs over its neighbors using tendrils, distinguishing it from milkvetches, which are all tendrilless. Yellowish Schmolls milkvetch forms hanging seedpods, which are reddish like its stems.

Complementary pairings such as purple lupine and gold mule's ears make a nice contrast for vividly pink **wild rose**. **Rocky Mountain penstemon** decorates its sturdy stalks with ultramarine tubes tending to one side, each suffused with a touch of violet. Every large tube contains five stamens, four working, one sterile.

Openings furnish more mule's ears and allow hikers a far view of Sleeping Ute Mountain to the west. Looking like miniature crab apples, **squaw apple** shrubs present peachy pink, applelike blossoms early in the bloom season along this sunny sector of trail.

SQUAW APPLE
Peraphyllum ramosissimum

When in brief bloom, the peach-tinged white flowers are fragrant. This southwest Colorado shrub is a member of the rose family, as is the cultivated apple. Growing up to 6 feet tall, branched, densely-leaved squaw apple is partial to open rocky soil in the foothills life zone. It is often in the company of scrub oak and serviceberry. Resembling miniature apples, the fruit is a bronzed yellow.

Soft dirt cushions Chicken Creek Trail as it winds through a wide grassy expanse, just the place to look for **leatherflower**, a member of the buttercup family also known as **sugarbowls** and **old maid's bonnet**. Its sepals are a velvety wine color inside and the plant is even showier in seed, with glistening swirls of pale plumes.

Vegetation closes in, led by **chokecherry** and juniper. Lifting slightly, the route comes upon pale lavender clumps **Colorado penstemon**, an endemic member of the snapdragon family.

Hawthorn and squaw apple flank the gently ascending trail, which passes some openings where **copper mallow** or, affectionately, **cowboy's delight** opens in orange sherbet hues. Line your boots between the sole and sock with the soft mallow leaves if your feet are prone to blisters. Look also for the lovely white cups of **sego** or **mariposa lily** swaying on thin stems over grasslike leaves.

Another junction revisits the Black Bear paw print, but Chicken

Creek Trail bears left to a sign sending it straight ahead into a meadow. Here, early-season hikers can spot wild iris blooming. From this vantage point, you can look southwest and see the long angled road that is the access to Mesa Verde National Park, with Sleeping Ute Mountain in the background.

Lofty **green gentian**, or **monument plant**, dots a meadow, sending up a thick, showy flowerstalk. **Scarlet gilia** adds its flaming, flared trumpets as the trail exits the meadow and rises.

The Mancos Valley opens over your shoulder as dry, bare soil supports **tufted evening primrose**, a fragrant, white-petaled beauty that opens late in the day, turning soft pink as it withers the following day.

Heading downhill over a stony tread, the path takes you to a gate. Head right (north) until you reach a Forest Service sign pointing Chicken Creek Trail left. American vetch grows near showy Rocky Mountain penstemon. The complementary combination of larkspur, wild iris, and mule's ears decorates an opening on the right.

Chokecherry's creamy racemes and wild rose's fragrant blossoms arc over lupine along what is likely an old wagon road. An aspen copse features purple peavine and white-umbelled **Porters lovage**, signaling a little more moisture, which also suits the vermilion and yellow blooms of **western red columbine**.

A bank of wild rose in a particularly rich pink makes the cool shade even more pleasant. As the descent increases, the tread grows rockier, bypassing an piece of lichen-covered sandstone that slid into the track.

The grade eases as you get closer to Chicken Creek. **Blue violet** and winsome western red columbine accompany the creek crossing, which is helped by a huge narrowleaf cottonwood log someone adzed to make the top flat. Stepping stones are another choice. **Redtwig dogwood** likes streamside life, as do golden banner, mountain parsley, wild iris, and lupine.

Find a log to enjoy a snack and watch butterflies. This quiet spot marks the turnaround point for this hike description. For a longer hike, Chicken Creek Trail continues on to meet the Colorado Trail. Another possibility is to add the Black Bear loop in Mancos State Park, accessed and exited along the return, adding 2 miles to the total length. That choice also adds some elevation gain and the bright pink **Coltons milkvetch** early in the loop.

*Wildflower
Hike 44*

Rim Trail/Box Canyon Trail/Transfer Loop Trail

Follow the West Mancos River in the inspired company of aspens and blue lupine.

Trail Rating   easy to moderate

Trail Length   3.7-mile loop

Location   San Juan National Forest, north of Mancos

Elevation   8,920 to 8,200 feet

Bloom Season   late May to August

Peak Bloom   mid-June

Directions   On US 160 heading west from Durango, turn right (north) at Mancos onto CO 184, then, in approximately 0.4 mile, turn right again onto CR 42/FR 561. Continue 11.5 miles to the trailhead parking on the right.

Located north of Mancos near the southwest boundary of San Juan National Forest, this hike makes a lovely loop in the montane life zone. Covering diverse ecosystems from scrub oak to riparian, the 3.7-mile route drops from a canyon rim down to the West Mancos River, then returns through aspen groves blanketed in mid-June with lush lupine spires. From the parking area, the eastern views of the snow-creased La Plata Mountains are breathtaking. Be sure to pick out Hesperus Mountain, a sacred place for the Dineh, or Navajo, which they call Debe'ntsa.

Switchbacks assist the elevation loss down to the river. After a segment paralleling the waterway, the trail climbs to the parking area. Sturdy boots are necessary.

Wildflowers are varied along the way, but it is lupine that steals the show in mid-June.

Parking is adequate on the rim at the Mancos Overlook.

Before heading to the trailhead at the west end of the parking area, be sure to peruse the interpretive signage for the La Plata Mountains. The West Mancos River rushes hundreds of feet below, while in the distance the La Platas are anchored by 13,231-foot Hesperus Mountain. Wildflowers start with **mule's ears'** sunburst heads and distinctive leaves. The yellow daisy heads of **New Mexico senecio** are diminutive in comparison. **Meadowrue**, **pussytoes**, and **spreading fleabane** also make an appearance before you have gone more than a few paces.

Perfumed **wild rose** unfurls smooth, pink petals. Under scraggly quaking aspens, **few-flowered false Solomon's seal** makes sparse flowers as does **white peavine**. Bushes of **snowberry**, a honeysuckle family member, dangle dusty pink tubes, and **golden banner**, a pea relative, glows against the white bark of the aspens.

The Rim Trail begins down, boxed in by scrub oak interspersed with **chokecherry**. Its creamy, thick racemes will

AMERICAN VETCH
Vicia americana

Climbing vetch and wild vetch are two more names for this native. Terminal tendrils, which may be single or forked, top leaves with 8 to 14 leaflets. The casual, one-sided raceme of 3 to 9 magenta-pink, pea-type flowers originates in the leaf axils of square stems that may be up to 30 inches long. Root-nodule bacteria fix nitrogen in the soil, enriching it. The Latin genus name comes from *vincio*, meaning "to bind." American vetch grows from Alaska to Mexico.

become drooping clusters of purple-black fruit when ripe. Bright yellow snow-flakes of mountain parsley outshine **bastard toadflax**, or **comandra**.

A Douglas fir provides entrance to a sunny opening right before a gate featuring panoramic views of the majestic La Platas. Where competition is slim, scented **tufted evening primrose** spreads its wide, white petals. In the vicinity, wild rose offers its fragrance as well. Woody **buckthorn** also has scented flowers, which, though tiny, have a cloying smell. Dark blue-purple tubes make **Rocky Mountain penstemon** easily recognizable. **Serviceberry** forms blueberry-like fruits amongst its bluish-green, serrated leaves.

Meandering, the trail follows a south aspect where tufted evening primrose opens fragrantly in late afternoon. Broken ledge rock leads to ponderosa pines and the common groundcover **kinnikinnick**, or **bearberry**; both the trees and shrubs thrive in lithic soil. Early-season hikers see kinnikinnick dangling tiny blushed bells in the company of **creeping grapeholly**.

Ponderosa shade shelters vermilion **narrowleaf paintbrush** and nearby **scarlet gilia**, sometimes called **sky rocket**. Evergreen needles whisper overhead as the trail approaches the varnished leaves of golden mule's ears and late-blooming serviceberry, waving ribbony white petals.

Another gate finds fragrant wild rose heralding a flat sector featuring lots of midnight blue **early larkspur**, sometimes known as **Nuttalls larkspur**; it is especially toxic to livestock, sheep in particular. **Mountain** or **fleabane daisy** adds subtle hues to a garden of blues and golds. The purple flowers of **American vetch** twine about near **wild iris**. **Yarrow** raises white umbels above aromatic, ferny, gray-green foliage. Plush clumps of **lupine** accent these gardens.

At a spur road, you have come 1 mile. Turn left for Box Canyon, the next trail segment in the loop. Mule's ears welcomes you with its bright blooms and heavily veined, upright leaves. Descending brings light purple wild iris and more wild rose. Loose rock underfoot heralds scarlet gilia.

Scarlet gilia accompanies the drop to the West Mancos River. Lupine and wild iris join tiny-flowered white umbels of **Porters lovage**. **Wild onion** and **cinquefoil** lead to **aspen sunflower**, and a curve in Box Canyon Trail.

Entering the dappled shade of aspens brings **white geranium**, golden banner, **beauty cinquefoil**, and snowberry. **Northern bedstraw** prepares its frothy white clusters. Another switchback passes American vetch sending out tendrils through the understory. Scrub oak flanks the trail, along with **small-flowered puccoon**, the tubes a pale lemon color.

A sunny downward curve takes hikers past aspen sunflower and wild iris to a moist area featuring golden banner, Porters lovage, and **tall chimingbells**. Decorating a tiny seasonal watercourse, mule's ears completes the picture.

A hillside opening showcases the blues of Rocky Mountain penstemon and **wild blue flax**. Switchbacks help you traverse a steep slope as Box Canyon Trail continues on a sunny south aspect, passing in and out of cool conifer and aspen shade. A little dip discloses tall chimingbells in the company of Rocky Mountain maple. **Ivory thistle** appears as well.

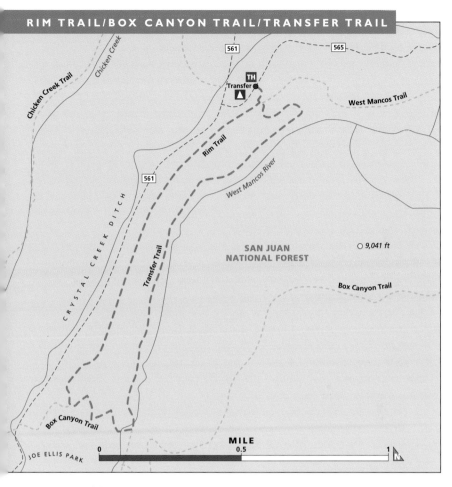

Thimbleberry enjoys the shade, along with **tall coneflower** and **giant lousewort**; both tower over little **blue violet** and subdued **waterleaf**. Arrival at the bottom sends hikers left (north) on a lumpy portion of trail where a sign points the way to the Transfer Trail section of the loop, 1.5 miles upstream. Out of sight but not sound, the West Mancos River rushes headlong to join the San Juan River. Displaying various shades of gold, **dandelion** and golden banner are early bloomers; later gold examples include cinquefoil and mountain parsley. Look nearby for the delectable fruits of **wild strawberry**.

A gate signals a left heading as hikers skirt a water diversion enclosure. Uphill, white trunks frame wild iris and lupine. White geranium and violet accompany a lift in the route, where the next shady sector may turn up **spotted coralroot orchid**. Similar to a red asparagus spear, this plant produces no chlorophyll. The wet environs also support **alpine veronica**, **cowbane**, and **bittercress**.

Now heading east on a soft footbed paralleling West Mancos River, look for lingering white flowers of **mountain candytuft**. Continue riverward to spot **western red columbine** under willows.

As the river rushes over its cobbled bed, check the bank for **heartleaf arnica** blooms, sheltered by **redtwig dogwood**. Spruces make a natural cathedral lit by luminous western red columbine. Alders, willows, narrowleaf cottonwoods, and small aspens line a level area where **wild raspberry** puts forth thorny canes.

The trail soon reaches a damp spot where tall chimingbells are guarded by **stinging nettles**—beware your legs around these plants! Runoff volume creates whitewater as **false Solomon's seal** presents creamy racemes of starry flowers. A star-shaped blossom also helps define dainty **starflower**.

A steep pitch up from the West Mancos sends the trail above the river. Few-flowered false Solomon's seal arrives before you come to a mossy bank. Pass into conifer shade for a closer look at upfacing starflower, collared by a whorl of dark green leaves. Drift down, passing pussytoes and heartleaf arnica under mixed aspen, alder, and evergreen shade.

An eroded riverbank forces the trail over an uptick, where **fireweed** will bloom in the sun. The trail passes primitive horsetails, signaling a pitch up a steep bank under spruces. As you drift down into welcome shade, watch the trail for the hoof prints of elk and mule deer.

The trail coils up under an arch of serviceberry sheltering western red columbine, each spurred head unveiling a shock of protruding yellow stamens. The pyramidal face of Hesperus Mountain rises in a U-shaped gap. A handy planked footbridge takes the hiker across a little ravine, where the trail then switchbacks down to river level. Lofty by the time it blooms, tall coneflower presents a cone-shaped mound of disk flowers.

Nearly touching the trail, the river nurtures **twistedstalk**, its split, recurved bells hanging under parallel-veined leaves, each on a thread of kinked stalk. Wild iris signals a rise in the route, taking hikers to a sign confirming you are on the Transfer Trail sector.

A left at this juncture begins the return to the rim. A bit of **hawthorn** amongst scattered aspens joins **wild geranium** and wild blue flax. A rising path passes white geranium, along with bracken fern and **tall scarlet paintbrush**. Fleabane daisy and purple **smooth aster** announce the appearance of **many-flowered puccoon**.

The trail curves on a slow ascent where fireweed sends up magenta-pink spires. Arrive at a sign where east-headed West Mancos Trail switchbacks to the west. Continue straight ahead through lupine to reach a metal gate that is supported by an aspen-log fence. More bright tall scarlet paintbrush and lupine add color to your ascent.

A sign giving you the mileage of the Transfer trail system is a signal to turn left along the main road. Walk a few paces to access a gravel pathway between two rusty stones on the left. Follow the brief, scrub oak–lined route back to your parked vehicle.

Indian Trail Ridge via Highline and Colorado Trails

Wildflower Hike 45

Wildflowers reign supreme on this La Plata Mountains Hike.

easy to moderate	*Trail Rating*
4.4 miles out and back	*Trail Length*
San Juan National Forest, northwest of Durango	*Location*
11,340 feet to 12,270 feet	*Elevation*
July to August	*Bloom Season*
late July to early August	*Peak Bloom*
From Durango, head west on US 160 approximately 6 miles to La Plata Rd./CR 124. Turn right (north) and continue approximately 12.5 miles to the junction with FR 571, bearing left for the trailhead. The last few miles of FR 571 that lead to the Kennebec Pass area and the Colorado Trail require a four-wheel-drive vehicle.	*Directions*

INDIAN TRAIL RIDGE VIA HIGHLINE AND COLORADO TRAILS

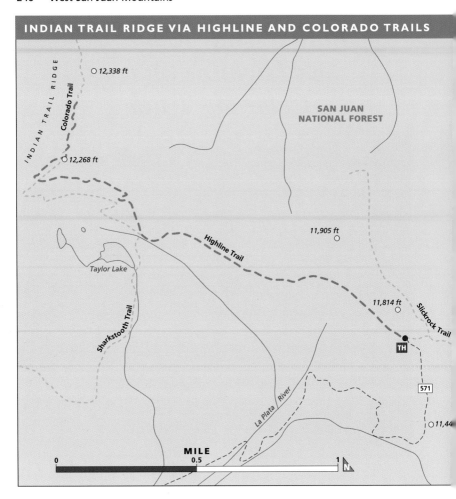

The Highline Trail No. 520 to Indian Trail Ridge is the stuff of postcards. Spectacular wildflowers, a serene lake, and open-skied mountain views make this one of the most scenic hikes in the La Plata Mountains. The only hitch is the access road. By all accounts, a high-clearance, four-wheel-drive vehicle best suits the last few miles of road, beginning at mile 10.4. But though the route is rough and rocky, it is not particularly challenging, with no stretches of shelf road. Plan appropriately before heading out on this trip and make sure your vehicle is up to the challenge.

The trail passes through level acres of wildflowers to Taylor Lake at mile 1. Then it rises easily on approach to a stiffer climb that pushes above the lake to Indian Trail Ridge. Again the route eases, reaching a spectacularly set causeway as the turnaround point.

Parking is generous at the flat trailhead, once drivers have negotiated the rugged access road.

Begin by heading west across the parking area to join the Colorado Trail on the Highline portion. Wildflowers begin with the golds of **thickbract senecio** and **orange sneezeweed** and the yellows of **alpine avens** and **tall pale agoseris**. Long-stemmed white **American bistort** waves over petite, blue **alpine veronica**. Powder blue **tall chimingbells** grow alongside swabs of **rosy paintbrush**. A spruce on the right reveals **Whipple** or **dusky penstemon**'s wine-colored tubes, looking like vintage port in a dusty bottle. **Porters lovage**, a member of the parsley tribe, presents hemispheric umbels made of myriad white flowers.

False hellebore leads to a signboard stating Taylor Lake is 1 mile, Denver 450 miles. This route is part of the 470-mile Colorado Trail from Denver to Durango. Abundant wildflowers include **subalpine larkspur**, **white geranium**, and Porters lovage. At their feet, look for winsome **Coulter daisy**'s fine white rays and odd-looking **Ritter kittentails**, a San Juan Mountains endemic that blooms pale yellow early in the season and by mid- to late summer is green with plump seedpods crowding the thick stalk.

Legions of **aspen sunflower** act as casual compasses, with most of the yellow heads facing east. **Rayless senecio**'s tuck-and-roll heads accompany plain **edible valerian** and deepest red **king's crown**. The red dirt track cruises through a sea of wildflowers, adding **beauty cinquefoil**'s cheery golden yellow hue. Off to the east, a talus ridge holds squared-off Kennebec Pass. In the foreground, note **bracted lousewort**'s creamy-beaked flowerstalks. A torchlike flare in the crowd proves to be **tall scarlet paintbrush**. Dominating trailside is thick-bract senecio, with **subalpine arnica** nearby in nearly the same gold. Bare-stemmed American bistort's packed inflorescences show numerous stamens.

You are enjoying the grand gardens of Cumberland Basin. Even the dull green, six-petaled flowers of false hellebore, reportedly poisonous even to pollinators, add to the colorful array. As you proceed, a pale ridge rises some 12,000-plus feet before you, framing rugged thirteeners curving up behind. An occasional **pink-headed daisy** or **wild onion** contributes rosy touches.

LITTLE ROSE GENTIAN
Gentianella acuta

Like most Rocky Mountain gentians, winsome little rose gentian is a late-season bloomer, typically peaking in late July and August. Upright, paired flowers show a dainty fringe, which may be absent in very late flowers. The satiny rose-colored blossoms can be found from montane to alpine life zones.

Momentarily decreasing vegetation allows tall scarlet paintbrush and **Colorado blue columbine** to flourish. The pathway narrows on a gentle ascent where **triangleleaf senecio** grows tall. Where more earth appears, Whipple penstemon, king's crown, and Coulter daisy take advantage of the space. Porters lovage is profuse everywhere you look.

A spruce gateway announces the lesser lights of **Parry goldenweed**, **yarrow**, and wiry-stemmed **rock primrose**. **Mountain parsley** stands out in a display of gold, white, and blue. A distant cascade courses down a bowl of beautiful mountains as the downhill side of the trail shines with aspen sunflower.

Where the route enters a flat meadow, willows and tall chimingbells make their stand. Tracking through willows brings about **marsh marigold**, **buttercup**, **cowbane**, and **pink willowherb**. On the right, familiar flowers vie for your attention, including alpine avens. A swath of rosy paintbrush contributes to the floral patchwork quilt.

Lanky orange sneezeweed complements regal larkspur. Purple-cowled **monkshood** and wide-rayed **subalpine daisy** precede **little pink elephants** farther along. King's crown's massed florets collectively form an impressive head as the trail reveals a small cascade pouring down Cutler Formation sandstone.

The route passes wild onion, Whipple penstemon, **fireweed**, and **harebell**. Less crowded spaces nurture cool yellow **northern paintbrush**, as well as its fiery cousin, tall scarlet paintbrush.

Looking left reveals a slash of Cutler Formation rock—the same sandstone that forms Monument Valley's famous sculpted buttes. A waterway lined with bright **Parry primrose** carves a path, while downstream the steep bank supports graceful Colorado blue columbine complemented by pale northern paintbrush.

As your eye travels up the far bank, check the hot pink of Parry primrose, which casts a purplish tinge when compared with rosy paintbrush. A meadow studded with waving bistort shows early-season hikers the creamy whorls of **Parry lousewort**. Its name, like that of Parry primrose, honors a 19th-century physician-botanist.

A bank of Whipple penstemon points the way to trail signs. Highline Trail No. 520 heads to the right to Indian Trail Ridge. Parry lousewort decorates the sign's base, while **different-leaved senecio** sporadically pops up on the left.

Though Indian Trail Ridge is not specified on the next Highline Trail sign, it is traveled en route to other hiking destinations. Willows sheltering monkshood flank the way. The pointy emerald leaves of **alpine** or **Bakers parsley** cradle yellow umbels.

Glancing left offers a good view of lovely Taylor Lake, actually a pair of lakes anchored by beaver lodges. Having come a well-flowered mile, those not wishing to climb to Indian Trail Ridge may turn around here.

For those ready to ascend the ridge, the trail begins with a curving rise. Willows fall behind where switchbacks lift the route to a good view of Taylor and its sublake. Rosy and tall scarlet paintbrush keep competitive but amiable company.

As the ascent increases, late-season hikers may find the funnels of **little rose gentian**, a delicate fringe in each rose-colored throat. **Golden aster** accompanies a switchback turn leading to lots of **slender-tipped clover**, a rosy-headed member of the pea family found often in the San Juans. Early-blooming **purple fringe** likes lithic soil and grows right beside the track. Sandworts, including grassy-leaved **Fendler**, present a constellation of little white stars.

Krummholz spruces flank the trail. Adapting to a harsh environment, krummholz bends from prevailing winds and grows horizontally by rooting where its branches touch the earth. Northern paintbrush flourishes along the slope, as does Colorado blue columbine and pink-headed daisy, with its refined rays and soft-haired buds. **Pussytoes** cling to the earth with creeping mats of gray-green leaves.

The route changes from dirt tread to rock as **twinberry honeysuckle**, sometimes called **black twinberry**, struggles to survive. Purple harebell dangles blooms on wiry stems. To conserve energy on this uptick, take small steps. Slender-tipped clover favors rocky places and this steep slope is ideal.

Little rose gentian flourishes on the slope's cutbank, offering you a chance to peer into its corolla, where its cilia fold in daintily. Shoulder your way through red, white, blue, and gold as the grade eases. **Meadowrue** shares space with fireweed.

The rocky trail switchbacks past a worn wall, its crevices sporting plush wild onion heads, along with Fendler sandwort, **mountain death camas**, and Colorado blue columbine, among other plants. Early-season hikers might note the purple-blue funnels of **sky pilot**.

Before another switchback, look on the left for **Brandegee clover**, each magenta-red floret individually displayed like a pendant jewel. Clumps of **black-tipped senecio** thrive in the lithic soil where the trail turns. Purple fringe, showing neon gold stamens, is happy here as well.

Prepare for a more challenging trail. Brassy buttercup and quiet

SLENDER-TIPPED CLOVER
Trifolium attenuatum

A Western Slope endemic that favors rocky soil and ledges, slender-tipped clover's gray-green leaves are indeed tapered to a point. It tends to form clumpy, loose mats in open areas around timberline. The Latin genus name is derived from *tres*, "three," and *folium*, "leaves"; the species name describes the tapered leaves.

wallflower, a pleasantly scented mustard, grow near your fingertips at a broken outcrop. Fendler sandwort thrives here, as does **goldenrod** and slender-tipped clover. Early-season hikers enjoy the sight and scent of **alpine phlox** and, up higher on the outcrop, mats of **dotted saxifrage**.

Pull up the last pitch toward a sign stating that you are 1.75 miles from the trailhead. Look nearby for aspen sunflower. Like other sunflowers, it favors facing east, toward the rising sun and away from prevailing winds.

As you make a turn to the right, inspect upcoming paintbrush, noting the subtle difference between luminous **Haydens paintbrush** and bright rosy paintbrush. Haydens' bracts tend to almost dusty purple-pink, with lower reaches tinted reddish-gray. Alpine parsley grows in the vicinity of sky pilot.

Curve around to enjoy high-mountain vistas and deep glacial valleys. Light purple **pinnate-leaf daisy** and more aspen sunflower join **beetleaf senecio**, a high-elevation endemic.

With drop-offs on both sides, a rock-studded causeway leads Indian Trail Ridge north. After absorbing the spectacular 360-degree panorama, turn around and retrace your steps.

A summer storm lifts along the Highline Trail.

Vallecito Trail

Colorado blue columbine flanks the Vallecito Trail.

moderate	*Trail Rating*
6.8 miles out and back	*Trail Length*
San Juan National Forest/Weminuche Wilderness, north of Bayfield	*Location*
7,900 to 8,400 feet	*Elevation*
late May to September	*Bloom Season*
late June to early July	*Peak Bloom*
From Durango, head east on US 160 approximately 13 miles to Bayfield. Turn right (north) on CR 501 and continue 18.8 miles. Turn left on CR 500 for the final 2.8 miles to the trailhead.	*Directions*

By Colorado standards, Vallecito Creek is really more of a river, especially during spring runoff. A lovely, translucent Jade color, this waterway parallels a beautiful hike. During peak bloom, Vallecito Trail No. 529 is a treat, though the going can be a bit of a push, with more elevation gain and loss than the start and finish elevations would indicate. Located at the far north end of Vallecito Reservoir at the entrance to Vallecito Campground, the trail takes you to a gorge still in the making.

Wildflowers abound in the mostly lithic soil. In addition, the trail features over a half-dozen fern species. Parking is generous at the trailhead, but remember that this is a very popular hike, especially on weekends. Horses and packers use Vallecito Trail as well.

Begin Vallecito Trail at the southwest corner of the parking area. Though you cannot see it from the trail, the extensive Missionary Ridge Fire area extends just over the hill. Nearby, **fireweed** shoots up spires of showy blossoms. This member of the evening primrose family thrives in burned areas, aiding the healing process. Also showing pink blooms is lovely **wild rose**.

The trail skirts the northern edge of the campground as it approaches **few-flowered false Solomon's seal** and **thimbleberry**, with its large white flowers. Occasional specimens of **twinberry honeysuckle** and **baneberry** appear, the latter bearing shiny, toxic fruits. **Northern bedstraw** is a minuscule bloomer, displaying frothy, scented clusters.

Granitic cliffs rise to the left, featuring **false Solomon's seal**, its creamy racemes maturing into round berries. Curving around the east periphery of the campsites brings you to a Weminuche Wilderness signboard.

Using a footbridge, immediately cross Fall Creek. With Fall Creek on the left, note **spreading dogbane** flaunting dainty pink bells in season. A trickle is damp enough to support **cow parsnip** and **tall coneflower**. More of thimbleberry's big, wide, maplelike leaves frame roselike blossoms that mature into edible, if rather tasteless, drupes, or berries. **Twistedstalk** may appear as well; a peek under the parallel-veined leaves shows splayed, off-white bells that turn into red-orange fruits popular with area wildlife.

Rising along Fall Creek, the route comes up to the official Weminuche Wilderness sign where a junction briefly separates hikers from horses; hikers go straight ahead, while horses head left. Twinberry honeysuckle bushes produce paired black fruits, shawled by red bracts. Both varieties of **wild strawberry**—one with smooth, blue-green leaves, the less common with matte foliage—are close enough to compare. Look also for two forms of **pussytoes**, growing with rhomboid, soft leaves on the right, and in gray, felty mats on the left.

Fall Creek mixes with the sound of Vallecito Creek as the trail climbs gently but steadily. **Buckthorn** exhibits thorny branchlets and whitish flower clusters. Early-season hikers encounter **serviceberry**'s ribbony petals; later in the season, blueberry-like fruits form.

Overhead, pines shade **Fendler sandwort**, **golden aster**, and **common evening primrose**. The route turns sharply to take you up on the rim above the gorge, where you might see **silvery cinquefoil** and, in rockwall crevices, **harebell**, which will keep blooming most of the summer. **Pearly everlasting** tucks its prolific foliage against a rock wall that also harbors a couple of young limber pines.

The trail clings to the granitic wall along a rocky sector where, under abbreviated scrub oak, **aspen daisy** readies for bloom. A short forest section ends with the merging horse trail. **Yellow stonecrop**'s succulent leaves and brassy stars show up in rock crevices.

Prolific **fleabane daisy** follows turns in the route. Arrow-leaved **sheep sorrel**'s sour leaves curve the trail up bedrock. Almost bushlike in shape, herbaceous **pale-flowered hyssop**, a mint, prepares terminal inflorescences of barely pink flowers. A cleft in the granitic rock gives you a close look at the yellows of stonecrop, golden aster, and common evening primrose. Thriving in lithic soil, rockbrake fern sprouts fronds below and crowded, fertile "antennas" above.

By following a brief spur onto a worn outcrop, hikers get a sneak preview of scenic Vallecito Creek. Bedrock tread brings more distinctive rockbrake fern in trailside crevices. Dividing horses and hikers once again, a sign steers all foot traffic to the right.

After rejoining the horse trail, look overhead at a lichen-covered outcrop draped with **dotted saxifrage**, its needly mats sending up piano-wire stems and spotted, white stars. Crevices sport **early blue daisy**, a fleabane. Look in crevices here for more fern species.

A fairly even section takes you to a broken outcrop harboring hyssop and pearly everlasting. **Meadowrue**, or **false columbine**, comes next, before more moisture grows **redtwig dogwood** and **chokecherry**. In drier soil, **umbrella-wort** shows dusty pink flowers. A steep jumble of rock sends the trail down a switchback through scrub oak, serviceberry, and chokecherry. A second switchback offers conifer shade framing a view of powerful Vallecito Creek.

TASSELRUE
Trautvetteria carolinensis

Membership in the buttercup family gives tasselrue a giant's status, as it grows chest high. The deep green palmate leaves collaring sturdy stalks that are rather rank-odored when rubbed. Its interesting buds are folded in, like an old-fashioned leather coin purse. When open, they spill out a fountain of creamy white staminal filaments. Also called false bugbane, the plant is named after Russian botanist E. R. von Trautvetter. Tasselrue is found in montane and subalpine life zones.

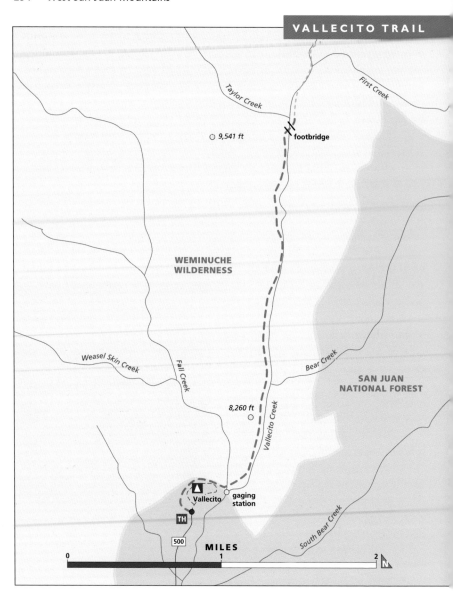

The grade eases though the tread remains stony as, at last, the hiker is formally introduced to Vallecito Creek. Black and white Wiedemeyer's admirals and tiger swallowtails flutter about, announcing more twinberry honeysuckle and umbrellawort.

Waterbars assist your descent to an outcrop wall for another look at baneberry. Greeting hikers here are early-blooming **western red columbine** and **alumroot**, with its scalloped basal leaves and yellowish-green flowers. The outcrop's mossy side is just right for mats of dotted saxifrage.

Ascending, you pass redtwig dogwood, thimbleberry, and Rocky Mountain maple, its sap reportedly sweeter than that of sugar maples. Pockets of aged forest duff are good places to locate **spotted coralroot orchid**. The trail follows another rock cleft, where harebell, sheep sorrel, Fendler sandwort, and a couple of mints congregate, including **self-heal**, or **prunella**. This short mint sports small, two-tone, two-lipped flowers. The upper lip is purple with hairs attached; the lower is pale lilac. Check for the square stems and fragrant foliage of the mint clan.

Look in bedrock soil pockets for pale pink **Geyer onion**, then squeeze between an old Douglas fir and an outcrop draped with dotted saxifrage. Check near the bottom of the lichen-encrusted outcrop for several species of fern.

Wolf currant and baneberry both make appearances. Watching your step as you approach a rockfall, look at the mossy base for rosettes of **rock primrose** and mustard family member **golden draba**, configuring its four petals in a cross shape. **Wild geranium** and a **tall chimingbells** or two accompany a rockfall covered in so much lichen that it looks like a map of an unknown planet.

Damp soil helps nurture bracken fern as **wild raspberry** displays a barely noticed bloom. Round an outcrop area that looks straight down on the roaring Vallecito. As the outcrop peters out on the left, keep an eye out for western red columbine. **Heartleaf arnica** presents sunflower brightness in evergreen shade as the track flattens. Joining it is yellow **mountain parsley**.

Vallecito Creek rushes past an outcrop framing Colorado blue columbine.

Hikers are next to the river now as it drops noisily over a short falls. When you've had your fill of river, turn to a vest pocket glen featuring **Colorado blue columbine**. This special spot has boulders perfect for resting and enjoying the solitude. Nearby, white **Canada violet** and tall chimingbells neighbor several fern species. This is another place to check for spotted coralroot orchid.

The trail lifts over bedrock and finds **beauty cinquefoil**, alumroot, and harebell. Geyer onion shares its lithic habitat with some reluctantly blooming dark red **king's crown**. Flat and sandy for a bit, the tread passes western red columbine and arnica. Starting up again, look upriver for a view of high peaks.

Rocks define the route as you pass **elderberry** and cow parsnip. Moisture supports **monkshood** and a lush stand of **tasselrue**, a tall member of the butter-cup clan displaying flowers bursting with white, staminal filaments. Terminal heads of fringy white flowers, small balls of buds, and palmate leaves combine to make tasselrue a robust, distinctive plant. Glance down at two-lipped self-heal, its dainty flowers cradled by no-nonsense bracts. A bit more tasselrue offers the chance to examine its flowers up close.

Over the large heads of cow parsnip and tall coneflower, a lovely view of the Vallecito opens up. **Alpine hawkweed** stands above basal leaves, its hanging head comprised of dull gold rays. **Rams-horn** accompanies its cousin **Indian warriors**, the latter displaying typical ferny lousewort leaves.

Another ascent brings **narrowleaf paintbrush** for a dash of red. A mixed aspen and conifer wood above the river shelters **tuber starwort**'s white flowers, growing just before the Taylor Creek crossing.

Head left upstream using logs to reach the far side, which is decorated with twistedstalk and **larkspur**. Next, the trail crosses roaring Vallecito Creek. Fortunately, it's done on a grand footbridge spanning the waterway. On the far side of the two-part bridge, an overhanging outcrop shows off Colorado blue columbine against a dark wall.

This is an excellent place to turn around, though the trail continues on, reaching First Creek in another 0.3 mile and presenting a real crossing challenge. So the description for this hike ends at mile 3.4 at Taylor Creek Bridge, which actually crosses not its namesake, but gorgeous Vallecito Creek.

Knife Edge Trail

*Wildflower
Hike 47*

The Knife Edge Trail is a great way to see Mesa Verde flora.

easy	*Trail Rating*
1.5 miles out and back	*Trail Length*
Mesa Verde National Park, Morefield Campground	*Location*
7,800 feet	*Elevation*
late May to July	*Bloom Season*
June	*Peak Bloom*
On US 160, go 7 miles west of Mancos or 9 miles east of Cortez to the Mesa Verde National Park entrance. Head 4 miles south to the Morefield Campground entrance. Turn right and drive to the farthest trailhead parking lot on the left. There is a national park fee for use.	*Directions*

A precarious route along the side of a steep canyon, this 1914 road was once the principal access to Mesa Verde National Park. Now abandoned, its upper reaches serve as an easygoing hike with a far view over the Montezuma Valley. The amiable 0.75-mile trail features some wildflower species you might not encounter on other park hikes. A trail guide helps you identify them with numbers that correspond to like-numbered posts. You can find the guides at the trailhead, located at Morefield Campground's far west end in the designated parking area.

The short trail follows the roadbed along a northern exposure that escaped recent fires, leaving intact a community of plants that includes some Douglas firs. The trail heads downhill almost indiscernibly, passing lush glades and raw shale slopes before culminating at a casual signed stopping point.

HAYDENS GILIA
Gilia haydenii

Haydens gilia is around all season long, blooming from late spring to summer's close. This member of the phlox family has five-petaled flowers that come in rose shades from hot pink to barely blushed. At first glance, Haydens gilia's wiry stems practically disappear into the landscape. The species name commemorates Ferdinand Vandiveer Hayden who, from 1867 to 1879, led the U.S. Geological and Geographical Survey of the Territories, employing quite a number of botanists.

Before heading west from the trailhead, pick up a brochure for reference as you hike. Ahead of you is Point Lookout to the right, reportedly used by the U.S. Cavalry as a vantage point when monitoring Indian movement. To the left is Prater Ridge, formed of the same sandstone as Point Lookout. Between these two promontories is a meadow, its grasses growing so lushly as to overwhelm most wildflowers.

The Knife Edge brochure numbers start with Gambel oak, also known as scrub oak. This hardwood used by the Ancestral Puebloans, or Anasazi, starts off the hike. Your wildflower search begins with **clustered sandwort**, also called **ballhead sandwort** due to the semiround head of tiny white flowers. Blooming from late spring to fall, **golden aster** grows low, sporting hairy, gray-green leaves.

The trail, never much for elevation gain, barely ascends through an open grassy meadow where the vibrant violet tubes of **Rocky Mountain penstemon** are lifted high. In comparison, check under an upcoming piñon pine for small clumps of **Colorado penstemon**, its pale lavender tubes marching up through narrow, gray-green leaves. Behind it, look for **broom snakeweed**, with its delicate yellow bloom. This composite was a veritable pharmacy for regional Indians and, probably, the Ancestral Puebloans.

Thistles are typically considered robust, but ivory-floreted **Tweedys thistle** is refined, as these prickly plants go. Long ago, thistles were found to have appreciable sugar content in the stems and flowers—artichokes are a prime example. Up next is **many-lobed groundsel**, with a splayed head of yellow-rayed daisies towering over basal leaves cut like those of dandelions.

Hikers walking in the morning or on a cloudy day will see the ephemeral azure petals of **wild blue flax** open wide. The day's warmth causes them to drift to earth, though myriad pointy buds are ready to take their place. **Yarrow**, a great medicinal plant, sets its many-flowered white heads above soft, ferny foliage. Reportedly, that strongly aromatic foliage was once rubbed on horses to repel mosquitos.

A Utah juniper looks over an occasional golden **mule's ears** peeking out of deep grasses. **Silvery lupine** pops up its light purple spires here and there, while trailside, lavender **fleabane daisy** grows humbly. Numbered posts call attention to various kinds of sagebrush as you continue.

A sign points the Prater Ridge connector trail back to the left. Knife Edge continues straight ahead to a small group of oaks also on the left. As gravel crunches underfoot, watch up on the right for brief-blooming **cliff Fendlerbush**, its four pristine white petals set against dark foliage. A member of the hydrangea family, this shrub pokes through short scrub oaks.

Look up a few hundred vertical feet to the summit of Point Lookout and imagine riders with the U.S. Cavalry scanning the vast Montezuma Valley for Ute action. A tall, scraggly Douglas fir, a species preferring north-facing slopes, draws attention to short piñon pines, whose protein-charged, oily nuts—delivering 5,000 calories per pound—were surely valued by Ancestral Puebloans. Today's tribes collect pine nuts as well.

More palmate-leaved lupine keeps company with ballhead sandwort as the trail continues evenly along the old roadbed. Brightening the landscape, **narrowleaf paintbrush** presents vivid scarlet bracts. Views of the Montezuma Valley are framed by **serviceberry**, used by indigenous peoples for food and roofing material. The whites of sandwort and yarrow mingle under evergreens. All along the way, plush, glaucous-leaved clumps of **blueleaf** or **glaucous aster** produce late-season pale lavender daisies.

Near post 12, look for a less common juniper, Rocky Mountain red juniper or red cedar, a member of the cypress family. An occasional leafy clump of **dryland fleabane** presents fine-rayed, light purple daisies in late June.

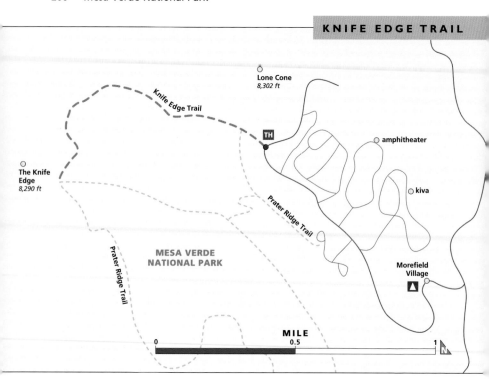

Conspicuous wands of rich blue Rocky Mountain penstemon team up with hot-hued narrowleaf paintbrush for a dash of primary colors.

Note the Point Lookout capstone as your eyes travel up the steepening slope of Prater Ridge. Mountain mahogany's seed plumes dry into corkscrews, augering into the soil by straightening when wetted. Montezuma Valley spreads out below Knife Edge Trail's steep slopes, with the Abajo Mountains 60 miles northwest. Well-named Lone Cone dominates the middle distance, while farther to the east the San Miguels present a trio of fourteeners—the two Wilsons and El Diente.

At post 16, **chokecherry** shrubs grow under serviceberry. Chokecherries were mixed with fat and powdered dried meat and incorporated into pemmican. Regional tribes also used them as a cough remedy.

Late-blooming **goldeneye** has lance-shaped, dark green leaves. Its gold-rayed daisy heads bloom until frost, but the plant is reportedly toxic under the right circumstances. Pass an arrow-shaped block of sandstone pointing downtrail to note **littleleaf mock orange**, its soft, lemony fragrance wafting from white, four-petaled blossoms. Shale soil supports shrubs discussed earlier and soon presents whole slopes of **Haydens gilia**, its little pink flowers suspended on stiff, wiry, gray-green stems. This member of the phlox family grows profusely, if not noticeably at first glance, in its preferred environment—bare, clayey earth.

Ranging from strong pink to barely pink, the diminutive five-petaled flowers grow by the thousands all summer long.

Post 23 offers a lesson in local geology. Some of the rock formations have fallen in chunks, landing by the trail. Here, you can examine the Point Lookout sandstone up close instead of craning your neck to the heights of Prater Ridge. In the vicinity, look for delicate pink **shale thistle**, its florets gathering upright like the bristles of an old-fashioned shaving brush. It is said that some American Indian tribes chewed the peeled stems for their sugar content.

Continue on in the direction of a lush glade while crossing pale, fine soil underfoot. Note nearby Rocky Mountain maple, a tall shrub with many trunks emanating from the base. Looking up to the heights, watch for indentations and cavities in the cliffs that provide homes for wildlife, from raptors to ringtail cats, a graceful nocturnal raccoon cousin. This habitat supports big **wild rose** bushes, each as luxuriantly leafy and fragrant as any old-fashioned shrub rose found in Grandmother's garden. Five pink petals encircle a boss of many stamens that, once pollinated, may become vitamin C–rich hips.

Resume your walk, passing fruited shrubs. Back out in the open, pale shale soil supports a small, healthy Douglas fir marking an eroded slope where a collection of **Coltons milkvetch** thrives. The rounded, compact clumps sport upright stalks of magenta-rose, pea-type flowers. More pink, bouncy Haydens gilia shares the slope as well.

The brow of Prater Ridge looms over familiar trailside shrubs. If watching the sun set over Montezuma Valley and Sleeping Ute Mountain is your goal, keep going until you end up at chunky boulders where a Mesa Verde ridge pokes out to the south, with Sleeping Ute Mountain rising to the west. Nearby, a little wild rose may offer delicate color. A sign in the decrepit roadbed warns you to go no farther, ending Knife Edge Trail.

Wildflower Hike 48 Petroglyph Point Loop

Stone steps along the Petroglyph Point Loop

In 2006, Mesa Verde National Park celebrated its centennial. For a century, it has preserved the distinctive cliff dwellings that have made it world renown, but this unique area also shelters unusual flora that thrives in the transition zone between slickrock desert and the southern Rocky Mountains. Displaying a wide variety of blooming plant life, including cacti, shrubs, and herbaceous bloomers, Petroglyph Point Trail affords a fascinating 2.8-mile tour of Mesa Verde's floristic and architectural wonders, including a panel of petroglyphs and a short sidetrip to Spruce Tree House.

The trail begins by descending on pavement to a junction, where it then continues downhill on natural surface. Sandstone walls and some brief

Trail Rating	easy to moderate, rough in places
Trail Length	2.8-mile loop
Location	Mesa Verde National Park, Chapin Mesa
Elevation	6,990 to 6,660 feet
Bloom Season	May to July
Peak Bloom	mid-June
Directions	On US 160, go 7 miles west of Mancos or 9 miles east of Cortez to the Mesa Verde National Park offramp. Follow the road into the park 21 miles south to Chapin Mesa Museum parking. The trailhead is located at the south end of the museum bookstore. There is a national park fee for use.

climbs follow the canyon's often shaded contours. This is a fairly rugged trail that includes stone stairs, and sturdy hiking boots are recommended.

If red blooms were the criteria for choosing a wildflower hike, then the trail to Petrogylph Point would win hands-down in June. Firecracker and scarlet bugler penstemons and claret cup cactus are most vivid, but many other species, including citrus-scented littleleaf mock orange and yellow prickly pear, offer their petals as well.

Parking is shared by the many, many people who visit Chapin Mesa's fabulous museum and Spruce Tree House. Come early to secure a close space in the paved lots.

Begin Petroglyph Point Trail at the Chapin Mesa Museum, which, itself, is not to be missed. The museum tells the history of the Ancestral Puebloans, who built a complex civilization here before abandoning their cliff dwellings late in the 13th century. The building contains a fine bookstore as well.

In front of the museum's entry, a small garden features **broadleaf** or **banana yucca**, forming generous fruits in mid-June from earlier whitish, lily-like pendant blossoms. Neighboring **prickly pear cactus** tops its spiny pads with silky yellow blossoms that belie its sharp nature, and **sego lily** sends up three-petaled white cups. **Bitterbrush** resides here as well.

Directly south of the museum, a descending paved path leads visitors down a branch of Cliff Canyon over sandstone ledges. A rail curves you around to meet long-blooming **golden aster** complementing gray-green, fine-leaved clumps of lavender **Colorado penstemon**. **Cowboy's delight**, or **copper mallow**, displays sherbet orange flowers.

The slender tubes of bright red **firecracker penstemon** call for attention. Passing through a gate (it closes at evening), look for another red penstemon,

scarlet bugler, blooming slightly later in the season. It sends up slim wands dressed with linear, opposite leaves and vermilion tubes.

Interpretive signs begin with **serviceberry**, whose fruit and wood were used by the Ancestral Puebloans. Just beyond the gate are the shining, swirled seedheads of **Rocky Mountain** or **blue clematis**.

The canyon opens to display stately Douglas firs that Richard Wetherill, discoverer of the Mesa Verde cliff dwellings in the late 1880s, mistook for spruce, hence the name Spruce Tree House for the cliff dwelling ahead. Prickly pear cactus clings to rocks as you follow the asphalt path left to Spruce Tree House. Since this elegant ruin does not require a tour ticket, it is understandably popular. The trail rejoins Petroglyph Point Trail farther down.

An early morning visit to Spruce Tree House is cooler and less crowded, and you might hear birdsong instead of a cacophony of human voices. **Wild rose** presents perfumed pink petals surrounding a boss of yellow stamens. Also nearby is Gambel oak, a rich resource for the Ancestral Puebloans.

After exploring Spruce Tree House, take the stairs past a rock carved with the initials JW, standing for Richard Wetherill's brother John. The pathway passes a sign for the museum and crosses a footbridge where a big Douglas fir provides shade for both wild rose and **creeping grapeholly**.

CLIFF FENDLERBUSH
Fendlera rupicola

In mid-June, Mesa Verde puts on a cliff fendlerbush show. Though the bloom time is brief, it is memorable due to the shrub's snowy blossoms. Tall, upright, and stiffly branched, this member of the hydrangea family has dark leathery leaves and four white, unevenly toothed petals on slim necks. The pretty, squarish, blushed buds resemble those of apple blossoms. *Fendlera* honors Augustus Fendler, the German who collected widely in the West in the mid-1800s.

Zigzag up to a junction where Petroglyph Point Trail takes off to the left, followed soon by a trail register offering a sign-in and brochure. **Three-leaf sumac** points toward some firecracker penstemon and broadleaf yucca as the natural-surface trail heads downhill.

Another junction arrives, sending Petroglyph Point Trail to the left. Stepping up, pass **snowberry** and serviceberry. The sandstone cliffs are striped with desert varnish, formed by rain, manganese oxide, and black lichen.

Native bedrock closes in to create a narrow gap, one of

the features making this hike fun for adventurous older children. Having slid through the split sandstone, enjoy the views of Spruce Canyon and the Mesa Verde tableland. **Wild buckwheat** blooms in latter June and eye-catching firecracker penstemon colors the pale rock ledges.

Stone steps take hikers steeply down through another squeeze, calling for cautious foot placement. Ahead are the airy yellow spires of **golden prince's plume**, a member of the mustard family. This tall, showy wildflower is an indicator of soil containing toxic selenium. Nearby are bitterbrush and red-stemmed **painted milkvetch**, with small magenta flowers and inflated, red-streaked pods.

Looking like desert papayas, broadleaf yucca's substantial fruits were appreciated by the Ancestral Puebloans. Growing from cracks in the crumbling sandstone, the wiry foliage of late bloomer **skeleton-weed** produces only sporadic flowers that resemble a single pink dianthus. Soil in eroded areas grows creeping grapeholly and **chokecherry**.

Passing more varnished rock, look to the right for pale blue **western stickseed**. Soon, the yellow heads of

Petroglyphs

many-lobed groundsel mark a brief, even section. Next is **aletes**, a fine-foliaged, yellow early bloomer in the parsley clan. More golden prince's plume decorates the terrain near sign 14.

The view opens as the trail coils around to meet scarlet bugler penstemon. Sticky, red-orange berries of threeleaf sumac lend this plant the refreshing alternate name of **lemonade bush**. A switchback lifts the route up to present an alcove, showing walls and soot from ancient dwellers. Check the grooves in sandstone boulders indicating a place where stone tools were sharpened. Then look for **purple rockcress**. Descend on uneven bedrock steps to once again see blue clematis, while fragrant **littleleaf mock orange** blooms nearby in white.

A quick squeeze between rock and a patriarch Douglas fir takes you to rock crevices where **alumroot** presents unremarkable flowers atop thin stems. Rounding a corner sends you up more steps, passing western stickseed and a lichen-encrusted rock wall with an aging line of Douglas firs. **Rock clematis'** four pale purple sepals take you to the canyon edge for distant views.

A flight of descending steps takes you to **cliff Fendlerbush**, which has four white petals configured like a cross and centered by eight stamens. Nearby, draping a shaggy old juniper, is littleleaf mock orange, its petals encircling a boss of many stamens. As it nears a cantilevered sandstone face, the trail once again shows golden prince's plume and scarlet bugler penstemon. In the vicinity, check out grasslike, leaved clumps of **perky Sue**, each thin stalk topped by a yellow daisy.

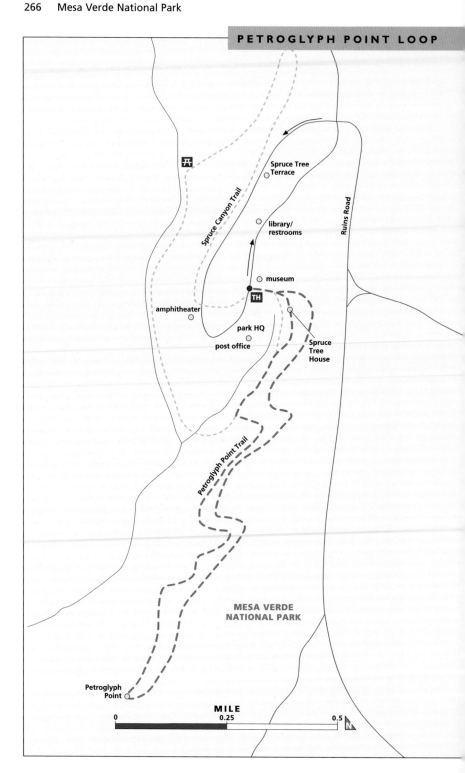

PETROGLYPH POINT LOOP

Spruce Canyon Trail

Ruins Road

Spruce Tree Terrace

library/restrooms

museum

TH

amphitheater

park HQ

post office

Spruce Tree House

Petroglyph Point Trail

MESA VERDE NATIONAL PARK

Petroglyph Point

MILE

0   0.25   0.5

N

Pause to crane your neck at the sandstone walls, the bases supporting wild buckwheat and **bladderpod**, whose seedpods are as round as bloated peas. Look here also for **claret cup**, a stunning hedgehog cactus species with flowers the color of ripe strawberries.

Where the canyon opens to reveal an old trail along the bottom, prepare for a sweet whiff of littleleaf mock orange. Prickly pear cactus sets its buds to unfurl into yellow silk. **Scarlet gilia**, a biennial in the phlox family, sets flared, vermilion trumpets high above a snowflakelike rosette. Early-season hikers see stubby **early purple lousewort**'s short spike that blooms from a rosette of crenellated leaves.

A "Do Not Touch" sign prepares hikers for Mesa Verde's largest panel of petroglyphs. The panel, Petroglyph Point's main feature, is in some nice, cool shade. When you've explored the petroglyphs, use the directional sign for the museum and prepare for another adventure. The continuing loop sends hikers up a ledge via toe- and handholds of Ancestral Puebloan influence.

Follow a ledge and arrow signs to attain the rim of the canyon, where a fairly gentle walk sends you through gardens of pale yellow prickly pear cactus punctuating the piñon-juniper forest, here called a pygmy forest. Early purple lousewort rosettes form patches in advance of the small, hemispherical mounds of **early Townsendia**, or **stemless Easter daisy**, each lavender-tinged, white-rayed head tight against linear gray leaves. Look for them near a rusted chain barrier.

Perky Sue and **pincushion**, with its off-white heads, lead you to broadleaf yucca and yellow groundsel. Tucked into a boulder crevice, mounded claret cup may offer its bright red blossoms. Watch for an occasional sego lily.

Heartleaf twistflower is a somewhat less common early bloomer with clasping, warm-hued leaves. Bladderpod displays yellow, cross-shaped flowers while needly mounds of **carpet phlox** bloom fragrantly for early-season hikers.

Crossing the head of a slick-rock canyon and an old stone dam returns you to the Chapin Mesa Museum, winding up your trek to Petroglyph Point and its fascinating desert and canyon habitats.

GOLDEN PRINCE'S PLUME
Stanleya pinnata

A member of the mustard clan with a penchant for collecting the toxic mineral selenium from the soil, golden prince's plume is a handsome flower. Also called bushy prince's plume, its absorption of selenium makes it poisonous to livestock. Airy sprays of yellow flowers, delicate looking because of the slender petals, protruded stamens, and a stalked pistil, rest atop sizable bushes with pinnate, gray-green leaves. The genus name commemorates Lord Stanley, a 19th-century British statesman.

*Wildflower
Hike 49*
Spruce Canyon Loop

*Spruce Tree House offers a view into
13th-century life in the Southwest.*

Trail Rating	easy to moderate
Trail Length	2.1-mile loop
Location	Mesa Verde National Park, Chapin Mesa
Elevation	6,900 to 6,600 feet
Bloom Season	May to July
Peak Bloom	early to mid-June
Directions	On US 160, go 7 miles west of Mancos or 9 miles east of Cortez to the Mesa Verde National Park offramp. Follow the road into the park 21 miles south to Chapin Mesa Museum parking. The trailhead is located at the south end of the museum bookstore. There is a national park fee for use.

Mesa Verde National Park is like none other, and draws thousands of visitors each year. Few people turn to Mesa Verde for solitude, but there is another side to the park, quieter and more private. By leaving the congested, man-made places for natural ones, you can discover lesser known aspects of this region. For example, try the 2.1-mile Spruce Canyon Loop.

This trail includes a brief side trip to the famed Spruce Tree House, one of the main cliff dwellings, which can be visited without a ticket. After exploring Spruce Tree House, continue to a junction for the Petroglyph Point and Spruce Canyon Trails (see p. 262).

Descending on a natural surface, the Spruce Canyon Loop drops through slickrock contours to arrive at the bottom of a drainage. After a level segment, it then rises through an old burn to step up to the canyon rim, then travels gently back to Chapin Mesa Museum's parking lot.

Special flowers include firecracker and scarlet bugler penstemons. Parking is shared with visitors to the Chapin Mesa Museum, a marvelous resource.

The Spruce Canyon Loop begins with a shared paved path to Spruce Tree House, Mesa Verde National Park's third-largest cliff dwelling—and one of its most popular, as it requires no ticket. Start your hike at the museum.

The museum's front garden offers an array of local vegetation, including **broadleaf yucca, mariposa** or **sego lily, prickly pear cactus**, and low-growing **sand lupine**. Locate the trailhead at the museum's south end, following signs for Spruce Tree House (see Petroglyph Point Loop, p. 262, for description). As you bear right, passing the turnoff trail for Spruce Tree House, consider including this beautiful cliff dwelling as part of your hike; it doesn't require a ticket to enter, and a path exits on the far end to rejoin the route to the Spruce Canyon Loop.

FIRECRACKER PENSTEMON
Penstemon eatonii

Found within Mesa Verde National Park and in regions to the southwest, firecracker penstemon shows broad, slightly wavy, leathery leaves paired sparingly on a slender stem. Early in its flowering phase, the stem is bent over, straightening as the stalk gathers strength to produce a show of brilliant red, slender tubes. This pretty penstemon's lower lip lobes aren't reflexed, unlike scarlet bugler penstemon's, a slightly later bloomer, though the two have a short period of simultaneous blooming in mid-June. The species name refers to Daniel Cade Eaton, a plant collector in the last half of the 19th century.

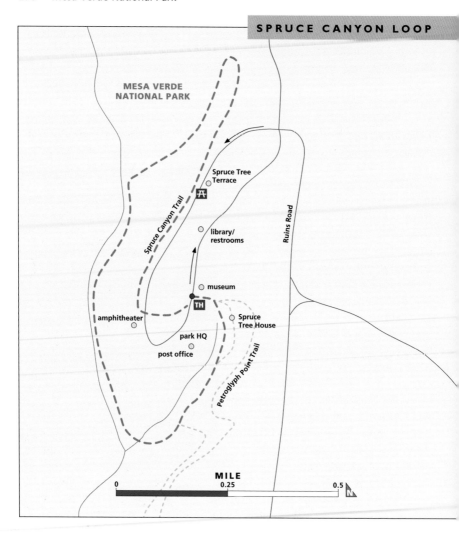

MESA VERDE
NATIONAL PARK

Spruce Tree
Terrace

Spruce Canyon Trail

library/
restrooms

Ruins Road

museum

amphitheater

TH

Spruce
Tree House

park HQ

post office

Petroglyph Point Trail

MILE

0   0.25   0.5

N

If you have visited or will visit the cliff dwelling at a different time, continue along the current trail and look for **threeleaf sumac**, named for its trilobed leaves. It is also known as **skunkbrush**, **squawbush**, and **lemonade bush** for the sticky, orange-red berries that made a refreshing beverage.

Continue dropping to encounter eye-popping **firecracker penstemon**. Watch for the speedy fence lizard as the descent increases on the way to a switchback, anchored by broadleaf yucca. The lilylike pendant blossoms will morph into edible plump pods the size of small mangoes.

Scrub oaks and Douglas firs, which may be up to 300 years old here, shade the drainage where pink **wild rose** bestows a whiff of perfume. Listen for the call of the spotted towhee as it scratches up larvae and insects under the trees. The male sports a ruby red eye.

The next juncture has Petroglyph Point Trail going left and up, while the Spruce Canyon Loop continues down. Maintaining the descent, you pass some spillover pools along a seasonal waterway. A tiger swallowtail butterfly floats in the limpid air, ready to taste pale blue **western stickseed**. **Creeping grapeholly** forms very sour blue-black berries from clusters of bright yellow flowers.

Hikers should be aware that poison ivy appears here and there. Keep in mind the saying "leaves of three, leave them be." Recross the canyon over a little bridge where box elders represent the maple family, then pass under a cantilevered chunk of sandstone.

The next span brings on sprawling **painted milkvetch**, a member of the pea clan with red-streaked, inflated pods. Another wooden bridge leads to the hairy seed plumes of **Rocky Mountain clematis**, its divided leaves clinging to woody stems that scramble over neighboring vegetation.

Take time to look around the ledgy sandstone for soft yellow prickly pear cactus blooms, which, when pollinated, form edible fruits known as tunas. The sea urchin–like mass of stamens surrounding the pistil are tactile reactive, meaning the lightest touch, such as that of a pollinating insect, causes them to slowly bend inward, temporarily trapping the pollinator in the same manner as a sea urchin closes its tentacles.

The view opens as you pass over rock that was once an ancient seabed. Occasional tufts of light lavender **Colorado penstemon** flower freely. Watch your head around the next corner, which leads to layered sandstone showing white lime. Gambel or scrub oaks shade the Spruce Canyon Loop as it bottoms out near western stickseed, whose burred seeds catch rides on passersby.

A juniper-post gate reveals more Colorado penstemon as well as **many-lobed groundsel** little gold stars. Keep a watch out for **scarlet gilia**, whose flared red tubes attract hummingbirds. A level area supports tall grasses as well as **Indian lomatium**, a member of the parsley clan.

SCARLET BUGLER PENSTEMON
Penstemon barbatus

Populating a wide area of southern Colorado, this red penstemon can grow up to 4 feet tall. Its bloom time briefly overlaps with firecracker penstemon. Often found on sandstone ledges and in bare soil, the vermilion floral tubes are narrow and long and the trilobed lower lip is reflexed. Narrow, opposing leaves grow on a slim, darkish stalk. Daniel Eaton first collected this outstanding penstemon in 1869.

A railing turns the trail, with a sign directing Spruce Canyon Loop up to the right. Tansy mustard and spreading fleabane accompany snowberry. Dry, sandy places are just right for the generous white petals of tufted evening primrose, which wilt into a soft pink color the following day. Blooming late in the day, this sweet-scented wildflower is also known as gumbo lily, referring to its ability to adapt to different soils.

Prepare to cross the drainage in view of the paper white blossoms of cliff Fendlerbush. At this point, what was a downhill hike becomes an uphill trek. A borage family member, white cryptantha brandishes prickly, low-growing foliage. In flat spots, mustard clan member golden prince's plume sports airy yellow spires; it thrives where selenium accumulates in the soil, collecting the toxin in its gray-green leaves.

As you continue, search the right side for a plant that looks almost tropical, with wide, leathery leaves that are smooth and heavily veined. Piñon four o'clock, with thick stems terminating in rose-pink clustered funnels, grows on a clay bank under its namesake pine.

The trail evens out as it passes firecracker penstemon. Note big specimens of broadleaf yucca pointing toward an alcove carved by exfoliating sandstone. Viewed through low-angled afternoon sun, the ballooned pods of double bladderpod are translucent. The pale green clusters nearly cover a rosette of gray-green leaves.

A young Douglas fir grows right out of the middle of a sandstone rock in the sharp company of broadleaf yucca. Yarrow makes an appearance, surviving from plains to alpine zones to slickrock high desert.

Continuing along the drainage takes you past cleavers, a forerunner of Velcro that sticks together without matting, making it good for coarse mattress stuffing. Douglas firs shade tansy mustard. Scarlet gilia, also called sky rocket, adds a bright touch. Snowberry shrubs bloom in dusty pink, while gooseberry presents bristly fruit.

Alumroot wands overlook the minuscule blossoms of rock jasmine and blue-eyed Mary. Cross a boggy area watered by a still seep to enter a boulder-strewn drainage that sets the trail on an ascent. A turn initiates a more serious climb as the trail moves from shade to open skies. A bedrock-based switchback leads to mustard family member purple rockcress. Guarded by a pair of venerable Douglas firs, a pool signals another turn in the trail as it doubles back to pull out of Spruce Canyon.

Pushing toward the rim, you may encounter many-lobed groundsel as well as xeric Colorado penstemon. Sandstone steps help you reach the canyon's rim, passing serviceberry en route.

Mormon tea's long thin stems gather chlorophyll in lieu of leaves. Nearby, look for orange-tinted copper mallow. A break from climbing comes when you reach an old burn, marked by stark, black tree skeletons. The exposed area suits bright scarlet bugler penstemon, while cousin Colorado penstemon seems retiring in contrast. Airy Indian ricegrass grows thicker here, but imagine how many seeds it would have taken to provide one meal, let alone a winter's worth.

Rock forms exposed by fire culminate near the rim by a pool where **fleabane daisy** huddles. On the last ascent, look for both firecracker and scarlet bugler penstemon, early-blooming yellow **bladderpod, pincushion, golden aster,** copper mallow, and pale Colorado penstemon.

A sign points the way back to the museum, which takes you right, through the burn area and past masses of alien **musk** or **nodding thistle**, an invasive species from southern Europe. Cryptantha and **broom snakeweed**, medicinally

important to early peoples, send the trail to the road. Follow the road until a crossing where a sign points the way to the museum.

An asphalt path takes you left, through piñon-juniper forest teeming with one of the earliest bloomers, **early purple lousewort**. In spring, this locally abundant member of the snapdragon family pushes up a short amethyst spike over a flat rosette of crenellated leaves. **Silvery lupine** lends blues to the next asphalt sector, while **perky Sue**'s gold daisies serve as complement. Here, you should be able to see the museum complex.

Broadleaf yucca

*Wildflower
Hike 50*
Step House Loop

The Step House ruins feature slickrock views and a variety of flora.

Trail Rating	easy to moderate
Trail Length	0.75-mile loop
Location	Mesa Verde National Park, Wetherill Mesa
Elevation	6,900 to 6,750 feet
Bloom Season	late May to July
Peak Bloom	early to mid-June
Directions	From the park entrance off US 160, head 15 miles south to the Far View Visitor Center. Go right on the Wetherill Mesa Rd., which opens at 9 a.m. from Memorial Day through Labor Day. Continue approximately 12 miles to the end of the road. The trailhead is located at the northeast end of the parking lot and is marked by a large sign. There is a national park fee for use.

It isn't just anywhere that hikers can combine wildflowers and ancient cliff dwellings, but Mesa Verde's Step House Loop, located on Wetherill Mesa, offers a chance to explore both. This part of the park is only open seasonally, from about Memorial Day to Labor Day. But the drive, winding and somewhat narrowly paved, is well worth it, traveling through some of the most floriferous areas in Mesa Verde.

In addition, the Step House ruins don't require a tour ticket. Visitors are free to make the short loop—just 0.75 mile—from the Wetherill Mesa parking area. Please note that a ticket to the park's second-largest cliff dwelling, Long House, is worth procuring. This nearby and approachable cliff dwelling is situated on very different terrain, meaning different flora as well.

The trail to Step House begins and ends on gravel, but the main portion is paved as it descends into the upper reaches of Long Canyon. A brief sector takes you to the rim before steps and zigzags take you into the Step House cliff dwelling; switchbacks take you up through colorful sandstone ledges and little flower gardens to regain the rim.

This is the transition zone between high slickrock desert and the tail of the Rocky Mountains, making flora a crossover affair. Several penstemons and a variety of shrubs, such as fragrant littleleaf mock orange, are prominent in mid-June.

The road to Wetherill Mesa is a wildflower pageant in itself, lined by the golden suns of **mule's ears**, spires of blue-purple **lupine**, the occasional flare of **narrowleaf paintbrush**, wands of deep purple **Rocky Mountain penstemon**, and low clumps of lemon yellow **wild buckwheat**, or **sulphurflower**. Flowers are especially showy in the green acres following the sign noting an 1989 fire. In fact, fire has affected most of Wetherill Mesa in the last century—even as recently as 2000, when the Pony Fire blackened Utah junipers and piñon pines. The effect is eerie, but the result is good for wildflowers, as the fire opened up and fertilized the area.

This description begins at the mini-train waiting area, where visitors board for the loop around the end of Wetherill Mesa. The signed trail, opened by rangers just before 10 a.m., begins on gravel and introduces rich orange **copper mallow**. **Golden aster**—an aster by common name only—stays low, while tall, graceful **sego lily** dots the 2000 Pony Burn area.

Guarded by burned junipers and piñons, **Colorado penstemon** forms clumps of thin, grayish leaves with pale lavender tubes marching up wiry stems. **Silvery lupine** also contributes to the purple hues with pea-type flowering spires on bushy foliage. **Yellow sweet clover** is another pea family member, but this one is a nonnative, as is **salsify**, a pale yellow, daisylike bloomer whose seed heads resemble large, dingy dandelion heads. But the most invasive alien is **musk** or **nodding thistle**, a magenta-headed plant that pops up in the burn areas and spreads to unburned spaces.

Natives return with narrowleaf penstemon, each warm lavender tube marked with wine-colored nectar guidelines for pollinators. Growing up to 2 feet tall, the stems sport slim, opposite leaves. Clumps of delicately flowered, yellow-green **broom snakeweed** appear here and there.

As the trail drifts down, passing white **fleabane daisy**, early-season hikers see another lupine, this one growing low and broad with wide, dark, velvety green palmate leaves. **Sand lupine** blooms in bright blue, producing typical pea-type pods.

LITTLELEAF MOCK ORANGE
Philadelphus microphyllus

This citrus-scented member of the hydrangea family is a late-spring and early-summer bloomer. Its four clean, barely toothed white petals surround a boss of a dozen stamens or more. Slim, shiny, opposite leaves emerge from opposite branching. The shrub's deep brown outer bark peels back to reveal pale underbark. It is reportedly named for an ancient Egyptian king.

Gravel turns into asphalt as the route prepares for a steepening descent to meet the rim of Long Canyon. **Dusty maiden**, also called **pincushion**, blooms to the right in off-white. As the trail heads down, note the shrubland community, led by scattered scrub oak, mountain mahogany, **cliff Fendlerbush, bitterbrush**, and **squaw apple**, an early bloomer with peach-colored flowers. **Serviceberry** is also very prevalent on the mesa, along with **snowberry**, its blushed, dangling tubes present here in early June.

A plethora of grass species help heal the burn, including Indian rice grass, with its airy, branched seed heads. It was collected as a cereal grain to be consumed immediately or stored for winter provisions. More clumps of Colorado penstemon flank the trail, as do golden aster's little brassy suns.

Just beyond a small bush of mountain mahogany are the gray-green, arrowhead-shaped leaves of **arrowleaf balsamroot**, which the Ancestral Puebloans harvested for medicinal uses. Where the rim appears before you, check trailside for the citrus-scented **littleleaf mock orange** shrub, its four pristine white petals surrounding a boss of many stamens.

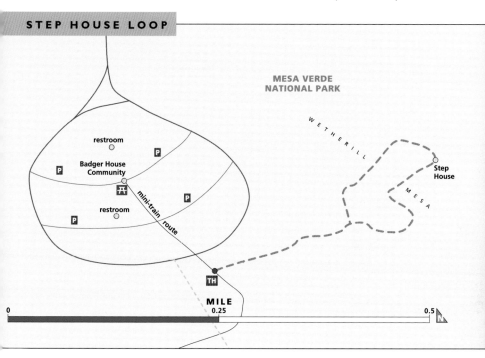

Follow a paved switchback to pass between more littleleaf mock orange bushes before treading over a bit of the sandstone. **Broadleaf yucca** anchors the transition from man-made to natural surface and back again.

Sandstone bedrock overhangs a set of concrete steps; at the last step, look right for **clustered sandwort**'s head of tiny white flowers. The sandstone that forms the wall on the left shelters **alumroot**. Long Canyon opens to view as you approach another set of descending stairs. Serviceberry hangs over snowberry, while **creeping grapeholly** and alumroot are tucked into rock fissures.

Chokecherry shrubs add dark leaves as cantilevered sandstone overhead leads to **skunkbrush**, more kindly called **threeleaf sumac** or **lemonade bush**. On the left, **western stickseed** has pale blue, forget-me-not-like flowers that mature into Velcrolike seeds. Mustards are prolific along here.

Step House is visible, with its masonry walls tucked in an alcove. You might spot swallows, swifts, or a rock wren accessing the alcove roof above the ruins. Running the length of Step House's ceiling is a seep spring crack that nurtures poison ivy; none is in the ruin itself.

With plush stands of chokecherry on the right, proceed down into the cool overhang to explore the 700-year-old ruins. In fact, in Step House you can go back another six centuries to the Basketmaker period, brought to the present by a mock-up pithouse. Look for moki steps, carved toeholds reaching a second story. Another set of moki steps at the far end of the ruin gives this dwelling its name. Mounting a short sturdy ladder takes you up to a view of

Mesa Verde National Park's most easily seen petroglyph panels. A ranger is on duty to answer questions.

Exiting the ruin and resuming the paved path, watch for **scarlet bugler penstemon**'s slender vermilion tubes, just the right shape for the long bill and tongue of a hummingbird. Up on the left, broadleaf yucca's pendant, lilylike flowers mature into edible green fruits.

Stained with iron oxide, sandstone ledges are good spots to observe the conical fruits forming on cliff Fendlerbush. Early-season hikers enjoy its snowy white petals arranged in foursomes like a pinwheel. Rounding a corner and looking up left, note a rocky garden where linear-leaved scarlet bugler penstemon competes with the red of the sandstone. Littleleaf mock orange and **scarlet gilia**'s flared trumpets contrast with the yellow daisy heads of **many-lobed groundsel**.

Switchbacks lift the trail past **sky blue penstemon**'s generous tubes. With wands rising about 2 feet high, this lavender penstemon grows in Colorado's southern counties. Up next, a sign points out **prickly pear cactus**, which served many uses, including as food and as a gluey binder for plaster.

Steadily pulling up, the path takes you past more serviceberry, then **rabbitbrush**, a late-summer bloomer with golden flowers. Scarlet gilia also makes an appearance as the trail continues to rise until it is right above Step House. Here, the trail reenters the Pony Burn of 2000, passing little gardens of pale lavender Colorado penstemon and its complement, golden aster, which is accented by rich orange-hued copper mallow. Sego lily's tuliplike blossoms wave on slender stems here and there.

Early-season hikers enjoy sand lupine, a low-growing member of the legume or pea family that sports broad palmate leaves in a dark blue-green. Often appearing in wide splashes of spring color along the returning pathway, sand lupine also marks the completion of the loop trail to Step House.

Split sandstone on the Petroglyph Point Loop

APPENDIX A: *Hikes by Elevation* (IN FEET)

FOOTHILLS

8. Upper Box Piedra River	7,650–7,500
43. Chicken Creek Trail	7,900–7,600
47. Knife Edge Trail	7,800
48. Petrogylph Point Loop	6,990–6,660
49. Spruce Canyon Loop	6,900–6,600
50. Step House Loop	6,900–6,750

FOOTHILLS TO MONTANE

34. Purgatory Trail	8,700–7,700
42. Goble Creek Loop	7,900–8,900
46. Vallecito Trail	7,900–8,400

MONTANE

2. Big Meadows Reservoir Loop	9,350
7. West Fork San Juan Trail to West Fork Bridge	8,400–8,900
9. Williams Creek Trail	8,400–9,300
10. Weminuche Trail via Poison Park Trailhead	9,210–8,500
11. Squaw Creek Trail	9,400–10,000
12. Ivy Creek Trail	9,200–10,000
33. Potato Lake via Spud Lake Trail	9,360–9,800
38. Bear Creek Falls	8,760–9,800
41. Fish Creek Trail	8,400–9,000
44. Rim Trail/Box Canyon Trail/ Transfer Trail	8,920–8,200

MONTANE TO SUBALPINE

3. Hope Creek Trail	9,550–10,300
37. Bilk Creek Upper Falls	9,800–10,900
39. Lower Blue Lake	9,400–11,000

MONTANE TO ALPINE

28. Ice Lake Basin	9,850–12,257

SUBALPINE

15. North Clear Creek Falls Loop	10,030
16. Rito Hondo Reservoir Loop	10,120
17. Tumble Creek via Skyline Trail	10,280–11,200
18. Brush Creek Trail	10,200–10,400

SUBALPINE continued

21. Upper Henson Creek from the Thoreau Cabin	11,200–11,400
24. Boulder Gulch/South Fork Animas River	10,600–11,200
30. Molas Pass East/ Colorado Trail	10,600–10,200
31. West Lime Creek Trail	10,000–10,400
36. Lizard Head/Wilson Meadows Trail	10,280–11,000

SUBALPINE TO ALPINE

4. Hunters Lake Loop	11,400–12,100
5. Continental Divide Trail North from Lobo Overlook	11,750–11,000
6. Continental Divide Trail South	10,857–11,770
13. Creede Trail to San Luis Pass	11,200–11,940
19. Grizzly Gulch Trail	10,425–11,900
20. American Basin	11,300–11,600
25. Highland Mary Lakes Trail	10,800–12,000
29. Rico-Silverton Trail	10,650–11,600
32. Pass Trail to Engineer Mountain	10,680–11,750
35. Lake Hope Trail	10,800–11,880
40. Wetterhorn Basin Trail from the West Fork Cimarron River	10,500–12,600
45. Indian Trail Ridge via Highline and Colorado Trails	11,340–12,270

ALPINE

1. Crater Lake Trail	11,600–12,100
14. Table Mountain Saddle via Crystal Lake Road	11,500–11,750
22. Horsethief Trail via American Flats	12,300–12,500
23. Placer Gulch	11,720–11,940
26. Bullion King Lake	11,550–12,600
27. Clear Lake	11,600–12,000

APPENDIX B: *Contact Information*

GRAND MESA, UNCOMPAHGRE, and GUNNISON NATIONAL FORESTS
2250 Highway 50
Delta, CO 81416
(970) 874-6600
www.fs.fed.us/r2/gmug

Gunnison
216 North Colorado
Gunnison, CO 81230
(970) 641-0471

Gunnison Ranger District at Lake City
P.O. Box 89
Lake City, CO 81235
(970) 641-0471 or (970) 944-2500

Ouray
2505 South Townsend
Montrose, CO 81401
(970) 240-5300

RIO GRANDE NATIONAL FOREST
1803 West Highway 160
Monte Vista, CO 81144
(719) 852-5941
www.fs.fed.us/r2/riogrande

Divide
13308 West Highway 160
Del Norte, CO 81132
(719) 657-3321

Divide Ranger District at Creede
3rd and Creede Avenue
Creede, CO 81130
(719) 658-2556

SAN JUAN NATIONAL FOREST
15 Burnett Court
Durango, CO 81301
(970) 247-4874
www.fs.fed.us/r2/sanjuan

Columbine East
367 South Pearl Street
P.O. Box 439
Bayfield, CO 81122
(970) 884-2512

Columbine West
110 West 11th
Durango, CO 81301
(970) 884-2512

Dolores
100 North 6th
P.O. Box 210
Dolores, CO 81323
(970) 882-7296

Pagosa
180 2nd Street
P.O. Box 310
Pagosa Springs, CO 81147
(970) 264-2268

Silverton
San Juan Mountains Center
(joint FS/BLM office, closed in winter)
1246 Blair Street
P.O. Box 709
Silverton, CO 81433
(970) 387-5530

MESA VERDE NATIONAL PARK
P.O. Box 8
Mesa Verde, CO 81330
(970) 529-4465
www.nps.gov/meve/index.htm

Index

Note: Citations with the letter "p" denote photos.

About the Author and Photographer

AUTHOR PAMELA IRWIN has been a volunteer naturalist at Roxborough State Park since the early 1980s. Her extensive background in and love of wildflower identification has earned her the certified title of Native Plant Master from Colorado State University. Pamela is also a member of the Rocky Mountain Nature Association, the Rocky Mountain Chapter of the American Rock Garden Society, Windflowers Garden Club, and the Audubon Society.

PHOTOGRAPHER DAVID IRWIN purchased his first 35mm SLR camera as a teenager and has been behind a lens ever since. His favorite subjects include people of foreign lands, the remnants of past civilizations, and the textures of western terrains.

Avid hikers, Pamela and David enjoy combining their talents to produce beautiful hiking guidebooks to their home state. Previous

collaborations include *Colorado's Best Wildflower Hikes Volume 1: The Front Range, Colorado's Best Wildflower Hikes Volume 2: The High Country*, and *100 Best Day Hikes: Denver Area & Front Range*. The Irwins also maintain an extensive slide library and have given slide-illustrated talks for various organizations including the Colorado Mountain Club. Additionally, many of David's photographs and Pamela's watercolors are now in private collections.